A CRITICAL DECADE
China's Foreign Policy (2008–2018)

Series on Contemporary China (ISSN: 1793-0847)

Series Editors: Joseph Fewsmith *(Boston University)*
Zheng Yongnian *(East Asian Institute, National University of Singapore)*

This series will include books on state-of-the-art developments in computational and experimental methods in structures, and as such it will comprise several volumes covering the latest developments. Each volume will consist of single-authored work or several chapters written by the leading researchers in the field. The aim will be to provide the fundamental concepts of experimental and computational methods as well as their relevance to real world problems.

The scope of the series covers the entire spectrum of structures in engineering. As such it will cover both classical topics in mechanics, as well as emerging scientific and engineering disciplines, such as: smart structures, nanoscience and nanotechnology; NEMS and MEMS; micro- and nano-device modelling; functional and smart material systems.

Published*

Vol. 46   *A Critical Decade: China's Foreign Policy (2008–2018)*
by Zhiqun Zhu

Vol. 45   *China's Omnidirectional Peripheral Diplomacy*
edited by Jianwei Wang & Tiang Boon Hoo

Vol. 44   *Reform and Development in China: After 40 Years*
edited by Wei Shan & Lijun Yang

Vol. 43   *The South China Sea Disputes and the U.S.–China Contest International Law and Geopolitics*
by James C Hsiung

Vol. 42   *The South China Sea Disputes: Historical, Geopolitical and Legal Studies*
edited by Tsu-Sung Hsieh

Vol. 41   *Moralization of China*
by Xin Liu

Vol. 40   *Social Construction in Contemporary China*
edited by Xueyi Lu

Vol. 39   *China's Economic Statecraft: Co-optation, Cooperation, and Coercion*
edited by Mingjiang Li

Vol. 38   *The Domestic Dynamics of China's Energy Diplomacy*
by Chi Zhang

*To view the complete list of the published volumes in the series, please visit:
http://www.worldscientific.com/series/scc

Series on Contemporary China – Vol. 46

A CRITICAL DECADE
China's Foreign Policy (2008–2018)

Zhiqun Zhu
Bucknell University, USA

NEW JERSEY • LONDON • SINGAPORE • BEIJING • SHANGHAI • HONG KONG • TAIPEI • CHENNAI • TOKYO

Published by

World Scientific Publishing Co. Pte. Ltd.

5 Toh Tuck Link, Singapore 596224

USA office: 27 Warren Street, Suite 401-402, Hackensack, NJ 07601

UK office: 57 Shelton Street, Covent Garden, London WC2H 9HE

Library of Congress Cataloging-in-Publication Data
Names: Zhu, Zhiqun, author.
Title: A critical decade : China's foreign policy (2008–2018) / by Zhiqun Zhu
　　(Bucknell University, USA).
Description: New Jersey : World Scientific, 2019. | Series: Series on
　　contemporary China ; volume 46 | Includes bibliographical references.
Identifiers: LCCN 2019013761 | ISBN 9789811200779 (hc)
Subjects: LCSH: China--Foreign relations--1976–
Classification: LCC DS779.27 .Z4893 2019 | DDC 327.51009/0512--dc23
LC record available at https://lccn.loc.gov/2019013761

British Library Cataloguing-in-Publication Data
A catalogue record for this book is available from the British Library.

Copyright © 2020 by World Scientific Publishing Co. Pte. Ltd.

All rights reserved. This book, or parts thereof, may not be reproduced in any form or by any means, electronic or mechanical, including photocopying, recording or any information storage and retrieval system now known or to be invented, without written permission from the publisher.

For photocopying of material in this volume, please pay a copying fee through the Copyright Clearance Center, Inc., 222 Rosewood Drive, Danvers, MA 01923, USA. In this case permission to photocopy is not required from the publisher.

For any available supplementary material, please visit
https://www.worldscientific.com/worldscibooks/10.1142/11291#t=suppl

Desk Editors: Aanand Jayaraman/Lixi Dong

Typeset by Stallion Press
Email: enquiries@stallionpress.com

Printed in Singapore

Preface

This book is a preliminary study of Chinese foreign policy during the critical decade of 2008–2018. This decade witnessed China's rapid rise from a regional power to a global power, beginning with the extravagant Summer Olympics in Beijing and ending with fierce economic and strategic rivalry between the United States and China. So many significant and impactful events happened in the world between 2008 and 2018 that this decade is going to be a focus of study by international relations scholars, historians, and others for years to come.

It was during this decade that China's role in global affairs became more prominent, generating both fear and admiration. This original study of China's external affairs during the important decade attempts to highlight some major characteristics of Chinese foreign policy. It is not a typical research monograph with a principal argument or theoretical innovation; rather, it includes my scholarly and policy writings and observations about Chinese foreign policy, taking stock of changing domestic and international environments. A central question that runs throughout the book is what major challenges China faced during the decade and is likely to face in the years ahead. The book does not study Chinese foreign policy comprehensively, but offers a unique and hopefully interesting perspective from a serious student of international relations on some of the key issues and challenges

vi *Preface*

related to Chinese foreign policy. I do not intend to break new ground or propose a novel theory, but the book may serve as a supplement to other rigorous scholarly research on Chinese foreign policy and could be a useful reference for readers who study Chinese politics and foreign policy during the critical decade of 2008–2018.

As an English major at the prestigious Shanghai International Studies University (SISU) in the mid-1980s, I did not plan my future career to be a Professor of International Relations and Political Science. Most SISU graduates in the 1980s were directly recruited by Chinese central and provincial governments, working in fields that required proficiency in foreign languages, such as the Ministry of Foreign Affairs, Ministry of State Security, Ministry of Commerce, Ministry of Education, provincial or municipal offices of foreign affairs, state banks, major state-owned import and export companies, and national media organizations. As a top graduate, I was fortunate to be offered a teaching position at my alma mater when I finished my BA degree in 1988. (Nowadays it is virtually impossible to secure a teaching position at Chinese universities without a PhD or other terminal degrees.) While teaching English reading and grammar, I also served as SISU's secretary for international cooperation from 1988 to 1991, responsible for the University's international exchange programs with universities in English-speaking countries including the United States, the United Kingdom, Canada, Australia, and New Zealand. This was the period during which I developed a strong interest in educational and cultural exchanges between China and other countries. Such "low politics" are often neglected when one looks at state-to-state relations in international politics, yet they are a crucial component of any bilateral relationship. My experience with people-to-people exchanges frequently reminds me of the solid bonds at the societal level between China and Western societies, especially when bilateral relations at the governmental level tend to fluctuate as political atmospheres change.

From 1991 to 1994 I worked at the U.S. Consulate General in Shanghai as the senior assistant to the Public Affairs Officer (Consul for Press and Cultural Affairs). It was during those years that I became immensely interested in Chinese foreign policy and U.S.–China relations. Highlights of my experience at the Consulate included welcoming various U.S. Congressional delegations that were in China to promote bilateral exchanges and hosting President Richard Nixon during his final, private visit to China in April 1993 before he passed away a year later. I vividly remember Nixon's recount to the Consulate staff of his decision to visit China and sign the Shanghai Communiqué in 1972. The Consulate's Public Affairs Section used to be part of the U.S. Information Agency (USIA), which was responsible for "public diplomacy" to promote American culture, values, and policies abroad through the American Centers or libraries. The USIA ceased to exist in 1999 and many of its functions and staff were merged into the U.S. Department of State.

In the early 1990s when I was involved in public affairs at the U.S. Consulate General in Shanghai, the Chinese government knew and did little about "public diplomacy." The pendulum has swung to the other side. Today the Chinese government spends billions of dollars a year in an effort to enhance its international image and shape global opinions of China. China established its first Confucius Institute in Seoul, Korea in 2004 to promote Chinese language, culture and soft power; the number of Confucius Institutes around the world had reached over 500 by the mid-2010s. In addition, major news outlets of China are broadcasting non-stop in major foreign languages or operating directly in different parts of the world to tell "the China story."

I moved to the United States in summer 1994 as a special non-degree graduate student in English at Slippery Rock University in Pennsylvania. I fell in love with this beautiful country and its kind people right away. I did not realize then that I would return to the great Commonwealth and make it my home 14 years later. Spending my first year in rural Pennsylvania gave me a fresh perspective of observing politics and international relations from the grassroots level. While politicians in Washington, DC like to talk about national security, local people care more about jobs. Between 1995 and 2003, I completed my Master's and Doctoral degrees in political science at Indiana State University and the University of South Carolina in Columbia, respectively. I began teaching at the college level in the viii *Preface*

United States in 2001, from the University of South Carolina to Hamilton College and then to the University of Bridgeport.

With an endowed chair professorship, I joined Bucknell University as the MacArthur Chair in East Asian Politics in 2008, returning to Pennsylvania with my family. Bucknell University is an elite liberal arts college about 3 hours away from Philadelphia, New York City and Washington, DC. The University has become more diverse and globally oriented while maintaining its academic and athletic excellence. In the 10 years I've been at Bucknell University, the total number of enrolled Chinese students has exploded from a single digit to well over 150. In contrast, the number of Bucknell students studying in China has remained small, reflecting the national trend in the past decade with most American universities and colleges seeing an exponential increase of Chinese students (from 81,127 in 2007–2008 to 363,341 in 2017–2018), while the number of American students studying in China has stayed flat at around 12,000–13,000 a year.[1] Clearly, much needs to be done to raise Americans' awareness of China's development and influence in the world today, and more importantly, to turn that awareness into action. Though my first book, *US–China Relations in the 21st Century: Power Transition and Peace*, which is based on my doctoral dissertation, was published in 2005, most of my scholarly research and writings were conducted after 2008. It has been an enriching, exciting, and rewarding experience teaching at a top liberal arts college.

The decade from 2008 to 2018 is undoubtedly a critical period in China's contemporary history and its relations with the outside world. It began with China's "coming out" as a great power through hosting the spectacular Beijing Olympics and culminated in Xi Jinping's

---

[1] This is based on the *Open Doors* data published by the Institute of International Education (https://www.iie.org/en/Research-and-Insights/Open-Doors/Data). Chinese students accounted for 33.2 percent of all international students in the United States in 2017–2018. The number of American students studying in China peaked in 2011–2012 with 14,887 and declined to 11,910 in 2016–2017. Every year an additional 2,500 or so American students study in Hong Kong and Taiwan. The number of American students studying in China is roughly about one third of American students studying in the United Kingdom each year.

elevation to be the most powerful leader since Mao Zedong. As China leapfrogged to become the second largest economy and a global power, its leadership and public have become more confident, hence a more active and even assertive foreign policy today. Meanwhile, China faced tremendous internal and external challenges, from declining economic growth to strained relations with major powers, particularly the United States. My writings during the decade — some of which were obviously not fully developed — largely reflect my thinking about the changes and continuities in Chinese foreign policy at the time. Whether one agrees with my views or not, one can learn about some of the major issues and challenges in China's foreign policy during the decade.

The book is divided into three parts, preceded by the Preface and a chronology of major events related to China's foreign relations from 2000 to 2018. Part I contains the introductory chapter about China's foreign policy in a rapidly changing world and an extensive annotated bibliography of recent English and Chinese publications on Chinese foreign policy. Part II is a collection of selected policy commentaries and short scholarly writings of mine between 2008 and 2018 on key issues in Chinese foreign policy, including chapters on U.S.–China relations, the Korean Peninsula, India and Japan, Taiwan, and global and regional cooperation. Most pieces in Part II were originally published by international media outlets and scholarly online journals such as *The Diplomat, e-International Relations, U.S. News & World Report, The Globe and Mail, The National Interest, Policy Forum*, and *The Christian Science Monitor.* They were only slightly modified where necessary to be included in this book. Part III deals with some key challenges in Chinese foreign policy during the critical decade and beyond, including chapters on the Belt and Road Initiative, Chinese investment in the West, and China's soft power deficiency. In lieu of a conclusion, the final chapter addresses problems and challenges in China's efforts to promote soft power abroad and suggests some ways for China to do a better job moving forward.

I greatly appreciate the opportunity provided by the World Scientific Publishing to publish this book. Senior editor Lixi Dong is instrumental in turning a book idea into the final product.

x *Preface*

She strongly encouraged me, a "veteran" author (her word) with the World Scientific Publishing, to publish with them once again. She offered a publishing contract to me even as I was still working on the book and only had the faintest idea of what it would look like. Who can turn down such a wonderful and sincere invitation? I thank Aanand Jayaraman for working tirelessly on the book at the production stage.

I also want to thank the Oxford University Press and *Asian Perspective*/Institute for Far Eastern Studies, Kyungnam University for granting the permissions to use my previously published works for Chapters Two and Nine in this book. The original articles have been revised and updated for the book.

Chinese foreign policy is a complex field of study, with different approaches, theories, analyses, and observations. Each decade or time period also has its unique features in the history of contemporary China. China's foreign relations reach every corner of the globe, covering countries big and small. Since my main interests are East Asia and U.S.–China relations, I do not thoroughly study Chinese foreign policy toward every part of the world; I only briefly touch upon China's relations with Africa, Russia, Western Europe, the Middle East, Latin America, and other regions in this book. The book does not engage in theoretical debate about Chinese foreign policy although Chapters One and Two concisely examine such theoretical explorations by Chinese and non-Chinese scholars in recent years. It is my ambition and hope that this book will contribute to the study of Chinese foreign policy in general and the 2008–2018 decade in particular, with a focus on major issues and challenges facing China during the period and beyond. If readers will gain a better and deeper understanding of Chinese foreign policy and politics after reading the book, I will be extremely and eternally satisfied. Of course, all the errors in the book are mine only.

Zhiqun Zhu
Lewisburg, Pennsylvania
January 2019

About the Author

Zhiqun Zhu is Professor of Political Science and International Relations at Bucknell University, USA. He was Bucknell's inaugural Director of the China Institute (2013–2017) and MacArthur Chair in East Asian politics (2008–2014). In the early 1990s, he was the Senior Assistant to Consul for Press and Cultural Affairs at the American Consulate General in Shanghai. He is currently a member of the National Committee on United States–China Relations.

Dr. Zhu's teaching and research interests include Chinese politics and foreign policy, East Asian political economy, and US–China relations. He has authored and edited over 10 books, including *Understanding East Asia's Economic "Miracles"* (Association for Asian Studies, 2016), *China's New Diplomacy: Rationale, Strategies and Significance* (Ashgate, 2013), *New Dynamics in East Asian Politics: Security, Political Economy, and Society* (Continuum International, 2012), and *US–China Relations in the 21st Century: Power Transition and Peace* (Routledge, 2006).

Contents

Preface		v
About the Author		xi
Chronology: Major Events Related to China's Foreign Relations (2000–2018)		xv
Part I	**Overview**	**1**
Chapter 1	Chinese Foreign Policy in a Rapidly Changing World: An Introduction	3
Chapter 2	Chinese Foreign Policy: A Bibliographical Review	27
Part II	**Selected Essays on Chinese Foreign Policy (2008–2018)**	**71**
Chapter 3	U.S.–China Relations	73
Chapter 4	The Korean Peninsula	105
Chapter 5	China's Relations with India and Japan	137
Chapter 6	The Taiwan Issue	167
Chapter 7	Global and Regional Cooperation	191

xiv Contents

Part III Challenges and Prospects

221

Chapter 8 Geostrategic Challenges of the Belt
and Road Initiative

223

Chapter 9 Going Global 2.0: China's Growing Investment
in the West and Its Impact

247

Chapter 10 Pitfalls in China's Soft Power Promotion

273

Index

291

Chronology: Major Events Related to China's Foreign Relations (2000–2018)

2000
- The first China–Africa Cooperation Forum is held in Beijing.
- U.S. President Bill Clinton grants China permanent normal trade relations status, paving the way for China to join the World Trade Organization (WTO).
- The Vatican canonizes 120 "saints" that were "martyred" in China between 1648 and 1930.
- First inter-Korean summit between South Korean President Kim Dae-jung and North Korean leader Kim Jong-il.
- Kuomintang (KMT) loses power to the pro-independence Democratic Progressive Party (DPP) in Taiwan.

2001
- A U.S. EP-3 reconnaissance plane collides with a Chinese fighter jet near Hainan, creating a crisis in U.S.–China relations.
- China, Russia, Kazakhstan, Kyrgyzstan, Tajikistan, and Uzbekistan form the Shanghai Cooperation Organization (SCO).

xv

xvi *Chronology*

- Terrorist attacks on the United States; China supports U.S. anti-terrorism campaign.
- China becomes a member of the WTO.
- China launches Boao Forum for Asia.

2002
- U.S. President George W. Bush visits China.
- Hu Jintao replaces Jiang Zemin as General Secretary of the Chinese Communist Party (CCP) at the Party's 16th National Congress.

2003
- SARS outbreak in Hong Kong and Guangdong.
- Hu Jintao becomes the President of the PRC.
- The Six-Party Talks over North Korea's nuclear program are launched in Beijing.
- China and the EU form the "Comprehensive Strategic Partnership."

2004
- China signs agreement with Russia settling long-lasting border disputes.
- The first China–Arab Cooperation Forum is held in Cairo.
- At a national meeting on diplomatic work, President Hu Jintao reiterates that China will continue its "independent foreign policy of peaceful development."

2005
- First joint military maneuvers of China and Russia.
- China passes Anti-Secession Law against Taiwan independence.
- Anti-Japanese protests in Chinese cities, sparked by a Japanese textbook which glosses over Japan's World War II record.
- CNOOC, one of China's largest oil and gas producers, fails to buy U.S. oil company Unocal as U.S. lawmakers stage a campaign against the deal on national security grounds.
- Deputy U.S. Secretary of State Robert B. Zoellick calls on China to serve as a "responsible stakeholder" in international affairs.

2006	• CNOOC buys a stake in a Nigerian offshore oil and gas field.
	• China surpasses the United States in carbon dioxide emissions due to fossil fuel use and cement production.
	• China's foreign currency reserves, already the world's biggest, top US$1 trillion.
2007	• Yahoo! is accused of providing information that led to the imprisonment of civil rights activists in China.
	• China unseats Germany as the world's third largest economy.
	• Financial crisis starts in the U.S. and begins to spread globally.
2008	• The Summer Olympic Games are held in Beijing.
	• China surpasses Japan to become the largest foreign holder of U.S. debt at around $600 billion.
	• KMT's Ma Ying-jeou is elected President of the Republic of China (ROC) in Taiwan, retaking power from the DPP.
	• Chinese mainland and Taiwan start direct air and sea transport and postal services for the first time since 1949.
	• China sends naval ships to the Gulf of Aden to join international fight against piracy in the first modern deployment of Chinese warships outside the Pacific.
2009	• The UN Climate Change Conference is held in Copenhagen, with China, the United States and other economies promising to cut greenhouse gas emissions significantly by 2020.
	• Nearly 200 people die and over 1,700 are injured in ethnic violence in Xinjiang.
	• China becomes the world's largest automobile market.
	• New gas pipeline is opened between Turkmenistan and China.

xviii *Chronology*

2010
- China overtakes Japan as the world's second largest economy.
- Diplomatic row with Japan when a Chinese fishing trawler collides with two Japanese Coast Guard patrol boats near the disputed Diaoyu/Senkaku Islands.
- Liu Xiaobo wins Nobel Peace Prize.
- The World Expo is held in Shanghai.

2011
- U.S. Secretary of State Hillary Clinton outlines a U.S. "pivot" to Asia.
- North Korean leader Kim Jong-il dies. His youngest son Kim Jong-un assumes power.
- China unveils new J-20 stealth jet.

2012
- Xi Jinping replaces Hu Jintao as General Secretary of the CCP at the Party's 18th National Congress.
- China's first aircraft carrier *Liaoning* is commissioned into the People's Liberation Army Navy (PLAN).
- Diplomatic crisis with Japan as the Japanese government purchases three islets in Diaoyu/Senkaku areas from a private Japanese citizen, triggering anti-Japanese protests in major Chinese cities.
- China launches the first strategic dialogue with 16 Central and Eastern European countries (16+1 Cooperation).

2013
- Xi Jinping becomes President of the PRC.
- "One Belt, One Road" is proposed by Xi Jinping.
- President Barack Obama hosts Xi Jinping for a "shirt-sleeves summit" at the Sunnylands Estate in California, where Xi defines U.S.–China relations as a "new type of great power relations."
- China declares an Air Defense Identification Zone (ADIZ) in the East China Sea.

2014
- China and Russia sign a $400 billion energy deal for Russia to supply China with 38 billion cubic meters of natural gas annually for 30 years through pipelines.

Chronology xix

- China hosts the Conference on Interaction and Confidence-Building Measures in Asia (CICA) in Shanghai and the Asia-Pacific Economic Cooperation (APEC) summit in Beijing.
- China and the United States issue a joint statement on climate change.
- "Umbrella Revolution" in Hong Kong and "Sunflower Movement" in Taiwan.

2015
- Asian Infrastructure Investment Bank (AIIB) is established.
- The BRICS Development Bank becomes operational.
- *Renminbi* joins the International Monetary Fund (IMF)'s Special Drawing Rights basket of reserve currencies.
- China holds a massive military parade to mark the 70th anniversary of the end of World War II and the war against Japanese invasion.
- Xi Jinping and Ma Ying-jeou meet in Singapore, the first meeting between top leaders from the two sides of the Taiwan Strait since 1949.
- The Paris Agreement on climate change is reached.

2016
- Donald Trump is elected President of the United States.
- China hosts G-20 summit in Hangzhou.
- An international tribunal case on the dispute in the South China Sea, titled *Philippines v. China*, is ruled in favor of the Philippines.
- Tsai Ing-wen from the DPP is elected President of the ROC, replacing the mainland-friendly Ma Ying-jeou from the KMT.

2017
- Xi Jinping is reelected General Secretary of the CCP at the 19th Party Congress.
- "Xi Jinping Thought" is written into the Party Constitution.
- China–India border standoff in Donglang/Doklam.

xx *Chronology*

- Donald Trump hosts Xi Jinping for a 2-day summit in April at the Mar-a-Lago estate in Florida.
- The first Belt and Road Forum is held in Beijing.
- China's first military base overseas opens in Djibouti.
- President Donald Trump visits China in November.

2018
- The National People's Congress (NPC) removes a two-term limit on the presidency from the Chinese Constitution, allowing Xi Jinping to remain in office for longer than the conventional decade for Chinese leaders since Mao Zedong.
- Donald Trump and Kim Jong-un meet in Singapore.
- Kim Jong-un visits China three times.
- The Trump administration announces sweeping tariffs on Chinese imports. Trump and Xi meet in Buenos Aires in December during the G20 Summit to reach a temporary truce on the trade war.
- President Trump signs "Taiwan Travel Act," "Reciprocal Access to Tibet Act," and "Asia Reassurance Initiative Act" into law.
- Chinese Premier Li Keqiang and Japanese Prime Minister Shinzo Abe exchange visits, improving the strained Japan–China relationship.
- China's first Import Expo is held in Shanghai.

Part I
Overview

Chapter

1

Chinese Foreign Policy in a Rapidly Changing World: An Introduction

The decade from 2008 to 2018 is a significant period in contemporary Chinese history and politics. It was during this critical decade that China emerged as a major economic, diplomatic, and military power in the world. China's rise is fundamentally shaping the 21st century world history.

In 2008, Beijing successfully hosted the Summer Olympics, with splendid opening and closing ceremonies. Dubbed the "coming out party" for China, the Olympics greatly boosted national pride at home and prestige abroad. By then the People's Republic of China (PRC) had become a major player in international political economy. In 2010, it replaced Japan as the second largest economy and was projected to catch up with the United States within a decade or two. During the critical decade of 2008–2018, President Xi Jinping proposed "One Belt One Road" (一带一路) or the Belt and

4   *A Critical Decade: China's Foreign Policy (2008–2018)*

Road Initiative (BRI), the "Chinese Dream" (中国梦), and "a community with a shared future for mankind" (人类命运共同体), which would all have long-term impacts for China and the rest of the world. China also made progress toward achieving the "Two Centenary Goals" (两个一百年奋斗目标) — to finish building a moderately prosperous society by the time the Chinese Communist Party (CCP) celebrates its centenary in 2021, and to turn China into a modern socialist country that is prosperous, strong, democratic, culturally advanced, and harmonious by the time the PRC celebrates its centenary in 2049. China is not a sleeping giant anymore; it has risen. Though it faces tremendous domestic challenges such as a widening income gap, a deteriorating environment, and growing public discontent, China continues to impress the world by making one achievement after another, which has added much confidence to policymakers in Beijing while causing concerns in other capitals. Undoubtedly, Chinese politics and foreign policy will have significant influence on international politics, economics, and security in the decades ahead.

Chinese foreign policy has been undergoing major transformations since the beginning of the 21st century. The emergence of Xi Jinping as a strong leader brought about many changes in Chinese politics and foreign policy. Deng Xiaoping's dictum *Tao Guang Yang Hui* (韬光养晦, roughly translated as "keeping a low profile") seems to be a thing of the past, giving way to *You Suo Zuo Wei* (有所作为, roughly "getting some things done"). Xi became General Secretary of the CCP at the 18th Party Congress in fall 2012 and President of the PRC in spring 2013. He consolidated power at the 19th Party Congress in fall 2017, adding the Xi Jinping Thought into the CCP Constitution. In March 2018, the Chinese Constitution was amended at the annual National People's Congress (NPC) meeting, removing the two-term limit for presidency which was introduced during the Deng era and followed by Xi's predecessors Jiang Zemin and Hu Jintao. Meanwhile, Chinese foreign policy has become more active and assertive. On issues regarding China's sovereignty, such as the South China Sea and Taiwan, China's policies have become more forceful. China remains adamant and uncompromising on such issues related to its "core interests."[1]

China is more involved in global governance now. It first proposed the establishment of the Asian Infrastructure Investment Bank (AIIB) in 2013. In 2015, the AIIB went operational with headquarters in Beijing and has provided valuable support for development projects in many Asian countries since then. The AIIB has quickly emerged as a dynamic international financial institution with members from countries in every continent. Even Japan and the United States, which initially did not support the new bank, have been working with China and other members of the bank. Also in 2015, China cooperated with other BRICS nations and established the BRICS Development Bank with headquarters in Shanghai, which promotes further financial and economic cooperation among the five major emerging economies.

China's most ambitious foreign policy project during the decade is undoubtedly the BRI. First unveiled by Xi Jinping in 2013, the BRI has become one of the largest infrastructure and investment megaprojects in human history, covering over 70 countries, equivalent to 65 percent of the world's population and 40 percent of the global GDP as of 2018. The BRI consists of the land-based Silk Road Economic Belt and the ocean-going 21st century Maritime Silk Road (丝绸之路经济带和 21 世纪海上丝绸之路) and aims to enhance connectivity and cooperation among countries along the routes, particularly Eurasian and African countries. Countries in faraway places such as Latin America, the Caribbean, and South Pacific have also been included in this massive development plan. The Chinese government asserts that the BRI idea may have come from China, but the dividends of cooperation are for all participating countries to share.

---

[1] According to the White Paper "China's Peaceful Development 2011," China's core interests include: (1) state sovereignty; (2) national security; (3) territorial integrity; (4) national reunification; (5) China's political system established by the Constitution and overall social stability; (6) basic safeguards for ensuring sustainable economic and social development.

6 A Critical Decade: China's Foreign Policy (2008–2018)

China continues to play a leadership role in the Shanghai Cooperation Organization (SCO), which is a major multilateral organization on Eurasian political, economic and security affairs and which expanded in 2017 to include India and Pakistan. In big power diplomacy, China has proposed "a new type of great power relations" (新型大国关系), particularly with the United States, but also with Russia, the EU, Japan, and India, in an attempt to promote cooperation and friendly competition and avoid conflict associated with the global power transition, or the so-called "Thucydides' Trap."[2]

Despite China's enhanced power and growing influence globally, China faces some daunting challenges in its foreign policy. When China was weak, no one seemed to see it as a threat since it caused no discomfort among its smaller neighbors, let alone a superpower like the United States or an industrial power like Japan. But as an economic and military giant now, China has stoked anxieties among rivals and neighbors. As a result, its relations with the United States, Japan, India, Vietnam, Australia, and several other countries have all become more difficult and even deteriorated in recent years.

On balance, China's bilateral relations with most countries are largely positive, but in its neighborhood, the PRC continues to be frustrated by disputes in the South China Sea and East China Sea and developments on the Korean Peninsula.[3] In cross-Taiwan Strait relations, Beijing remains disappointed at no major breakthroughs despite its charm offensives and preferential economic policies toward Taiwan. The United States is unlikely to give up the Taiwan card any time soon, which is evidenced by the unanimous passage of the

---

[2] The term "Thucydides' Trap" was popularized by Harvard Professor Graham Allison in his book *Destined for War: Can America and China Escape Thucydides's Trap?* (Houghton Mifflin Harcourt, 2017). However, international relations scholars especially those working on the power transition theory have presented the same concept long ago. For an analysis of how the power transition theory can be applied to US–China relations, see for example, Zhu (2006) and Chan (2007), For the original power transition theory, see Organski (1968).

[3] Tensions on the Korean Peninsula were lowered to some extent as a result of inter-Korean reconciliation and the Trump–Kim summit in Singapore in 2018, however, the future of the Korean Peninsula remains uncertain.

Chinese Foreign Policy in a Rapidly Changing World: An Introduction   7

"Taiwan Travel Act" by both houses of U.S. Congress in 2017 and 2018, respectively. The Act was signed into law by President Donald Trump in March 2018. At the end of 2018, Trump signed another pro-Taiwan bill, the Asia Reassurance Initiative Act, into law. With a pro-independence party in power in Taiwan that refuses to abide by the so-called "1992 Consensus," whereby both sides agree there is one China, but the exact meaning of one China is open to interpretation, cross-Taiwan Strait relations are unlikely to improve in the short term.[4]

India and China had a 70 plus day military standoff in the Doklam/Donglang area in the summer of 2017 before tensions were finally defused through diplomacy. Today India remains concerned about the BRI, especially the China–Pakistan Economic Corridor (CPEC) that passes through the controversial Kashmir region. Despite moderate improvement in Japan–China relations by the end of 2018 with Prime Minister Shinzo Abe's official visit to Beijing after a long hiatus of top-level exchanges, Japan has been uncomfortable about China's continued rise and has worked with India to propose an Asia–Africa Growth Corridor (AAGC) partially in response to China's BRI.[5] The United States, Japan, India, and Australia have formed the so-called "Quad" to promote security cooperation in the Indo-Pacific region. Though ostensibly not an anti-China club, many believe the Quad is shaping up to provide an alternate narrative to the China-centered development in the region.

Notably, China's international image remains mixed and even poor in some parts of the world. Various global opinion polls conducted by Pew and others suggest that in general China enjoys favorable views in many parts of the developing world but more negative views in the West. As far as the South China Sea controversy is

---

[4] For a brief overview of the "1992 Consensus" and why Taiwan should accept it in order to improve cross-Strait relations, see Hickey and Huang (2018).

[5] During Prime Minister Abe's visit in October 2018, China and Japan vowed to raise the relationship to a new level. Japan pledged to actively participate in the BRI, especially in developing infrastructure in third countries. This is encouraging, but due to historical and structural conflicts, Japan–China relations remain delicate.

concerned, China is perceived to be violating international law and bullying small countries in its neighborhood, and no country has stepped forward to defend China's position. In Africa and Latin America, China is often criticized for not helping promote governance, environment or human rights while focusing on trade and investment and extracting resources. In fact, the term "neocolonialism" is sometimes used to describe China's exploitative practices in Africa, Latin America, and elsewhere. Upon closer examinations, not all such charges against China hold water, but China does need to work harder and do a better public relations job in presenting its preferred image of an open, peaceful, caring and responsible global power. With a deficit in soft power, there will be a limit to what China can achieve in its foreign policy.

Internal and External Factors

The international security environment remains fragile and unpredictable even as China continues to benefit from the current international system. Meanwhile, China's domestic politics has become more complicated with multiple players vying for influence and with the reemergence of a strong leader. China's decision-making process remains opaque, but changing international and domestic conditions will continue to shape China's foreign policy. The Chinese government has to maintain a balanced foreign policy without succumbing to growing domestic pressures that demand tougher Chinese actions in international affairs. These external and internal factors will produce a dynamic, and sometimes inconsistent and contradictory, foreign policy in Beijing.

Pessimists tend to view China through the realist lens, while optimists often from a liberal perspective. China's foreign policy since the end of the Cold War has received diverse reactions. On one hand, many countries welcome China's growth and benefit from trading with its robust economy. China's efforts to help combat poverty in developing countries have been appreciated by these governments. Its commitment to a peaceful international environment has also contributed to global development. In many regional and global affairs such

Chinese Foreign Policy in a Rapidly Changing World: An Introduction 9

as North Korea and climate change, China has played a positive and responsible role. On the other hand, China's relations with the West and some of its neighbors remain delicate and even strained. Its practice in Africa and Latin America of focusing on expanding trade and snatching energy and commodity resources while paying little attention to other development issues has raised many eyebrows. Its human rights record, tight control in ethnic minority regions particularly Tibet and Xinjiang, and lack of transparency in military modernization continue to be sources of frictions in China's external relations.

Uncertain about China's long-term intentions, many of its neighbors have adopted a "hedging" strategy or a balanced approach. They remain engaged with China economically and diplomatically, but at the same time they reach out to the United States for security reassurance. For example, worried about big power rivalry in Asia, Southeast Asian nations have taken such a dual-track policy and have become some of the strongest advocates of strong relations with both the United States and China since they do not want to take sides between the two powers (Lemon, 2018). These countries also urge the two powers to maintain friendly ties and resolve differences peacefully.

Aspiring to be a global power, China seems aware of the need to balance its national interests and its increasing global responsibilities. Its foreign policy is not radical or ideological but more pragmatic, calculated, and sophisticated now. It is still in transition and will keep adjusting to the changing international and domestic conditions while upholding long-standing principles.

As the second largest economy, China is expected by the international community to play more leadership roles in world affairs, yet despite its expanding global reach, China considers itself a developing nation and does not want to shoulder too many responsibilities. China may be doing what it thinks is right to defend its national interests, but some of its behaviors are regarded assertive and even aggressive by other countries. These two contradictions will continue to characterize China's relations with other countries. A variety of external and internal factors will make conducting Chinese foreign policy more complicated in the years ahead.

Key External Factors

It appears that Deng Xiaoping's cautious "*Tao Guang Yang Hui*" policy no longer dominated China's strategic thinking in the 2010s. There have been calls, especially from the People's Liberation Army (PLA) and some nationalistic scholars, that China should and can play a bigger role in international affairs and be tougher in dealing with disputed issues. Increasingly, Chinese leaders were talking confidently about the "rejuvenation of the Chinese nation" by the mid-21st century.

China's rapid rise since the 1990s has triggered some concerns about how it is going to use its power. As a response to the growing "China threat" sentiment in some parts of the world, the Chinese government under Hu Jintao's leadership (2002–2012) proposed policies of "peaceful development" (*heping fazhan* 和平发展) and "harmonious world" (*hexie shijie* 和谐世界) to ease anxieties about China's global expansion of trade and influence. However, with the change of leadership in *Zhongnanhai* (中南海 the headquarters for the CCP) in 2012, such policies have been deemphasized somewhat, and external concerns about China's rise have grown.

Conflicts, wars, and revolutions in different parts of the world pose serious challenges to China as it tries to maintain a peaceful environment for continued domestic growth. Security challenges in Asia directly affect China's foreign policy outlook. East Asia is one of the most economically dynamic regions, yet it is also home to some of the world's potentially most dangerous hotspots — the Korean Peninsula, the Taiwan Strait, and the South China Sea. China has been directly involved in all these cases since the very beginning, and any conflict in East Asia will affect China's security and stability. In addition, China has unresolved territorial disputes with Japan, India, and several Southeast Asian nations. In 2016, almost 80 percent of China's oil imports passed through the South China Sea via the Strait of Malacca and nearly 40 percent of its total trade transited through the South China Sea,[6] yet China does not have a strong blue-water navy

---

[6] "How Much Trade Transits the South China Sea?" China Power Project, CSIS, Washington, DC, undated report. https://chinapower.csis.org/much-trade-transits-south-china-sea/. Accessed on November 15, 2018.

Chinese Foreign Policy in a Rapidly Changing World: An Introduction   11

to protect its energy transportation and overseas interests. This "Malacca dilemma" will continue to frustrate China in the near future. While China has improved relations with its Asian neighbors, its security environment is far from satisfactory.

As globalization widens and deepens, China has begun to embrace multilateralism, which it shunned in the past. Over the past 40 years, China has transformed itself from a "taker" of the norms and rules in the international system to a combination of both a "taker" and a "maker" of these norms and rules. In 2001, it became a WTO member after some 15 years of tough negotiations. China has been an active member since, both following the existing trade rules and helping make new ones as part of WTO reforms. China is a founding member of the SCO and has worked with Russia and several Central Asian nations to cooperate on economic, trade, and security issues in the region. China has been a strong advocate of peaceful conflict resolution and opposes the use of force in international affairs. It played a leadership role in convening the Six Party Talks in an attempt to resolve the North Korea nuclear issue peacefully in the 2000s.

While the "Five Principles of Peaceful Coexistence" remain guiding principles of Chinese foreign policy, over the years China's policies have been adapted to changing international conditions and its own capabilities.[7] In the past when China was weak, it opposed international intervention in a country's internal affairs as China itself was often the target of such intervention. Today as a major power in the world, it faces increasing pressure and demand for defending justice in international affairs and protecting its own interests overseas. China has been "free-riding" for long; now it is prepared to provide international public goods. For example, China has long been accused of ignoring genocide in Sudan. In response, China appointed a special envoy to Sudan in May 2007, helping to mediate between rebels in

---

[7] First agreed upon between India and China in 1954 to handle Sino-Indian relations, these five principles have guided Chinese foreign policy since. The Five Principles are: mutual respect for each other's territorial integrity and sovereignty, mutual non-aggression, mutual non-interference in each other's internal affairs, equality and cooperation for mutual benefit, and peaceful coexistence.

12 *A Critical Decade: China's Foreign Policy (2008–2018)*

Darfur and the Sudanese government. China has also appointed special envoys to the Middle East and Southeast Asia. By doing so, has China interfered in other countries' internal affairs? When China hosted the Six-Party Talks, was China interfering in North Korea's internal affairs? These are interesting policy questions to ask as we study changes and continuities in Chinese foreign policy.

China is still clumsy in public relations. Its reaction to Liu Xiaobo's winning of the 2010 Nobel Peace Prize is quite telling of China's poor public relations campaign. The Chinese government condemned the Nobel Committee and the Norwegian government for the award and exerted pressure on a dozen plus countries so that they would stay away from the award ceremony in Oslo. All this backfired and deeply hurt China's reputation. The empty chair reserved for Liu at the award ceremony served as a powerful reminder that the international community was disapproving of China's human rights record and its high-handed diplomatic approach.

China does not have much "power of discourse" or "pouvoir du discours" (话语权). Take the BRI as an example. This massive project will undoubtedly benefit China the most economically and diplomatically, but it will also obviously help many developing countries enormously in their development. It is a true opportunity for win–win cooperation in international political economy. However, Western media and governments have largely portrayed it in a negative light and focused on potential debt crisis in some developing countries and unsubstantiated assumption about China's ambition to replace the United States as the global hegemon. The Chinese responses so far have been weak and ineffective.

Among all external factors, the United States obviously remains the most important for China. The U.S. presence in Asia has a direct bearing on China's foreign policy. Since the end of the Cold War, the lone superpower and the emerging global power have developed a highly interdependent relationship. However, with the disintegration of their common enemy — the Soviet Union, the two countries have been struggling to find new common ground and they remain suspicious of each other strategically today. From anti-terrorism to climate change, and from trade to Asian security, none of the new shared

Chinese Foreign Policy in a Rapidly Changing World: An Introduction 13

interests have been strong enough to serve as the cornerstone of the relationship in the 21st century. Though China has expressed no intention to exclude the United States from Asia, it is concerned about renewed U.S. commitments in Asia. For example, the United States has reached out to countries including India and Vietnam, both of which feel uncomfortable living in the shadow of a giant neighbor. The publicly denied but widely understood rationale is that the United States wants to work with China's neighbors as a check on China's rise. This is reflected in the much touted new concept "Indo-Pacific," which has replaced "Asia Pacific" as a preferred term by the U.S. government and which clearly reveals America's intention to boost India's status *vis-à-vis* China.[8] The United States has also beefed up its alliance with Japan, South Korea, and Australia at the same time when its relations with China are experiencing some difficulties.

The United States has accentuated competition with the PRC while upgrading relations with Taiwan since Donald Trump was elected president in November 2016. In December 2017 and January 2018, the U.S. government published two documents regarding America's overall security stance toward the world: the National Security Strategy (NSS) and the Summary of the National Defense Strategy (NDS), respectively. Both documents mention China numerous times and portray China as a revisionist power and a strategic competitor that seeks to shape a world antithetical to American values and interests. In a public speech at the Hudson Institute in Washington, DC on October 4, 2018, Vice President Mike Pence blasted China for undermining U.S. interests, accusing China of meddling in America's democracy, stealing American technology, cracking down on religious freedom at home, and expanding global influence through "debt diplomacy."[9] Whereas President Bill Clinton

---

[8] For a discussion of "Indo-Pacific," see Zhu (2017). The article is also included in this book.

[9] Pence's speech transcript can be found on the White House website here at: https://www.whitehouse.gov/briefings-statements/remarks-vice-president-pence-administrations-policy-toward-china/.

14   *A Critical Decade: China's Foreign Policy (2008–2018)*

championed Beijing as a partner and President Barack Obama accepted China as a competitor, the Trump administration has publicly identified China a national security threat. The Trump administration is particularly sensitive to "Made in China 2025," which was unveiled by China's State Council in 2015 to transform China from a big manufacturing country to a powerful one in a decade. The United States considers this industrial plan a direct challenge to its technological leadership.

The 2018 "Taiwan Travel Act" allows U.S. officials "at all levels" to travel to Taiwan to meet with their Taiwanese counterparts and allows high-level Taiwanese officials to enter the United States and meet with U.S. officials. Meanwhile, the American Institute in Taiwan (AIT), the *de facto* U.S. embassy in Taiwan, completed its 14,934 square meter and $255.6 million new office building in Taipei in June 2018.[10] Many people realize that the U.S.–Taiwan relationship is perhaps officially "unofficial," but unofficially official. In Beijing's view, the United States has not abandoned its Cold War-style containment policy toward China and will continue to use Taiwan as a check on the PRC.

U.S.–China relations have always been marked by both cooperation and competition. Since President Richard Nixon's visit to China in 1972, the two countries have tried to expand areas of cooperation while controlling and managing areas of differences. As the Chines power continues to grow and as China becomes more assertive in foreign affairs such as island-building in the South China Sea, the United States has become increasingly frustrated. Many Americans have become disillusioned that after so many years of engagement and cooperation with China, the interests of the two countries remain divergent, and as a rising power, China, either intentionally or unintentionally, is challenging key U.S. interests from open market and fair trade to human rights and cybersecurity. Taken together, such concerns have fueled a new consensus in Washington that China is

---

[10] "AIT Dedicates New Office Complex in Taipei," *AIT News and Events*, June 12, 2018, from the AIT website at: https://www.ait.org.tw/ait-dedicates-new-office-complex-in-taipei/.

Chinese Foreign Policy in a Rapidly Changing World: An Introduction 15

not just a strategic competitor but very possibly America's major long-term adversary. Even long-time advocates of strong U.S.–China relations such as Henry Kissinger and Henry Paulson have become more pessimistic. At a speech in Singapore in November 2018, Paulson remarked that unless the United States and China seriously address the broad and deep issues that separate them, they will be in for "a long winter" in the relationship.[11] In the same speech, Paulson was critical of China's current direction. Seventeen years after joining the WTO, he said, China still "has not opened its economy to foreign competition in so many areas," using joint-venture requirements, ownership limits, technical standards, subsidies, licensing procedures and regulation to block foreign competition. "This is simply unacceptable." Apparently China's latest developments have even alienated moderates and some of its friends in the United States.

To a large extent, the trade war President Trump launched against China in 2018 reflects the U.S. frustration about China's rise and its challenge to U.S. dominance in the world. The growing rivalry between the United States and China is also an indication that neither of them is fully prepared for a new world in which China has evolved into a great power that does not necessarily share the same interests and values with the West. The bilateral relationship under the administrations of Donald Trump and Xi Jinping has become more conflictual in many ways, and the underlying structural problems and tensions between the two countries are unlikely to disappear any time soon.

Key Internal Factors

Contrary to the common perception that the Chinese state is monolithically controlled by the CCP, China has become an increasingly diverse and dynamic society, in which many players are competing for influence in national politics. While the Standing Committee of the CCP's Politburo still has the final say in Chinese politics and foreign policy decisions are made by the Leading Small Group on foreign

---

[11] Remarks by Henry M. Paulson, Jr., on the United States and China at a Crossroads, The Bloomberg New Economy Forum, Singapore, November 7, 2018.

16 *A Critical Decade: China's Foreign Policy (2008–2018)*

affairs, a growing number of players — from high ranking government officials and military officers to scholars, researchers, businesspeople, media, large state companies, and Internet users — are increasingly involved in China's policy discussions.

Various government departments and offices compete for power and influence in foreign affairs. The Foreign Ministry is now perceived as just one of the government agencies, and not necessarily a very powerful one, while other key government agencies such as the CCP Central Committee's International Department, the People's Bank of China, and the Ministry of Commerce are also active in dealing with political, financial, and economic relations with other countries. The CCP's Policy Research Office, the National Development and Reform Commission, and the PLA are some of the other powerful official actors vying to influence top leadership's decisions (Jakobson and Knox, 2010). The players that help ensure China's domestic stability, such as the PLA, People's Armed Police and Ministry of Public Security, often speak with a stronger voice in policy debate. The successful hosting of the 2008 Beijing Olympics and the 2010 Shanghai World Expo, as well as the need to maintain control in ethnic minority regions, particularly Xinjiang and Tibet, have led to more funds and prestige to these more hardline actors.

The PLA has always been a major force in Chinese politics. In fact, the PLA, together with the CCP and the state bureaucracy, is part of the powerful tripod of Chinese state apparatus. Mao Zedong cautioned that the Party must always control the gun. However, it does not mean the PLA will not attempt to influence the Party's decision-making. On issues regarding territory and national security, PLA generals tend to be more outspoken and hawkish than civilian leaders. In recent years, a few retired PLA generals such as Wang Hongguang and Luo Yuan have become very vocal and often appear in national media to comment on current affairs and discuss China's strategies and policy options.

China's foreign policy-related think tanks are also active in policy debate. The Chinese Academy of Social Sciences, China Institute of Strategy and Management, China Center for International Economic Exchanges, Institute for Strategic Studies of National Defense

University, China Institute of International Studies, Shanghai Institute of International Studies, Center for China and Globalization, and Pangoal Institution are just some of such prominent think tanks. In addition, scholars at foreign policy and international affairs research centers at major universities are already actively involved in policy debate. Other actors that influence China's foreign policy include state-owned enterprises which have become part of China's "*zou chu qu*" (走出去 going out) strategy by investing and purchasing abroad, state financial institutions such as the China Development Bank, large energy companies such as the China National Petroleum Corporation (CNPC) and the China National Offshore Oil Corporation (CNOOC), and local regions with booming economies or strategically important locations.[12]

On one hand, it is healthy to have diverse views on foreign affairs. China's foreign policies have become more calculated today, taking into account various options. On the other hand, these different views may complicate the policymaking process and send mixed messages to the outside world. The debate over what China can do with its growing power is a case in point. Some Chinese scholars take a neoliberal approach, advocating further integration with the world and more cooperation with the West, while others prefer a neorealist policy of aggressively defending China's national interests, especially in its trade or territorial disputes with other countries.

Public interest in world affairs is always high in China. As a joke goes, any taxi driver in Beijing could be a sharp current affairs analyst. The Chinese netizen population had reached over 800 million by the end of 2010s, creating the largest pool of online discussions and opinions. Chinese officials reportedly often surf the Internet to get a feeling of the public's sentiments and concerns. They need to carefully manage growing nationalism as a result of China's patriotic education in the 1990s and its remarkable economic performance in the past 40 years. While Chinese handling of disputed territories with Japan, India and in the South China Sea may be viewed as "assertive" or

---

[12] For an examination of how local governments affect China's foreign policymaking, see Hao and Lin (2006).

18 A Critical Decade: China's Foreign Policy (2008–2018)

even "aggressive" by foreign media and observers, Chinese netizens tend to blame Chinese leaders for not being tough enough to stand up against foreign governments. This perception gap highlights a dilemma Chinese leaders face in making foreign policy decisions.

Sometimes Chinese policy may be hijacked by the public opinion. Anger over perceived affronts to China's national honor or encroachment on vital Chinese interests often quickly turns to criticism of the Chinese government's failure to defend the country's interests. For instance, in September 2010, when a Chinese fishing boat collided with Japanese patrol boats in the disputed Diaoyu/Senkaku area, the Chinese public got extremely agitated and nationalistic, which made the government's calm handling of the case very difficult. Partially under heavy pressure from the Chinese public, the Chinese government took a strong approach to Japan, who was forced to release the Chinese fishing boat captain without formal charges. China also briefly imposed a ban on shipments to Japan of rare-earth metals that are crucial for Japan's economy. Although Chinese netizens might think that China won, China's relations with Japan and its efforts to become a peacefully rising power suffered since the international media sympathized with Japan and considered Chinese behavior to be overbearing.[13]

In the future, China will have to maintain a balanced foreign policy without succumbing to public pressures at home. As Asia-Pacific security expert Denny Roy comments, the greatest single foreign policy challenge for the Chinese government is to balance two objectives that easily clash: to build a reputation as a responsible, principled great power that will be a force for peace rather than a regional bully, and to satisfy demands from the Chinese public and some Chinese elites that China begin to act like a powerful country and stand up more strongly for what they see as China's interests (Roy, 2010).

---

[13] See, for example, a *Washington Post* report of the incident, "Japan to Release Chinese Boat Captain," September 24, 2010, and a *BBC* report "Boat Collisions Spark Japan–China Diplomatic Row," September 8, 2010.

Chinese Foreign Policy in a Rapidly Changing World: An Introduction 19

It must be pointed out that under President Xi Jinping's forceful leadership, decision-making in China seemed to be more centralized once again after the 18th Party Congress in 2012. Xi is an assertive and ambitious leader with a strong sense of historical mission. He introduced some new concepts in China's foreign policy such as "a new type of great power relations" and "a community with a shared future for mankind." He ushered in a "new era" in China. If Mao made China independent (*zhan qi lai*), and Deng made it prosperous (*fu qi lai*), Xi will make it powerful (*qiang qi lai*). Chinese domestic and foreign policies experienced some significant transformations since Xi took power. While Deng loosened the Party's control on China's economy and society, Xi has resumed and strengthened the Party's dominance and leadership over all tasks. On May 15, 2018 at the first meeting of the newly established Central Foreign Affairs Committee, Xi emphasized the central leadership role of the Party in China's foreign affairs. At the Central Conference on Work Relating to Foreign Affairs on June 22, 2018, Xi reminded Chinese diplomats that they were first and foremost "Party cadres."

At the National Security Forum on February 17, 2017, Xi suggested that China should "guide the international community to jointly shape a fairer and more just new international order" and "guide the international community to jointly maintain international security." The "two guides" (两个引导) were clearest indication that Xi was no longer content with Deng Xiaoping's "*Tao Guang Yang Hui*" policy and intended to push China to the center stage of international affairs. "What we are seeing is the slow, steady emergence of a more integrated Chinese worldview which links China's domestic vision with its international vision — and a vision which very much reflects the deep views of China's paramount leader Xi Jinping."[14] As veteran journalist Cary Huang observed, "No Chinese leader, ancient or contemporary, has been as active as Xi in diplomacy (Huang, 2018)." No Chinese leader has done more globetrotting within such a short time: in his first 5-year term, Xi went on 28 overseas trips that

---

[14] Kevin Rudd on Xi Jinping, China and the Global Order, Speech at the Lee Kuan Yew School of Public Policy, National University of Singapore, June 26, 2018.

20 A Critical Decade: China's Foreign Policy (2008–2018)

took him to 56 countries across five continents. During his first term, Xi also hosted five major world summits. Chinese foreign policy will continue to be constrained by changing domestic and international conditions. The role of key internal and external factors, particularly that of President Xi, must he underscored in understanding China's foreign policy since 2012.

New Thinking on Chinese Foreign Policy

"The world thought it could change China, and in many ways it has. But China's success has been so spectacular that it has just as often changed the world — and the American understanding of how the world works," remarks *The New York Times*' Asia Editor Philip P. Pan (2018). China is widely seen as a major power today that is heavily involved in global affairs. As veteran China scholar David Shambaugh points out, Xi Jinping has taken a personal interest in global governance. Consequently, China is contributing much more to the United Nations operating budget, global peacekeeping, overseas development assistance and the Millennium Development Goals, and it is more active in a range of areas, from combating public health pandemics to disaster relief, energy and sea lane security, counterterrorism, and anti-piracy operations. While the BRI is encountering criticism of late, it is nonetheless illustrative of China's new foreign policy activism under Xi (Shambaugh, 2018).

China's expanded interests and enhanced capabilities call for new policies at home and added responsibilities abroad. New thinking is required for understanding the transformations in Chinese politics and foreign policy. International relations and foreign policy studies have long been dominated and shaped by Western scholars and Western theories. Among major international relations theories, realism and its variants still dominate international politics today with emphasis on conflict of national interests. The Chinese, however, believe countries with differences can live harmoniously (和而不同). In recent years, some scholars in China have been attempting to develop a "Chinese school of thought" in international relations. Qin Yaqing, a leading scholar at the China Foreign Affairs University in

Chinese Foreign Policy in a Rapidly Changing World: An Introduction 21

Beijing, defines "China's central question" as "how to peacefully integrate into international society" (Qin, 2005). According to Qin, a Chinese international relations theory is likely and even inevitable to emerge along with the great economic and social transformations that China has been experiencing. The *Tianxia* (天下) worldview and Tributary System in the two millennia of China's history, the radical thinking and revolutions in the 19th and 20th centuries, and the reform and opening-up since 1978 are the three milestones of China's ideational and practical development and therefore could provide rich fodder for a Chinese international relations theory (Qin, 2007). Other Chinese scholars such as Zhao Tingyang, Ren Xiao, Yan Xuetong, Wang Yizhou, Tang Shiping, Yu Xiaofeng, and Guo Shuyong have also attempted to propose innovative Chinese perspectives of the world and international politics.[15] Daniel A. Bell, Dean of the School of Political Science and Public Administration at Shandong University and professor at Tsinghua University (Schwarzman College and Department of Philosophy), suggests that China should promote Confucianism in its interactions with the outside world, especially meritocracy and a harmonious world view (Bell, 2010). In international political economy, it appears that the Chinese model of state-guided capitalism plus political meritocracy has some appeal, but whether it is sustainable is highly debatable.

Managing the complex U.S.–China relationship remains a most challenging diplomatic undertaking for both China and the United States. Many scholars have applied Western international relations theories, including variants of the power transition theory such as the "Thucydides' Trap," to analyze U.S.–China relations. Wang Jisi, a top U.S.–China relations scholar at Beijing University, proposes the "two orders" concept to examine the inherent U.S.–China conflict. He argues that Chinese leaders are most concerned with keeping the U.S. from upsetting their country's internal order under the Communist

---

[15] For example, Zhao (2005); Ren (2000); Yu (2014); and Guo (2005). For a general survey of developing a Chinese theory of international relations, see, for example, Noesselt (2015) and Feng *et al.* (2019). Also see "Theories of Chinese Foreign Policy" in Chapter Two of this book.

22 A Critical Decade: China's Foreign Policy (2008–2018)

Party leadership. The U.S., however, sees the relationship mainly in terms of the challenge that China poses to the international order, which the U.S. has been leading. This contradiction between the "two orders" or "two supremacies" lies at the heart of the fraught relationship between the two nations (Wang, 2015). It's essential that the two countries respect each other's key concerns and avoid actions that will trigger strong reactions. New perspectives such as Wang's are very helpful to understand Chinese foreign policy and U.S.–China relations.

More than 40 years after China rebuilt its social sciences at the conclusion of the Cultural Revolution, Chinese scholars in international relations are sophisticated enough to propose unique Chinese perspectives on international relations. The study of Chinese foreign policy must and can be raised to a higher level, with a more vigorous theoretical development. As Chinese society becomes more diverse, new actors will be shaping Chinese politics and foreign policy. China will continue to adapt to rapidly changing international and domestic environments. The real challenge is creating a parsimonious model to account for an ever-evolving policy.

One basic tenet of Chinese foreign policy remains unchanged as China continues to commit to the "Five Principles of Peaceful Coexistence" and insists on a narrative of "peaceful rise," no matter how the West and China's neighbors feel about its ascendancy. Amid concerns about growing Chinese power, the Chinese government has painstakingly reiterated that China is still a large developing country, and China's development benefits the rest of the world. Since China's "Reform and Opening up" started in the late 1970s, the twin themes of peace and development have guided Chinese domestic and foreign policies. In Deng Xiaoping's words: Development is the absolute principle (发展才是硬道理). Western experiences have yielded the so-called liberal or democratic peace model. The Chinese do not necessarily reject the Western model, but are becoming increasingly confident that China's "developmental peace" or "development for stability" model is a viable alternative for developing countries.

It is important for China to have a clear sense of self-identity: Is China a large developing nation or already a global superpower?

Is China punching above its weight by ditching "*Tao Guang Yang Hui*" too early? Is China suffering from imperial overstretch? Through various initiatives and programs, China is attempting to create a new identity as a peaceful, inclusive, caring and responsible great power whose development contributes to the international community as a whole. How can China successfully form, consolidate and project such an identity? Will it be accepted by the international community? In this regard, some modified version of social constructivism could help us understand the changes and continuities in Chinese foreign policy.[16] Eventually, perhaps some fusion of Western and Chinese philosophies may emerge as a distinct Chinese theory of international relations. China's domestic transformations and its evolving foreign policy are already shaping the global landscape of the 21st century. For this reason alone, extra efforts are needed to study China's foreign policy — its rationale, implementation, contradictions, major challenges, and significant impact on the world.

References

Bell, A. Daniel, "China Might As Well Boldly Promote Its Political Values" (Zhongguo Bufang Dadan Tuiguang Zhengzhi Jiazhi), *Global Times*, November 17, 2010.

Chan, Steve, *China, the US and the Power-Transition Theory: A Critique* (Routledge, 2007), Abingdon, UK.

Feng, Huiyun, Kai He and Yan Xuetong (eds.), *Chinese Scholars and Foreign Policy: Debating International Relations* (London and New York: Routledge, 2019).

Guo, Shuyong (ed.), *Guoji Guanxi Huyu Zhongguo Lilun* (*International Relations Calls for a Chinese Theory*) (Tianjin: Tianjin Renmin Chubanshe, 2005).

Hao, Yufan and Lin Su, *China's Foreign Policy Making: Societal Force and Chinese American Policy* (Ashgate, 2006).

---

[16] Constructivism, with its focus on norms, values, and identity, has been used by some to analyze China's foreign policy today. See, for example, Zhu (2010); Uemura (2015); Yeh (2010); and Jørgensen and Wong (2016).

Hickey, Dennis and Kwei-Bo Huang, "Taiwan Should Return to the 1992 Consensus," PacNet #78, *Pacific Forum*, November 27, 2018. https://www.pacforum.org/analysis/pacnet-78-taiwan-should-return-1992-consensus.

Huang, Cary, "Rising Giant Stretches Its Arms across the World," *The South China Morning Post*, November 12, 2018, pp. A4–A5.

Jakobson, Linda and Dean Knox, "New Foreign Policy Actors in China," SIPRI Policy Paper 26, Stockholm International Peace Research Institute, September 2010.

Jørgensen, Knud Erik and Reuben Wong, "Social Constructivist Perspectives on China–EU Relations" in Jianwei Wang and Weiqing Song (eds.), *China, the European Union, and the International Politics of Global Governance* (New York: Palgrave Macmillan, 2016), pp. 51–74.

Lemon, Jason, "U.S. or China? Asian Nations May Soon Be Forced to Choose, Singapore PM Warns," *Newsweek*, November 15, 2018.

Noesselt, Nele, 2015. "Revisiting the Debate on Constructing a Theory of International Relations with Chinese Characteristics." *The China Quarterly*, Vol. 222, pp. 430–448.

Organski, A.F.K. *World Politics*, 2nd edition (Alfred A. Knopf, 1968), New York.

Pan, P. Philip, "The Land That Failed to Fail," *The New York Times*, November 18, 2018.

Qin, Yaqing, 2005. "Core Problems of International Relations Theory and the Construction of a Chinese School" (Guoji Guanxi Lilun de Hexin Wenti yu Zhongguo Xuepai de Shengcheng). *Social Sciences in China* (Zhongguo Shehui Kexue), Vol. 3, pp. 165–176.

Qin, Yaqing, 2007. "Why Is There No International Relations Theory in China?" *International Relations of the Asia-Pacific*, Vol. 7, No. 3, pp. 313–340.

Ren, Xiao, 2000. "Lilun yu guoji guanxi lilun: yixie sikao" (Some Thoughts on Theory and IR Theory), *Ouzhou Yanjiu* (*Chinese Journal of European Studies*), Vol. 20, No. 4, pp. 19–25.

Shambaugh, David, "China Under Xi Jinping," *East Asia Forum*, November 19, 2018.

Uemura, Takeshi, 2015. "Understanding Chinese Foreign Relations: A Cultural Constructivist Approach." *International Studies Perspectives*, Vol. 16, No. 3, pp. 345–365.

Wang, Jisi "The 'Two Orders' and the Future of China–U.S. Relations," *ChinaFile*, Center on U.S.–China Relations, Asia Society, July 9, 2015.

Yeh, Hui-chi, "Norms and Their Implications for the Making of China's Foreign Aid Policy since 1949," PhD dissertation, April 2010, University of Sheffield.

Yu, Xiaofeng, 2014. "Gongxiang Anquan: feichuantong anquan yanjiu de zhongguo shijiao" (Shared Security: Chinese Perspectives on Nontraditional Security Studies), *Guoji Anquan Yanjiu* (*International Security Studies*), No. 1, pp. 4–34.

Zhao, Tingyang, *Tianxia tixi: shijie zhidu zhexue daolun* (*The Tianxia System: An Introduction to the Philosophy of a World Institution*) (Nanjing: Jiangsu Education Press, 2005).

Zhu, Zhiqun, *US–China Relations in the 21st Century: Power Transition and Peace* (Routledge, 2006), Abingdon, UK.

Zhu, Zhiqun, *China's New Diplomacy: Rationale, Strategies, and Significance* (Ashgate, 2010).

Zhu, Zhiqun, "Is Indo-Pacific the 'New' Pivot?" *The National Interest*, November 23, 2017. https://nationalinterest.org/feature/indo-pacific-the-new-pivot-23321.

Chapter

2

Chinese Foreign Policy: A Bibliographical Review[*]

Introduction

Since the late 20th century, China has been transforming itself from an isolated and backward agrarian society into a modern economic superpower with global interests and responsibilities. To adjust to changing international and domestic conditions, Chinese foreign policy has become more active, pragmatic, and flexible. With continued economic growth, China is expected to widen and deepen its global search for energy and other resources and to expand its investment, market, and political clout. China is vigorously projecting soft

---

[*]This chapter is based on an earlier version titled "China's Foreign Policy," which was published by the Oxford University Press in February 2018 as part of the Oxford Bibliographies (http://www.oxfordbibliographies.com/view/document/obo-9780199743292/obo-9780199743292-0025.xml). It contains works on Chinese foreign policy published in the West as well as a selected few from China. The use of the materials in the original article is by permission of the Oxford University Press.

power and presenting a peaceful image abroad by promoting cultural, educational, sports, tourism, and other exchanges. It has also become more active in global governance. In addition to its roles in existing international institutions, China has played a leadership role in establishing and expanding the Shanghai Cooperation Organization (SCO), setting up the Asian Infrastructure Investment Bank (AIIB) and the BRICS Development Bank. It has also proposed the "Belt and Road Initiative (BRI)" to enhance connectivity and cooperation in global development.

There is good reason to believe that China wants to regain its great-power status peacefully, as it serves China's fundamental interests. However, China will be a half-baked "responsible stakeholder" in the 21st century world if it does not help tackle global challenges such as climate change, terrorism, and international development. China remains a vulnerable nation surrounded by powerful rivals and potential foes. Understanding China's foreign policy means fully appreciating these geostrategic conditions. Although its foreign policy has become more sophisticated, China is still learning to become a peaceful, responsible, and respectable great power in the ever-changing world. Indeed, there is much to learn. In addition to traditional diplomatic challenges, China also needs to give more attention to non-traditional security threats such as infectious diseases, economic crises, cyber hacking, piracy, transnational crimes, natural disasters, and environmental degradation. China will need to boost cooperation with other countries and international institutions to deal with these challenges.

General Overviews

This chapter first provides an overview and history of China's foreign relations; it then addresses a few important aspects of the foreign policy of the PRC: foreign policy theories, foreign and security policymaking, the role of the People's Liberation Army (PLA), domestic–foreign policy nexus, soft power, new diplomacy, U.S.–China relations, relations with other major powers, China and Africa, China in other developing areas, and China's role in global governance. China follows an independent foreign policy and does not form political or military alliances with other countries. To understand China's foreign policy in the early 21st century, one needs to know of the so-called "Century of Humiliation" in Chinese history — roughly from 1839 to 1949, during which China was humiliated by and suffered from Western and Japanese domination. The "Century of Humiliation" has a profound impact on China's foreign relations. The PRC considers itself a country whose historical greatness was eclipsed by Western and Japanese imperialist aggressions. The Chinese public is constantly reminded that only the Chinese Communist Party (CCP) was able to "save China" and end the "Century of Humiliation." Knowing this history helps one understand why the Chinese are obsessed with issues of sovereignty, national unification, and territorial integrity. As China becomes more powerful, nationalism will continue to grow when foreign countries, especially those former invaders and colonizers, are perceived to be encroaching on China's sovereignty, such as supporting independence for Taiwan or Tibet. No matter how its foreign policies may change, China considers such "core interests" to be inviolable. To have a general understanding of Chinese foreign policy, one needs to study its objectives, guiding principles, and strategies.

The following books offer excellent overviews of Chinese foreign policy — its changes and continuities since 1949 as well as more recent issues and challenges. Lanteigne (2015) serves as an excellent introductory text on Chinese foreign policy. Rozman (2012) and Kornberg and Faust (2005) focus on the various actors and issues in China's foreign policy. Sutter (2012) and Wang (2012) highlight international and domestic constraints, whereas Hao *et al.* (2009) and Johnston and Ross (2006) underline challenges and directions in Chinese foreign relations. Cheng (2016) offers an overall framework of Chinese foreign policy before examining important bilateral ties and significant challenges, while Qu and Zhong (2018) chronicles China's diplomatic strategies since the 1980s to cope with complicated and changing international situations. Feng *et al.* (2019) addresses two fundamental questions: how does China see the rest of the world and to what extent do Chinese IR scholars influence Beijing's foreign policy and outlook? *Zhongguo Waijiao* (China's Foreign Affairs) has presented the official Chinese version of major issues in China's foreign affairs every year since 1987. The website of the Ministry of Foreign Affairs of the People's Republic of China (zhonghua renmin gongheguo waijiaobu wangzhan "ziliao" lan) is a rich source of useful information about the PRC's foreign relations and foreign policy.

- Cheng, Joseph Yu-shek, *China's Foreign Policy: Challenges and Prospects* (Singapore: World Scientific Publishing, 2016).

  Cheng examines the Chinese foreign policy framework and traces its evolution since the post-Mao era. The volume also looks at China's relations with other major powers and its management of various challenges.

- Feng, Huiyun; Kai He and Yan Xuetong (eds.), *Chinese Scholars and Foreign Policy: Debating International Relations* (London and New York: Routledge, 2019).

  The editors discuss fundamental aspects of China's foreign policy such as China's view of the international structure, soft power projection, maritime disputes, and the principle of non-interference.

- Hao, Yufan; George Wei C.X. and Lowell Dittmer (eds.), *Challenges to Chinese Foreign Policy: Diplomacy, Globalization, and the Next World Power* (Lexington: University Press of Kentucky, 2009).

  The contributors argue that the challenges in Chinese foreign policy remain daunting and that some of them come from within. They represent interesting perspectives of Chinese scholars.

- Johnston, Alastair Iain and Robert Ross S., *New Directions in the Study of China's Foreign Policy* (Stanford, CA: Stanford University Press, 2006).

  The authors draw on a wide range of materials to explore traditional issues, such as China's use of force since 1959, and new issues, such as China's response to globalization and the role of domestic opinion in its foreign policy.

- Kornberg, Judith F. and John Faust R., *China in World Politics: Policies, Processes, Prospects*, 2nd edition (Boulder, CO: Lynne Rienner, 2005).

  Introducing students to the history of China's foreign policy, the authors outline the political, security, economic, and social issues the country faces in the early 21st century. Each chapter familiarizes the reader with the Chinese framework for analyzing the issues in question.

- Lanteigne, Marc, *Chinese Foreign Policy: An Introduction*, 3rd edition (New York: Routledge, 2015).

  It explains how China's foreign policy is being reconstructed and who (and what) makes policy in the early 21st century, and examines the patterns of engagement with various domestic and international factors. It's an in-depth look at the key issues, problems, and trends of China's modern global relations.

- Ministry of Foreign Affairs of the People's Republic of China (zhonghua renmin gongheguo waijiaobu wangzhan "ziliao" lan. https://www.fmprc.gov.cn/web. 中华人民共和国外交部网站 "资料"栏).

  The website contains rich information on the PRC's foreign relations, including key speeches by Chinese leaders, a list of statements and communiqués, a list of treaties, diplomatic history, a list of China's diplomatic allies, and a directory of foreign diplomats in China.

- Qu, Xing and Zhong Longbiao, *Contemporary China's Diplomacy* (New York: Taylor & Francis, 2018).

  Written by two of the best Chinese scholars on international relations and foreign policy, this book gives a comprehensive and systematic introduction to the development of China's diplomatic strategies since the 1980s.

- Rozman, Gilbert (ed.), *China's Foreign Policy: Who Makes It, and How Is It Made?* (Seoul, South Korea: Asan Institute for Policy Studies, 2012).

  It's a collection of essays written by some of the leading China scholars. Topics include China's leadership, think tanks, national

32 *A Critical Decade: China's Foreign Policy (2008–2018)*

identity, and financial factors in Chinese foreign policymaking as well as China's foreign policy toward the Korean Peninsula.

- Sutter, Robert G., *Chinese Foreign Relations*, 3rd edition (Lanham, MD: Rowman & Littlefield, 2012).

  A nuanced analysis that shows that despite its growing power, Beijing is hampered by both domestic and international constraints. China's leaders exert more influence in world affairs but remain far from dominant.

- Wang, Zheng, *Never Forget National Humiliation: Historical Memory in Chinese Politics and Foreign Relations* (New York: Columbia University Press, 2012).

  This is a study of history education in China in the late 20th and early 21st centuries and how it affects China's worldview and foreign policy.

- *Zhongguo Waijiao, China's Foreign Affairs* 中国外交 (Beijing: World Affairs, 1987–2018).

  It's a comprehensive and authoritative account of major issues in Chinese foreign relations in the previous year, compiled yearly by the Policy Planning division of the PRC's Foreign Ministry.

History of Foreign Policy of the People's Republic of China

The Five Principles of Peaceful Coexistence have guided Chinese foreign policy since the early 1950s. Peace and development have become objectives of China's foreign policy in the post-Mao era. In the early 1990s the Chinese government launched a new wave of diplomacy, following both *yin jin lai* (引进来 bringing in) and *zou chu qu* (走出去 going out) strategies. China's foreign policy objectives remain the same: safeguarding national independence and state sovereignty and creating an international environment favorable to its reform, opening-up, and modernization efforts as well as maintaining world peace and promoting common development. The following books concentrate on the evolution of Chinese foreign policy since the mid-20th century. Womack (2010) and Wills (2010) provide a historical survey of Chinese foreign relations. Mark (2012) and Sutter (2013) are panoramic studies of the foreign relations of the PRC since 1949, whereas Liu (2004) stresses the post-Cold War era. Kissinger (2012) and Qian (2005) highlight some of the most dramatic events in China's foreign relations. Wang and Tan (2016) is an edited collection of articles by Chinese scholars about China's foreign affairs in the past 60 years. Xie (2009) and Zhao (2010) closely examine Chinese foreign policy decade by decade from 1949 to the early 21st century, whereas Niu (2013) deals with China's foreign affairs in the first few years after the PRC's founding. Qin and Chen (2016) covers some interesting but not well-known stories in the PRC's diplomatic history such as China's policies toward the Universal Postal Union and China's support for Albania.

- Kissinger, Henry, *On China* (New York: Penguin, 2012).

  Kissinger illuminates the inner workings of Chinese diplomacy during such pivotal events as the initial encounters between China and European powers, the formation and breakdown of the Sino-Soviet alliance, the Korean War, and President Richard Nixon's historic trip to Beijing.

- Liu, Guoli (ed.), *Chinese Foreign Policy in Transition* (New York: Aldine de Gruyter, 2004).

  This anthology helps deepen our understanding of the sources, substance, and significance of Chinese foreign policy, with a focus on the post-Cold War era. Contributors include academic specialists, researchers, and journalists.

- Mark, Chi-kwan, *China and the World since 1945: An International History* (New York: Routledge, 2012).

  It's a concise introduction to China's foreign relations from 1949 to 2012. It looks at the aims, features, and impact of China's interactions with the two superpowers, its Asian neighbors, and European and developing countries at political, military, economic, and cultural levels.

- Niu, Jun, (牛军). *Lengzhao yu xinzhongguo waijiao de yuanqi, 1949–1955* (冷战与新中国外交的缘起 1949–1955) (Beijing: Social Science Archives, 2013).

  The book covers major historical events from 1949 to 1955, including the establishment of the PRC, Chinese leaders' diplomatic activities, and China's bilateral and multilateral negotiations as well as its interactions with countries of the East and the West.

- Qian, Qichen, *Ten Episodes in China's Diplomacy* (New York: HarperCollins, 2005).

  Qian shows how global relationships are delicately maintained through rarely seen negotiations. His remembrance covers world-changing events, including the thawing of China's relationship with the Soviet Union, Nelson Mandela's visit to China, the normalization of Sino-Indonesian relations, and the handover of Hong Kong.

- Qin, Yaqing and Zhirui Chen (eds.), *Future In Retrospect: China's Diplomatic History Revisited* (Hackensack, NJ: World Century Publishing Corporation, 2016).

  Based on rich literature, including some newly declassified files from the Chinese Ministry of Foreign Affairs, this volume introduces some of the most interesting and significant, but lesser-known, episodes in the diplomatic history of the PRC.

- Sutter, Robert G., *Foreign Relations of the PRC: The Legacies and Constraints of China's International Politics since 1949* (Lanham, MD: Rowman & Littlefield, 2013).

  This is an assessment of the country's successes and advances as well as the important legacies and constraints that hamper its foreign relations, especially in Asia.

- Wang, Yizhou and Xiuying Tan, *Sixty Years of China Foreign Affairs* (Reading, UK: Paths International, 2016).

  A collection of essays by Chinese scholars and diplomats, this book chronicles how China has handled challenges in international affairs since 1949.

- Wills, John E., Jr., (ed.), *Past and Present in China's Foreign Policy: From "Tribute System" to "Peaceful Rise"* (Portland, ME: MerwinAsia, 2010).

  This volume presents a remarkable variety of approaches to issues of how the past influences policy in the early 21st century. Tribute, empire, asymmetry, China's peaceful rise, and the Chinese model for developing countries all enter into the discussion.

- Womack, Brantly (ed.), *China's Rise in Historical Perspective* (Lanham, MD: Rowman & Littlefield, 2010).

  Contributors explore the internal dynamic of China's rise since traditional times through the key themes of China's identity, security, economy, environment, energy, and politics.

- Xie, Yixian, (谢益显), (ed.), *zhongguo dangdai waijiaoshi* (中国当代外交史), 1949–2009 (Beijing: China Youth Press, 2009).

  It covers every major period in the PRC's diplomatic history, including the consolidation of independence after 1949, fighting against both superpowers in the 1950s and 1960s, promoting peace and development in the 1970s and 1980s, integrating into the global system, and pushing for multilateralism in the 1990s and 2000s.

- Zhao, Jinjun, (赵进军). 新中国外交60年 *China's Diplomacy 1949–2009* (Beijing: Peking University Press, 2010).

  It's a systematic summary of Chinese foreign policy practices since the PRC was established, with focus on the decades after the Reform and Opening Up. The chapters also attempt to develop foreign policy theories based on the practices.

Theories of Chinese Foreign Policy

No single theory can capture and explain China's evolving foreign policy. Western and Chinese scholars have attempted to offer their theoretical interpretations. Most of the scholarly works on China approach the question at a structural level by looking at the international system and the systemic impact on China's foreign policy.

36 *A Critical Decade: China's Foreign Policy (2008–2018)*

Traditional realist theorists define China as a revisionist power eager to address wrongs done to it in history, whereas some cultural and historical analyzes attest that China's strategic culture has been offensive, despite its weak material capability. Liberal and constructivist theorists tend to be more upbeat about China's external relations. Of particular interest in this section are efforts by some Chinese scholars to theorize policymaking in China. Zhao and Chen (2012), Yan (2011), and Ye (2011) are examples of such extraordinary endeavors. Liu (2016) summarizes recent efforts in promoting foundational research in China and building a Chinese school of foreign policy theory. Ni (2013) and Xin (2012) are fine Chinese-language publications on Chinese international relations theory building by leading Chinese scholars. Robinson and Shambaugh (1994) offers an overview of theory and practice in Chinese foreign policy, whereas Lampton (2001) and Callahan and Barabantseva (2011) theorize Chinese foreign policy in the context of China's reform and integration into the global system. Qin (2008), Feng (2009), and Lu (2000) challenge the conventional Western theories about foreign policymaking by introducing how Chinese culture and China's informal politics affect efforts to theorize Chinese foreign policy. Pu (2019) uses the metaphor of rebranding to analyze China's contradictory images as both a great power and a developing nation.

- Callahan, William A. and Elena Barabantseva (eds.), *China Orders the World: Normative Soft Power and Foreign Policy* (Baltimore: Johns Hopkins University Press, 2011).

  It's an examination of complex debates concerning the role of China's historical ideals in shaping its foreign policy. The contributors discuss how China's imperial past inspires a new generation of Chinese scholars and policymakers and their plans for China's future.

- Feng, Huiyun, *Chinese Strategic Culture and Foreign Policy Decision-Making: Confucianism, Leadership and War* (London: Routledge, 2009).

  Feng traces the historical roots of Chinese strategic culture and its links to the decision-making of six key Chinese leaders via their belief systems.

Chinese Foreign Policy: A Bibliographical Review **37**

- Lampton, David M. (ed.), *The Making of Chinese Foreign and Security Policy in the Era of Reform, 1978–2000* (Stanford, CA: Stanford University Press, 2001).

  The author examines the forces reshaping Chinese foreign and national security policymaking institutions and processes: bureaucratic politics and evolving organizations, changing elite views and skills, an altered domestic agenda; increasingly diverse social forces and public opinion, etc.

- Liu, Ming, (刘鸣). *Zhongguo guoji guanxi yu waijiao lilun qianyan: Tansuo yu fazhan* (中国国际关系与外交理论前沿: 探索与发展) (Shanghai Academy of Social Sciences Publisher, 2016).

  The book offers a survey of foundational research on Chinese foreign policy in China and a summary of recent efforts to construct a Chinese school or Chinese theory on foreign policy.

- Lu, Ning, *The Dynamics of Foreign-Policy Decisionmaking in China*, 2nd edition (Boulder, CO: Westview, 2000).

  Lu reveals the inner workings of the Chinese Foreign Ministry, introduces Chinese-language sources, and presents a series of case studies that challenge existing Western theoretical analysis of Chinese policymaking.

- Ni, Shixiong, (倪世雄). *guoji guanxi lilun tansuo wenji* (国际关系理论探索文集) (Shanghai, China: Fudan University Press, 2013).

  This is an exploration of the development of Chinese international relations theories based on a thorough examination of Western international relations theories and their practice in China.

- Pu, Xiaoyu, *Rebranding China: Contested Status Signaling in the Changing Global Order* (Stanford, CA: Stanford University Press, 2019).

  Drawing on a sweeping body of research, including original Chinese sources and interdisciplinary ideas from sociology, psychology, and international relations, this book puts forward an innovative framework for interpreting China's foreign policy.

- Qin, Yaqing, (秦亚青). "Reflections on the Development of Chinese Theory of Diplomacy." (关于构建中国特色外交理论的思考), *Foreign Affairs Review* (外交评论), Vol. 01, No. 101: pp. 9–17, No. 102, February 2008.

  This is a call by a leading Chinese international relations scholar to establish a Chinese theory of diplomacy, based on Marxism, Chinese traditional culture, and China's socialist system.

- Robinson, Thomas W. and David Shambaugh (eds.), *Chinese Foreign Policy: Theory and Practice* (New York: Oxford University Press, 1994).

  The book is a review of China's desire to ensure its security and to regain freedom of initiative in its foreign relations as the country searches for a redefined role in the multipolar world order.

- Xin, Yishan, (辛一山). *zhongguoshi guojiguanxi lilun* (中国式国际关系理论) (Beijing: Current Affairs, 2012).

  It critiques major Western international relations theories. Using case studies and following the constructivist approach, the author argues that the concepts of peace and morality are crucial for a nation's development.

- Yan, Xuetong, *Ancient Chinese Thought, Modern Chinese Power*, in Daniel A. Bell and Sun Zhe (eds.), Translated by Edmund Ryden (Princeton, NJ: Princeton University Press, 2011).

  Yan studies the lessons of ancient Chinese political thought and the development of a "Beijing consensus" in international relations. He asserts that political leadership is the key to national power and that morality is an essential part of political leadership.

- Ye, Zicheng, *Inside China's Grand Strategy: The Perspective from the People's Republic*. Edited and translated by Steven I. Levine and Guoli Liu (Lexington: University Press of Kentucky, 2011).

  Ye analyzes China's interactions with other world powers and neighboring countries and compares China's global ascension with the historical experiences of rising European superpowers, giving an insider look at China's growing global clout.

Chinese Foreign Policy: A Bibliographical Review   39

- Zhao, Jinjun and Zhirui Chen (eds.), *Participation and Interaction: The Theory and Practice of China's Diplomacy* (Hackensack, NJ: World Century, 2012).

  The book provides insightful theoretical perspectives on China's diplomacy and the international system written by outstanding Chinese scholars.

Foreign and Security Policymaking

Contrary to the common misperception that the Chinese state is monolithically controlled by the Communist Party, China has become an increasingly diverse and dynamic society, in which many players are competing for influence in national policy. Although the Leading Small Group on Foreign Affairs has the final say, a growing number of players — from high-ranking government officials and military officers to think tank scholars and researchers; from businesspeople to media; from large, state-owned companies to Internet users — are increasingly involved in China's foreign policymaking. Various government departments and offices compete for power and influence in foreign affairs. The Foreign Ministry is perceived as just one of the government agencies and not necessarily a very powerful one. Other key government agencies, such as the CCP Central Committee's International Department, the People's Bank of China, and the Ministry of Commerce, are also active in dealing with political, financial, and economic relations with other countries. The CCP's Policy Research Office, the National Development and Reform Commission, the People's Liberation Army (PLA), and the newly established National Security Committee are some of the other powerful official actors vying to influence top leadership's decisions. Ross (2009) is an excellent introduction to security policymaking in China. Sun (2013) complements the study by focusing on the three security policymaking models. Hao and Lin (2005), Linda and Knox (2010) and Zhu (2012) discuss the complexity in foreign and security policymaking by highlighting non-governmental players, such as interest groups and think tanks. Harris (2014) examines both domestic and international factors that shape China's policymaking. Kastner and Saunders (2012)

40 A Critical Decade: China's Foreign Policy (2008–2018)

ask a challenging question: Is China a status quo power or revisionist power, based on its foreign policy behavior? Kochhar (2018) looks at China's security policy from a historical perspective and analyzes how interactions of internal and external issues shape China's policymaking. Finally, Bush (2013) reminds readers that the Taiwan issue remains a key security challenge in China's foreign policy.

- Bush, Richard C., *Uncharted Strait: The Future of China–Taiwan Relations* (Washington, DC: Brookings Institution, 2013).

  The Taiwan Strait is uncharted water, with China fearing the island's permanent separation and Taiwan fearing subordination to an authoritarian regime.

- Hao, Yufan and Lin Su (eds.), *China's Foreign Policy Making: Societal Force and Chinese American Policy* (Aldershot, UK: Ashgate, 2005).

  The edited book examines various domestic factors and their increasing impact on China's policy toward the United States.

- Harris, Stuart, *China's Foreign Policy* (Cambridge, UK: Polity, 2014).

  This is an analysis of multiple domestic and international sources of Chinese foreign policy in the context of Chinese culture, history, and national interests as well as its improving economic and military capabilities and the patterns of behavior of other countries.

- Jakobson, Linda and Dean Knox, *New Foreign Policy Actors in China*. Institute Policy Paper 26 (Stockholm: Stockholm International Peace Research, 2010).

  In addition to the official foreign policy actors, the authors note that other actors are playing an increasingly influential role, such as the business sector, local governments, research institutions and academia, the media, and netizens.

- Kastner, Scott L. and Phillip Saunders C., 2012. "Is China a Status Quo or Revisionist State? Leadership Travel as an Empirical Indicator of Foreign Policy Priorities." *International Studies Quarterly*, Vol. 56, No. 1, pp. 163–177.

  Where Chinese leaders choose to travel can offer insights into whether China's behavior is more consistent with that of a revisionist or status quo state and into China's broader diplomatic priorities. The authors analyze the correlates of travel abroad by top Chinese leaders from 1998 to 2008 and conclude that China is more a status quo power.

- Kochhar, Geeta (ed.), *China's Foreign Relations and Security Dimensions* (New Delhi: Routledge India, 2018).

  It offers insight into China's historical security concerns and the linkages of internal issues with external diplomacy which reshape its relations with neighboring countries. The volume also examines President Xi Jinping's foreign policy orientations and aspirations for future.

- Ross, Robert S., *Chinese Security Policy: Structure, Power and Politics* (London: Routledge, 2009).

  The work integrates the realist literature with key issues in Chinese foreign policy and investigates China's strategic vulnerability, which has compelled Beijing to seek cooperation with the United States.

- Sun, Yun, *Chinese National Security Decision-Making: Processes and Challenges* (Washington, DC: Brookings Institution, 2013).

  This paper attends to three processes of China's national security decision-making: the decision-making at the top level, the policy coordination process conducted through the National Security Leading Small Group (NSLSG), and the informational process for national security decision-making.

- Zhu, Xuefeng, *The Rise of Think Tanks in China* (London: Routledge, 2012).

  The book, with comparative case studies and data from nationwide surveys, provides a comprehensive picture of think tanks in the country's political system.

The People's Liberation Army and Foreign Policy

China has evolved from a nation with local and regional security interests to a major economic and political power with global interests, investments, and political commitments. It now requires a military that can project itself around the world to protect its interests.

42 A Critical Decade: China's Foreign Policy (2008–2018)

The People's Liberation Army (PLA) is a major pillar of Chinese politics. The PLA plays a crucial role in both domestic and foreign affairs. Blasko 2012), Fisher (2008), Yoshihara and Holmes (2010), and Wortzel (2013) look at the latest developments of the PLA and how it affects China's foreign relations. Karmel (2000) points out the weaknesses of the PLA, whereas Kamphausen *et al.* (2010); Scobell (2003); and Howarth (2006) examine its capabilities, especially those of the People's Liberation Army Navy (PLAN) as China plans to project its power beyond its borders. Scobell *et al.* (2015) discusses how the PLA has expanded its overseas missions as China's international interests grow. Fravel (2019) delves into the security threats China has faced over the last seven decades. Finally, Du *et al.* (2015) is a rare textbook on the PRC's military diplomacy written by Chinese scholars for the PLA International Relations Institute.

- Blasko, Dennis J., *The Chinese Army Today: Tradition and Transformation for the 21st Century* (New York: Routledge, 2012).

  Written by a retired professional military officer, this text uses first-hand observation of the Chinese military and three decades of military experience to weave many disparate threads from official Chinese statements, documents, and media reports into an integrated whole.

- Du, Nongyi; Zhou Hui and Yang Kai, 杜农一, 周辉, 杨凯. 新中国军事外交与国际维和研究 (*Military Diplomacy of New China and International Peacekeeping*) (Beijing: National Defense University Press, 2015).

  This book discusses theories and practices of Chinese military diplomacy, especially peacekeeping missions, and emphasizes the significance of China's military diplomacy in terms of enhancing China's international image and promoting international peace.

- Fisher, Richard D., Jr., *China's Military Modernization: Building for Regional and Global Reach* (Westport, CT: Praeger Security International, 2008).

  The author shows how the PLA remains critical to the existence of the Chinese government and looks at China's political and military actions designed to protect its expanded strategic interests.

- Fravel Taylor M., *Active Defense: China's Military Strategy since 1949* (Princeton, NJ: Princeton University Press, 2019).

  The book offers the first systematic look at China's military strategy from the mid-20th century to today and explores the range and intensity of threats that China has faced through illuminating China's past and present military goals and how it sought to achieve them.

- Howarth, Peter, *China's Rising Sea Power: The PLA Navy's Submarine Challenge* (London: Routledge, 2006).

  Howarth offers answers to a plethora of questions, such as: Why does China place so much emphasis on its navy? What is the level of training of the PLAN's submarine crews? Are U.S. carriers truly vulnerable to Chinese submarines? The author also explains why Taiwan is so critical to China's national security.

- Kamphausen, Roy; David Lai and Andrew Scobell (eds.), *The PLA at Home and Abroad: Assessing the Operational Capabilities of China's Military* (Carlisle, PA: Strategic Studies Institute, US Army War College, 2010).

  The chapters illustrate that (1) Chinese and PLA leaders have a strong sense of mission, (2) the PLA is committed to continuing the transformation in military affairs with Chinese characteristics, (3) the PLA is eager to learn from the US military, and (4) the PLA has made progress in its transformation and operational capabilities.

- Karmel, Solomon M., *China and the People's Liberation Army: Great Power or Struggling Developing State?* (Basingstoke, UK: Palgrave Macmillan, 2000).

  The book follows established methods of military analysis to demonstrate that China's greatest threat to world peace is its poorly managed military bureaucracy.

- Scobell, Andrew, *China's Use of Military Force: Beyond the Great Wall and the Long March* (Cambridge, UK: Cambridge University Press, 2003).

  The book studies Chinese use of military force abroad, as in Korea (1950), Vietnam (1979), and the Taiwan Strait (1995–1996),

44 *A Critical Decade: China's Foreign Policy (2008–2018)*

and domestically, as during the Cultural Revolution and in the 1989 military crackdown in Tiananmen Square.

- Scobell, Andrew; Arthur Ding; Phillip Saunders and Scott Harold (eds.), *The People's Liberation Army and Contingency Planning in China* (Washington, DC: National Defense University Press, 2015).

  The edited book examines how China's rapidly expanding international interests are creating demands for the PLA to conduct new missions ranging from protecting Chinese shipping from Somali pirates to evacuating citizens from Libya.

- Wortzel, Larry M., *The Dragon Extends Its Reach: Chinese Military Power Goes Global* (Washington, DC: Potomac, 2013).

  Wortzel presents a clear picture of the PLA's modernization effort as it expands into space and cyberspace and as it integrates operations into the traditional domains of war.

- Yoshihara, Toshi and James Holmes R., *Red Star over the Pacific: China's Rise and the Challenge to U.S. Maritime Strategy* (Annapolis, MD: Naval Institute, 2010).

  The authors assess how the rise of Chinese sea power will affect US maritime strategy in Asia and argue that China is laying the groundwork for a sustained challenge to American primacy in maritime Asia.

The Domestic–Foreign Policy Nexus

China's foreign policy is increasingly constrained by both domestic and international factors. The range of participants in China's decision-making process has widened, with different societal actors playing an increasingly important role in the Chinese policymaking process. A major foreign policy challenge for China is to balance two seemingly conflicting objectives: to build a reputation as a responsible, principled great power that will be a force for peace rather than a regional bully and to satisfy demands from the Chinese public that China begin to act like a strong country and stand up more forcefully for China's interests. As China's political and economic influence in the world is rapidly increasing, it is essential to understand how

China's domestic politics affects its foreign political and economic policy. Whereas mainstream literature on international relations suggests that China's foreign policy is primarily determined by individual leaders such as Mao Zedong or Deng Xiaoping and external factors such as the international system and policies of other powers, the fact is that domestic factors profoundly shape China's foreign policy in the reform era. Lai (2010) and Shambaugh (2011) study domestic sources of China's decision-making. Shirk (2007) and Lampton (2008) highlight domestic constraints on China's conduct of foreign policy. Wang (2011); Wang *et al.* (2012); Clegg (2009); and Swaine and Tellis (2000) focus on China's search for a grand strategy as it becomes more confident in international affairs as a result of domestic growth. Turcsányi (2018) examines the domestic sources of Chinese policies in the South China Sea.

- Clegg, Jenny, *China's Global Strategy: Toward a Multipolar World* (New York: Pluto, 2009).

  Clegg shows that China is taking a multilateral approach, offering real assistance to developing countries and helping build the institutions required to run a multipolar world. She argues that China's international consensus-building strategy could lead to a more peaceful and equitable world.

- Lai, Hongyi, *The Domestic Sources of China's Foreign Policy: Regimes, Leadership, Priorities and Process* (New York: Routledge, 2010).

  Lai discusses how China's foreign policy is driven by the preservation of political and economic regimes, the political survival of the top leader, the top leader's vision for and skill in managing external affairs, the top leader's policy priorities, dramatic events, and the process of policymaking.

- Lampton, David M., *The Three Faces of Chinese Power: Might, Money, and Minds* (Berkeley: University of California Press, 2008).

  The book investigates the military, economic, and intellectual dimensions of China's growing influence.

46　*A Critical Decade: China's Foreign Policy (2008–2018)*

- Shambaugh, David, 2011. "Coping with a Conflicted China." *Washington Quarterly*, Vol. 34, No. 1, pp. 7–27.

  Shambaugh suggests that although there seems to be domestic agreement in the early 21st century, China remains a deeply conflicted rising power with a series of competing international identities.

- Shirk, Susan L., *China: Fragile Superpower* (New York: Oxford University Press, 2007).

  Shirk argues the real danger of Chinese politics lies in the deep insecurity of its leaders. China's leaders face a troubling paradox: the more developed and prosperous the country becomes, the more insecure and threatened they feel.

- Swaine, Michael D. and Ashley Tellis, J., *Interpreting China's Grand Strategy: Past, Present, and Future* (Santa Monica, CA: RAND, 2000).

  The book identifies and analyzes major factors determining China's grand strategy, past, present, and future.

- Turcsányi, Richard Q., *Chinese Assertiveness in the South China Sea: Power Sources, Domestic Politics, and Reactive Foreign Policy* (New York: Springer, 2018).

  It's a detailed account of the events in the South China Sea and power dynamics in the region. It studies the driving forces, both domestic and international, behind China's assertive foreign policy.

- Wang, Jisi, 2011. "China's Search for a Grand Strategy: A Rising Great Power Finds Its Way." *Foreign Affairs*, Vol. 90, No. 2, pp. 68–79.

  Wang points out that with China's clout growing, the international community needs to better understand China's strategic thinking.

- Wang, Jisi; Fang Gang; Jin Canrong, *et al. China at the Crossroads: Sustainability, Economy, Security and Critical Issues for the 21st Century* (San Francisco: Long River, 2012).

  This is a collection of essays by leading Chinese scholars on the reforms that are taking place in China and the types of responses needed by China to shift course and manage continued development, while addressing rising security and economic problems.

The New Diplomacy

The diplomacy of the PRC can be divided into two periods. In the first 30 years (1949–1978) the focus of China's diplomatic tasks was to oppose the threat from the two superpowers, consolidate national independence, and safeguard sovereignty and territorial integrity. Since 1978 China has reoriented its diplomacy to create an external environment conducive to its domestic economic development in the midst of the changing international situation. In the early 1980s, China's role in global affairs, beyond its immediate East Asian periphery, was decidedly minor, and it had little geostrategic power. In the early 21st century, however, China's expanding economic power has allowed it to extend its reach virtually everywhere. This second wave of diplomacy is driven by China's domestic need for energy, raw materials and market for continued growth as well as its intention to project the image of a peaceful and responsible power. This new diplomacy has brought about many development opportunities for other countries; it has also created concerns and challenges in some quarters. Shambaugh (2013) and Zhu (2013) offer comprehensive surveys of this wave of diplomacy around the world, whereas Gill (2010) focuses on the security dimension. Kerr *et al.* (2008) explores whether China's diplomacy is just a foreign policy instrument or a natural outcome of a learning process as China becomes more integrated into the international community. Johnston (2013) challenges the view that China's assertiveness represents a change and notes that one can find similar behaviors in the past, whereas Nathan and Scobell (2012) underlines the security challenges China faces from different fronts. Wang (2011) explains how and why China is moving from being passive to being more active in its foreign policy. Ellis (2009) and Karrar (2009) are careful studies of China's diplomacy in selected global regions. Rolland (2017) and Mayer (2018) study the impact of the BRI on the Eurasian political economy. Chan (2018) assesses the implications of China's new diplomacy for the global political economy, while Blackwill and Campbell (2016) suggest that U.S. must "rebalance" towards Asia in dealing with a more assertive China under Xi Jinping.

48 *A Critical Decade: China's Foreign Policy (2008–2018)*

- Blackwill, Robert and Kurt Campbell, *Xi Jinping on the Global Stage: Chinese Foreign Policy Under a Powerful but Exposed Leader* (New York: Council on Foreign Relations Press, 2016).

  In the Xi Jinping era, China's foreign policy may well be driven by the risk of domestic political instability. The authors identify the U.S. pivot or rebalance to Asia as "the indispensable ingredient in a successful U.S. policy" to deal with Chinese power and influence under Xi Jinping.

- Chan, Gerald, *Understanding China's New Diplomacy: Silk Roads and Bullet Trains* (Cheltenham, UK: Edward Elgar, 2018).

  The book argues that a new developmental path called "geo-developmentalism" is in the making: China plays a leading role in promoting growth and building connections across Eurasia and beyond.

- Ellis Evan R., *China in Latin America: The Whats and Wherefores* (Boulder, CO: Lynne Rienner, 2009).

  The author examines how the China–Latin America relationship has taken on distinct characteristics in various instances, such as the role of oil and other resources, the Taiwan issue, and the unique case of Cuba.

- Gill, Bates, *Rising Star: China's New Security Diplomacy* (Washington, DC: Brookings Institution, 2010).

  The book offers a coherent framework for understanding China's security diplomacy since the mid-1990s, with focus on Chinese policy in three areas: regional security mechanisms, non-proliferation and arms control, and questions of sovereignty and intervention.

- Johnston, Alastair Iain, 2013. "How New and Assertive Is China's New Assertiveness?" *International Security*, Vol. 37, No. 4, pp. 7–48.

  This article argues that the assertiveness meme underestimates the degree of assertiveness in certain policies in the past and overestimates the amount of change in China's diplomacy in 2010 and after.

Chinese Foreign Policy: A Bibliographical Review 49

- Karrar, Hasan H., *The New Silk Road Diplomacy: China's Central Asian Foreign Policy since the Cold War* (Vancouver: University of British Columbia Press, 2009).

  It's an overview of China's cooperation with Russia and the Central Asian republics to stabilize the region, facilitate commerce, and build an energy infrastructure to import the region's oil.

- Kerr, Pauline; Stuart Harris and Qin Yaqing (eds.), *China's "New" Diplomacy: Tactical or Fundamental Change?* (New York: Palgrave Macmillan, 2008).

  The authors highlight the view that diplomacy is both an instrument of foreign policy and a learning and socializing process that fosters positive and negative change. They assert that there is little to suggest that China's changed diplomacy has a tactical, revisionist agenda.

- Mayer, Maximilian (ed.), *Rethinking the Silk Road: China's Belt and Road Initiative and Emerging Eurasian* (New York: Palgrave Macmillan, 2018).

  The book deals with the central question of how China's expanding economic influence will transform the Eurasian political landscape.

- Nathan, Andrew J. and Andrew Scobell, *China's Search for Security* (New York: Columbia University Press, 2012).

  It's an analysis of China's security concerns on four fronts: at home, with its immediate neighbors, in surrounding regional systems, and in the world beyond Asia.

- Rolland, Nadège, *China's Eurasian Century? Political and Strategic Implications of the Belt and Road Initiative* (Seattle and Washington, DC: National Bureau of Asian Research, 2017).

  Rolland examines the origins, drivers, and various components of the BRI and argues that the new initiative has economic and geopolitical purposes and serves the Chinese leadership's vision of a risen China sitting at the heart of a Sinocentric regional order.

50 *A Critical Decade: China's Foreign Policy (2008–2018)*

- Shambaugh, David, *China Goes Global: The Partial Power* (New York: Oxford University Press, 2013).

  Shambaugh offers an enlightening look into the manifestations of China's global presence: its extensive commercial footprint; its growing military power; its increasing cultural influence, or soft power; its diplomatic activity; and its prominence in global governance institutions.

- Wang, Yizhou, (王逸舟). *Chuangzhaoxing jieru: zhongguo waijiao xinquxiang* (创造性介入:中国外交新取向) (Beijing: Peking University Press, 2011).

  In the early 21st century, China is gradually shifting away from "keeping a low profile," as Deng Xiaoping admonished, to exercising its increased power and becoming a more active and responsible player in international affairs. Using case studies, the book suggests that China is becoming more creative in its diplomacy.

- Zhu, Zhiqun, *China's New Diplomacy: Rationale, Strategies, and Significance*, 2nd edition (Farnham, UK: Ashgate, 2013).

  The book examines and evaluates Chinese initiatives in the Middle East, Latin America and the Caribbean, Africa, Central Asia, Southeast Asia, and the South Pacific since the early 1990s. It studies China's efforts to secure energy and other resources, to expand trade and investment, and to enhance soft power.

China's Soft Power

Since the beginning of the 21st century, the Chinese government has given attention to the importance of enhancing its soft power. Chinese leaders recognize the value of soft power in projecting China's image as a peaceful, reliable, and responsible great power and in reducing misunderstanding of its intentions as well as deflecting concerns about the "China threat." Soft power has become one of the most frequently used phrases among political leaders, leading academics, and journalists in China. The idea of soft power figures significantly in the story of China's reemergence as a global power. Likewise, China's soft power has attracted considerable attention in the early

21st century. Kurlantzick (2008) is perhaps the first book to examine the significance of soft power in China's foreign relations. Lai and Lu (2012), Wang (2011), Li (2009), and Hartig (2017) are excellent studies of how soft-power promotion has become a major Chinese foreign policy objective. Ding (2008) attempts to find the theoretical and empirical connection between soft power and China's rise. King (2013), Barr (2011), and Cardenal and Araújo (2013) stress the impact of China's growing influence in different parts of the world.

- Barr, Michael, *Who's Afraid of China? The Challenge of Chinese Soft Power* (London: Zed, 2011).

  The rise of China as an alternative model to Western liberalism has created a fear that developing countries will stray from Western values. Barr argues that the rise of China presents a fundamental challenge to ideas about modernity, history, and international relations.

- Cardenal, Juan Pablo and Heriberto Araújo, *China's Silent Army: The Pioneers, Traders, Fixers and Workers Who Are Remaking the World in Beijing's Image*. Translated by Catherine Mansfield (New York: Crown, 2013).

  This is a study of the unprecedented growth of China's economic investment in the developing world and its impact at the local level with a focus on the role of China's silent army — ordinary Chinese in the juggernaut that is "China Inc."

- Ding, Sheng, *The Dragon's Hidden Wings: How China Rises with Its Soft Power* (Lanham, MD: Lexington Books, 2008).

  The main questions addressed are: What are the theoretical and empirical connections between the soft-power concept and the rise of China? What are China's soft-power resources? How has Beijing used soft power to become a major player in the world? What opportunities and challenges does the use of soft power present to China?

- Hartig, Falk, *Chinese Public Diplomacy: The Rise of the Confucius Institute* (London: Routledge, 2017).

  This book examines the Confucius Institute as a tool of public diplomacy to promote soft power in China's foreign policy, with case studies of Confucius Institutes in different parts of the world.

- King, Kenneth, *China's Aid and Soft Power in Africa: The Case of Education and Training* (Woodbridge, UK: Boydell and Brewer, 2013).

  King offers hard evidence from Ethiopia, South Africa, and Kenya of the dramatic growth of China's soft power and increasing impact in capacity building.

- Kurlantzick, Joshua, *Charm Offensive: How China's Soft Power Is Transforming the World*, (New Haven, CT: Yale University Press, 2008).

  Kurlantzick reveals how China has wooed the world with a "charm offensive" that has largely escaped the attention of American policymakers and how Beijing's changed diplomacy has altered the political landscape in Southeast Asia and far beyond.

- Lai, Hongyi and Yiyi Lu (eds.), *China's Soft Power and International Relations* (London: Routledge, 2012).

  This volume covers the main areas in which China has made noticeable advances in its appeal and influence, including foreign policy discourse, international communication, cultural diplomacy, and foreign assistance.

- Li, Mingjiang (ed.), *Soft Power: China's Emerging Strategy in International Politics* (Lanham, MD: Lexington Books, 2009).

  Li's book provides an analysis of domestic and international views of China's soft power, its main strengths and weaknesses, and its application in China's international politics.

- Wang, Jian, *Soft Power in China: Public Diplomacy through Communication* (New York: Palgrave Macmillan, 2011).

  The book furnishes answers to a number of questions about China's pursuit of soft power through international communication, such as: What kinds of images does China want to project? What is the role of the government *vis-à-vis* that of other institutional and social actors? What kinds of tensions and pressures has China experienced?

U.S.–China Relations

Among all the external factors that affect China's foreign policy, the United States is obviously the most significant. Since the end of the Cold War, the lone superpower and the emerging global power have developed a highly interdependent relationship. However, the two sides have remained suspicious strategically. Although China has expressed no intention of driving the United States out of Asia, it is concerned about U.S. strategies and policies toward China. In the early 21st century the United States has reached out to India and Vietnam, both of which have experienced rocky relations with their giant neighbor. The United States has also beefed up its alliances with Japan, South Korea, and Australia and "unofficially" with Taiwan. Some in China feel that the United States has not abandoned its Cold War-style containment policy toward China. Just as China continues to grow in global importance, so, too, will the U.S.–China relationship, which will continue to be marked by cooperation and competition. Cohen (2010), Tao and He (2009), and Wang (2013) are historical surveys of U.S.–China relations from American and Chinese scholars, respectively. Sutter (2018) examines the domestic and international factors that have affected the relationship, whereas Zhu (2006) attempts to develop a working theory based on power transition to explain cooperation and conflict between the United States and China. Lampton (2001) is the most comprehensive study of the U.S.–China relationship in the 1990s. Shambaugh (2013) tackles the complexity of the relationship from multiple dimensions, whereas Friedberg (2011) provides a somber and perhaps alarming view of what will happen to the United States if it does not counter China's growing power. Moosa (2012) aims to dispel some of the myths and misunderstandings about trade between the two sides. Pomfret (2016) and Chang (2015) are remarkable historical accounts of the two-centuries-old relationship, while Allison (2017) carries on the power transition research and explores how the bilateral relationship can avoid the "Thucydides' Trap." Chan (2017) introduces trust, a key concept in international relations, into the study of Sino-American relations. Shobert (2018) explores how America's attitudes toward China have changed and how economic anxieties and political dysfunction have laid the foundation for turning America's collective frustrations away from acknowledging the consequences of its own poor decisions.

- Allison, Graham, *Destined for War: Can America and China Escape Thucydides's Trap?* (Boston: Houghton Mifflin Harcourt, 2017).

  Out of the 16 power transitions in the past 500 years, 12 led to war. Today, the seventeenth case looks grim. Unless China is willing to scale back its ambitions or Washington will accommodate China's rise, a conflict could soon escalate into all-out war.

- Chan, Steve, *Trust and Distrust in Sino-American Relations* (Amherst, NY: Cambria, 2017).

  Chan provides a systematic framework for analyzing the level of trust between the two countries and examining how ongoing trends and prospective developments may foster or undermine this relationship.

- Chang, Gordon H., *Fateful Ties: A History of America's Preoccupation with China* (Cambridge, MA: Harvard University Press, 2015).

  Through portraits of entrepreneurs, missionaries, academics, artists, diplomats, and activists, Chang demonstrates how ideas about China have long been embedded in America's conception of itself and its own fate.

- Cohen, Warren I., *America's Response to China: A History of Sino-American Relations*, 5th edition (New York: Columbia University Press, 2010).

  From the mercantile interests of the newly independent America to the early-21st-century changing international political economy, Cohen analyzes the concerns and conceptions that have shaped America's China policy and examines their far-reaching outcomes.

Chinese Foreign Policy: A Bibliographical Review   55

- Friedberg, Aaron L., *A Contest for Supremacy: China, America, and the Struggle for Mastery in Asia* (New York: W. W. Norton, 2011).

  Friedberg argues that America's leaders are failing to act expeditiously enough to counter China's growing strength and explains that the ultimate aim of China is to win without fighting, displacing the United States as the leading power in Asia, while avoiding direct confrontation.

- Lampton, David M., *Same Bed, Different Dreams: Managing U.S.–China Relations, 1989–2000* (Berkeley: University of California Press, 2001).

  The processes of globalization have brought America and China increasingly close in the global bed. At the same time, their respective national institutions, interests, and popular perceptions, and the very characters of the two peoples, ensure that the two nations continue to have substantially different dreams.

- Moosa, Imad, *The US–China Trade Dispute: Facts, Figures and Myths* (Cheltenham, UK: Edward Elgar, 2012).

  Moosa addresses contentious issues, including whether the Chinese currency is undervalued; whether the undervaluation of the yuan, should it exist, is the cause of the US trade deficit with China; and whether Chinese policies are immoral and illegal.

- Pomfret, John, *The Beautiful Country and the Middle Kingdom: America and China, 1776 to the Present* (New York: Henry Holt, 2016).

  Drawing on personal letters, diaries, memoirs, government documents, and contemporary news reports, Pomfret reconstructs the surprising, tragic, and marvelous ways Americans and Chinese have engaged with one another through the centuries.

- Shambaugh, David (ed.), *Tangled Titans: The United States and China* (Lanham, MD: Rowman & Littlefield, 2013).

  This is an in-depth exploration of the historical, domestic, bilateral, regional, global, and future contexts of this complex relationship by a team of top-notch scholars.

56 A Critical Decade: China's Foreign Policy (2008–2018)

- Shobert, Benjamin, *Blaming China: It Might Feel Good but It Won't Fix America's Economy* (Lincoln, Nebraska: Potomac Books, 2018).

  The United States harbors deep insecurities about its economic future, its place in the world, its response to terrorism, and its deeply dysfunctional government. Over the next several years, these four insecurities will be perverted and projected onto China in an attempt to shift blame for errors entirely of America's own making.

- Sutter, Robert G., *U.S.–Chinese Relations: Perilous Past, Pragmatic Present*, 3rd edition (Lanham, MD: Rowman & Littlefield, 2018).

  Tracing the history of Sino-American engagement, Sutter shows that strong differences and mutual suspicions persist, only partly overridden by mutual pragmatism that shifts with circumstances. He considers key domestic and international factors determining the evolution and status of the relationship.

- Tao, Wenzhao (陶文钊) and He Xingqiang, (何兴强). *Zhongmei guanxishi* (中美关系史) (Beijing: China Social Sciences, 2009).

  This book covers a complete history of U.S.–Chinese interactions, from the voyage of the *Empress of China* to Canton in 1784 to the first term of President George W. Bush, highlighting the complexity of the relationship.

- Wang, Dong, *The United States and China: A History from the Eighteenth Century to the Present* (Lanham, MD: Rowman & Littlefield, 2013).

  Wang examines the foundations and character of political, economic, military, social, and cultural relations and shows how these have come to shape domestic and international affairs.

- Zhu, Zhiqun, *US–China Relations in the 21st Century: Power Transition and Peace* (London: Routledge, 2006).

  Using a modified power transition theory, Zhu addresses bilateral relations on international, domestic, societal, and individual levels after 1989. This book discusses whether China and the United States can learn from history and manage a potential power transition peacefully.

Relations with Other Major Powers

In its "big power" diplomacy, China gives particular attention to Japan, India, Russia, the European Union (EU), and the Korean Peninsula. The rivalry between Japan and China has a long and sometimes brutal history, and they continue to eye each other warily as the balance of power tips toward Beijing. In the early 21st century, China and Russia have made efforts to strengthen bilateral ties and improve cooperation on a number of diplomatic fronts, although historical suspicion and the Russian concern over China's rapid rise may become obstacles for further ties. Relations between China and EU countries are generally positive, but disputes in trade, human rights, and weapons sanctions continue to exist. The Korean Peninsula is the venue where major powers compete for influence and where China has vital national interests. Bush (2010), Sun (2012), and Lam (2017) are some of the best studies on the difficult Japan–China relationship. Bellacqua (2010) focuses on China–Russia relations, whereas Ross *et al.* (2010) examines the China–US–EU triangle. Snyder (2009) is probably the most comprehensive study of China's relations with the two Koreas. Sidhu and Yuan (2003), Holslag (2010), and Ogden (2017) consider different aspects of the ever-growing but competitive relations between China and India. Fravel (2008) deals with China's territorial disputes with its neighbors, including Japan, Russia, India, and Vietnam.

- Bellacqua, James (ed.), *The Future of China–Russia Relations* (Lexington: University Press of Kentucky, 2010).

  A group of international scholars explore the state of the relationship between the two powers and assess the prospects for future cooperation and possible tensions in the new century.

- Bush, Richard C., *The Perils of Proximity: China–Japan Security Relations* (Washington, DC: Brookings Institution, 2010).

  Bush evaluates the chances of armed conflict between China and Japan, throwing into stark relief the dangers it would pose and revealing the steps that could head off such a disastrous turn of events.

58 *A Critical Decade: China's Foreign Policy (2008–2018)*

- Fravel, Taylor M., *Strong Borders, Secure Nation: Cooperation and Conflict in China's Territorial Disputes* (Princeton, NJ: Princeton University Press, 2008).

  Fravel contends that since the 1950s China has been more likely to compromise in conflicts with its Asian neighbors and less likely to use force than many scholars and analysts might have surmised.

- Holslag, Jonathan, *China and India: Prospects for Peace* (New York: Columbia University Press, 2010).

  Holslag argues that China and India cannot grow without a fierce contest. Despite a period of peace in the 1990s and early 2000s, mutual perceptions have become hostile, and a military game of tit-for-tat promises to diminish prospects for peace.

- Lam, Peng Er (ed.), *China–Japan Relations in the 21st Century: Antagonism despite Interdependency* (Singapore: Palgrave Macmillan, 2017).

  Focusing on power transition in East Asia, lack of a common enemy in the post-Cold War era, clash of nationalism, and lack of trust and shared values between China and Japan, this collection addresses the origins of a troubled bilateral relationship that could challenge stability and prosperity of East Asia.

- Ogden, Chris, *China and India: Asia's Emergent Great Powers* (Cambridge, UK: Polity, 2017).

  Ogden explores the extent to which domestic political and cultural values as well as historical identities and perceptions are central driving forces behind the common status, ambitions and worldviews of China and India.

- Ross, Robert S.; Øystein Tunsjø and Zhang Tuosheng (eds.), *US–China–EU-Relations: Managing the New World Order* (London: Routledge, 2010).

  It examines how a future global order will be developed by the interactions of these leading actors, and how they promote cooperation and manage conflicts on a wide spectrum of issues, including security challenges.

- Sidhu, Waheguru Pal Singh and Jing-dong Yuan, *China and India: Cooperation or Conflict?* (Boulder, CO: Lynne Rienner, 2003).

  The authors see a trend in Beijing and New Delhi toward a more pragmatic approach to managing differences and broadening common interests.

- Snyder, Scott, *China's Rise and the Two Koreas: Politics, Economics, Security* (Boulder, CO: Lynne Rienner, 2009).

  It offers an insightful, expert account of how China's economic ascension affects the balance of power on the Korean Peninsula and in Northeast Asia. Snyder studies the transformation of China's relations with both Koreas and assesses the likely consequences of those developments for the United States and Japan.

- Sun, Jing, *Japan and China as Charm Rivals: Soft Power in Regional Diplomacy* (Ann Arbor: University of Michigan Press, 2012).

  Instead of adopting a one-size-fits-all approach, the Chinese and the Japanese deploy customized charm campaigns for each target state. Sun evaluates the effectiveness of individual campaigns from the perspective of the target state.

China and the Developing World

This section covers China's diplomacy in Africa and other developing regions, such as the Middle East, Latin America, and the South Pacific. The China–Africa relationship has become a hotly debated topic since the late 20th century. The "China and Africa" part features several books dealing with the history, motivations, strategies, and significance of China's robust relations with African countries. The "China and Other Developing Regions" part treats China's relations with the rest of the developing world.

China and Africa

Africa–China relations have a long history. In the mid-20th century, Maoist China funded sub-Saharan African anticolonial liberation

60   A Critical Decade: China's Foreign Policy (2008–2018)

movements, and the PRC then assisted newly independent African nations. In the early 21st century, Africa and China are immersed in an era of heavy engagement, one that promises to do more for economic growth and poverty alleviation than anything attempted by Western colonialism or international aid programs. Nowhere in the world is China's rapid rise to power more evident than in Africa. From multi-billion-dollar investments in oil and minerals to the influx of thousands of merchants and laborers and of cheap consumer goods, China's economic and political reach is redefining Africa's traditional ties with the international community. Is China a neo-colonizer? Or is China helping the developing world pave a pathway out of poverty? What do ordinary Africans make of it? And how do China–Africa relations influence wider geopolitics? Such debates and discussions will continue and China will continue to be a significant player in Africa's political economy in the years ahead. Michel and Beuret (2009) and Power *et al.* (2012) focus on China's resource needs in Africa, whereas Alden (2007) and Taylor (2010) cover a wide range of activities in which China has been engaged in Africa. Jackson (1995) studies how China dealt with conflicts and revolutions in African countries in the 1970s. Brautigam (2011), Rotberg (2008), and Chan (2013) offer some thought-provoking assessments of China's multiple roles in Africa. Dent (2011) and Zhang (2013) look at the contributions of China–Africa relations to global development. Brautigam (2015) debunks some myths about China's agricultural investment in Africa.

- Alden, Chris, *China in Africa: Partner, Competitor or Hegemon?* (London: Zed, 2007).

  To understand Chinese involvement on the continent, one needs to recognize the range of economic, diplomatic, and security rationales behind Beijing's Africa policy as well as the responses of African elites; only then can the challenges and opportunities for Africa and the West be accurately assessed.

- Brautigam, Deborah, *The Dragon's Gift: The Real Story of China in Africa* (Oxford: Oxford University Press, 2011).

Brautigam explains what the Chinese are doing, how they do it, how much aid they give, and how it all fits with their "going global" strategy. Using hard data and a series of vivid stories ranging across agriculture, industry, natural resources, and governance, she offers a compelling assessment of China's role in Africa.

- Brautigam, Deborah, *Will Africa Feed China?* (Oxford: Oxford University Press, 2015).

  Few topics are as controversial and emotionally charged as the belief that the Chinese government is aggressively buying up huge tracts of prime African land to grow food to ship back to China. Brautigam probes the myths and realities behind the media headlines.

- Chan, Stephen (ed.), *The Morality of China in Africa: The Middle Kingdom and the Dark Continent* (London: Zed, 2013).

  This book analyzes the moral aspects of China–Africa relations. The work undermines existing assumptions concerning Sino-African relations, such as that Africa is of critical importance for China, that China sees no risk in its largesse toward Africa, and that there is a single Chinese agenda.

- Dent, Christopher M. (ed.), *China and Africa Development Relations* (Abingdon, UK: Routledge, 2011).

  The contributors investigate what is particularly special about the emerging development partnership and how it may evolve in the future. They concentrate on various development capacity issues and consider diverse debates on development and development ideologies.

- Jackson, Steven F., 1995. "China's Third World Foreign Policy: The Case of Angola and Mozambique, 1961–1993." *China Quarterly*, Vol. 142, pp. 388–422.

  This article examines the tensions and shifts of Chinese policy toward two essentially simultaneous revolutionary struggles and their post-independence governments: Angola and Mozambique. It reveals how China organizes its relations with Third World countries after their independence.

- Michel, Serge and Michel Beuret, *China Safari: On the Trail of Beijing's Expansion in Africa* (New York: Nation, 2009).

  Traveling from Beijing to Khartoum, Algiers to Brazzaville, the authors explore the possibility that China will help Africa direct its own fate and finally bring light to the "dark continent," making it a force to be reckoned with internationally.

- Power, Marcus; Giles Mohan and May Tan-Mullins, *China's Resource Diplomacy in Africa: Powering Development?* (Basingstoke, UK: Palgrave Macmillan, 2012).

  Using detailed case study material collected in Africa, the authors paint a picture of gains for some states, but losses for others. Looking beyond the state, the authors see an even more complex picture of evolving social relations between Chinese and Africans and a troubling ecological footprint.

- Rotberg, Robert I. (ed.), *China into Africa: Trade, Aid, and Influence* (Washington, DC: Brookings Institution, 2008).

  Among the specific topics tackled in this volume are China's interest in African oil, military and security relations, the influx of Chinese aid to sub-Saharan Africa, human rights issues, and China's overall strategy in the region.

- Taylor, Ian, *China's New Role in Africa* (Boulder, CO: Lynne Rienner, 2010).

  Taylor discusses in depth China's relations with the continent, the importance of oil, what Africa gets in return, human rights concerns, arms trading, and what it all means for world peace and the United States.

- Zhang, Chun, (张春). *Zhongfei guanxi guoji gongxianlun* (*中非关系国际贡献论*) (Shanghai, China: Shanghai People's Publishing House, 2013).

  The book addresses the international contributions of China–Africa relations from three angles: material benefits, strategic significance, and theoretical implications. The author maintains that Chinese scholars should take the leadership role in studying China–Africa relations.

China and Other Developing Regions

The "sleeping dragon" has wakened and is becoming a major political and economic force in regional and world affairs. In the early 21st century, China's reach covers every corner of the earth. China is signing investment agreements, building roads and pipelines, seeking strategic partnerships, and gaining membership in regional and international organizations. Developing countries are seen by China both as extremely important sources of energy and raw materials and as potential supporters to its multilateral approach to international affairs. Dittmer (2018) provides a broad account of China's Asia policy since the Cold War. Eisenman *et al.* (2007); Dittmer and Yu (2010); and Hickey and Guo (2010) offer an overview of China's relations with the developing world, whereas Currier and Dorraj (2011) examines China's energy diplomacy in the developing world. Lu and Fan (2017) examines China–Southeast Asia relations from the perspective of Chinese scholars. Olimat (2013) studies China–Middle East relations, whereas Garver (2006) focuses on China–Iran relations. Guo and Xu (2007) discuss the importance of and challenges to China's relations with the developing world. Hardy (2013) and Su and Zhao (2017) study China–Latin America relations, and Wesley-Smith (2013) makes the case that China offers island states in the Pacific economic and political opportunities not available under established structures of power and influence. Reardon-Anderson (2018) surveys China's expanding relations with the Middle East, while Fulton (2019) examines the dynamic relations between China and the Gulf Cooperation Council countries since 1949.

- Currier, Carrie Liu and Manochehr Dorraj (eds.), *China's Energy Relations with the Developing World* (New York: Continuum, 2011).

  This is a collection of essays that cover many developments in China's quest for energy security in the developing world.

- Dittmer, Lowell, *China's Asia*: *Triangular Dynamics since the Cold War* (Lanham, MD: Rowman & Littlefield, 2018).

Dittmer traces the PRC's policy toward its Asian neighbors in the context of the country's move from a developing nation to a great power, capable of playing a role in world politics commensurate with its remarkable economic rise.

- Dittmer, Lowell and George Yu, T. (eds.), *China, the Developing World, and the New Global Dynamic* (Boulder, CO: Lynne Rienner, 2010).

  A series of regional chapters showcases a quid pro quo relationship — variously involving crucial raw materials, energy, and consumers, on one hand, and infrastructure development, aid, and security, on the other.

- Eisenman, Joshua; Eric Heginbotham and Derek Mitchell (eds.), *China and the Developing World: Beijing's Strategy for the Twenty-First Century* (Armonk, NY: M.E. Sharpe, 2007).

  The book offers a broad overview of the strategies and accomplishments of China's diplomacy toward the developing world. Beginning in the early 1980s, China's foreign policy toward the Third World shifted from being political–ideological to pragmatic–economic.

- Fulton, Jonathan, *China's Relations with the Gulf Monarchies* (New York: Routledge, 2019).

  Growing relations between China and Gulf Cooperation Council countries are examined across diplomatic and political interactions, trade and investment, infrastructure and construction projects, people-to-people exchanges, and military and security cooperation.

- Garver, John W., *China and Iran: Ancient Partners in a Post-imperial World* (Seattle: University of Washington Press, 2006).

  Grounding his survey in the twin concepts of civilization and power, Garver explores the relationship between these two ancient and proud peoples, each of which considers the other a partner in its efforts to build a post-Western-dominated Asia.

- Guo Xinning, (郭新宁) and Xu Qiyu, (徐弃郁). *Cong lishi zouxiang weilai-zhongguo yu fazhanzhong guojia guanxi xilun* (从历史走向未来-中国与发展中国家关系析论) (Beijing: Current Affairs, 2007).

The book highlights the new challenges and opportunities facing China in its relations with the developing world.

- Hardy, Alfredo Toro, *The World Turned Upside Down: The Complex Partnership between China and Latin America* (Hackensack, NJ: World Scientific, 2013).

  The economic partnership between China and Latin America epitomizes the growing integration between emerging economies. Even if mostly benefiting from it, Latin America is under the double sign of threat and opportunity as a result of this complex relationship.

- Hickey, Dennis and Baogang Guo (eds.), *Dancing with the Dragon: China's Emergence in the Developing World* (Lanham, MD: Lexington Books, 2010).

  The edited book provides an analysis of China's increasing engagement with many of the less developed countries and looks at the current and future trends in Beijing's foreign relations.

- Lu, Jianren and Zuojun Fan, *China–ASEAN Relations: Cooperation and Development* (Singapore: World Scientific Publishing, 2017).

  This is an in-depth study on China–ASEAN cooperation and development, including the general introduction of China–ASEAN relations and China–ASEAN cooperation, achievements and problems in politics, economy, diplomacy, security, military affairs, and maritime and cultural aspects.

- Olimat, Muhamad S., *China and the Middle East: From Silk Road to Arab Spring* (London: Routledge, 2013).

  Olimat highlights important events and key areas of the relationship, including energy, trade, arms sales, culture, and politics. He explains why most Middle Easterners prefer China's engagement to Western engagement and explores the future of Sino-Middle Eastern relations.

- Reardon-Anderson, James, *The Red Star and the Crescent: China and the Middle East* (New York: Oxford University Press, 2018).

  It's an in-depth and multidisciplinary analysis of the evolving relationship between China and the Middle East. It examines the "big picture" of international relations, then zooms in on case studies and probes the underlying domestic factors on each side.

- Su, Zhenxing and Hongling Zhao, *China and Latin America: Economic and Trade Cooperation in the Next 10 Years* (Singapore: World Scientific Publishing, 2017).

  The book explores the prospect for Sino-Latin American economic and trade cooperation in the next 10 years by analyzing resource endowment, industrial structure, economic system, development pattern, economic policy, economic environment, and trade relations between China and Latin America.

- Wesley-Smith, Terence, 2013. "China's Rise in Oceania: Issues and Perspectives." *Pacific Affairs*, Vol. 86, No. 2, pp. 351–372.

  This paper identifies a broad context for assessing China's increased interest in the islands of the Pacific. The author contends that Beijing's policy toward the Pacific is not driven by strategic competition with the United States, nor is it reducible to a specific set of interests centered on natural resources and competition with Taiwan.

China and Global Governance

The expanding scope of China's international activities is one of the latest and most important trends in global affairs. Actively engaged in global governance in both traditional and new securities, China's global activism is continually changing and has so many dimensions that immediately raises questions about its near and long-term intentions. Observers have debated whether China would be a status quo power or a revisionist power and whether it would observe the rules and regulations of international institutions and regimes. Rather than simply reassuring others that its rise is peaceful, China has taken proactive steps to reduce possible conflicts. Beijing seeks to shape the emerging global governance order as both non-threatening to itself and productive in transnational problem solving. Chan *et al.* (2012) and Li (2012) are overviews of China's engagement in global

Chinese Foreign Policy: A Bibliographical Review   67

governance in the early 21st century. Kornberg and Faust (2005), Medeiros (2009), and Dellios and Ferguson (2013) look at the process and transition of China's involvement in global governance, whereas Kavalski (2009), Zeng and Liang (2013), and Chan (2011) consider selected areas of China's global involvement: regionalization, trade, and health, respectively. Kennedy (2017) suggests that while China is a defender of the status quo in some areas of global governance, it is a reformer in others, and occasionally a revisionist in still other spheres. Kastner *et al.* (2018) offers more case studies of China's involvement in global governance, ranging from global finance to climate change. Li (2019) examines how China joins other members of BRICS in shaping global governance. Finally, Wang (2016) represents the voice of Chinese public intellectuals who explain and defend the Belt and Road Initiative.

- Chan, Lai-Ha, *China Engages Global Health Governance: Responsible Stakeholder or System-Transformer?* (New York: Palgrave Macmillan, 2011).

  In scrutinizing China's evolving global role and its intentions for global governance, Chan argues that China is neither a system defender nor a system transformer of the liberal international order.

- Chan, Gerald; Pak Lee K. and Lai-Ha Chan, *China Engages Global Governance: A New World Order in the Making?* (London: Routledge, 2012).

  It examines and assesses whether China is capable of participating in multilateral interactions, if it is willing and able to provide public goods to address global problems, and what impact this would have on global governance.

- Dellios, Rosita and Ferguson, James R., *China's Quest for Global Order: From Peaceful Rise to Harmonious World* (Lanham, MD: Lexington Books, 2013).

  This book interprets China's quest for global order from Chinese perspectives and furnishes the relevant philosophical and historical background to engage the reader in the debates.

68 *A Critical Decade: China's Foreign Policy (2008–2018)*

- Kastner, Scott; Margaret Pearson M. and Chad Rector, *China's Strategic Multilateralism: Investing in Global Governance* (Cambridge University Press, 2018).

  It includes case studies of China's approach to security in Central Asia, nuclear proliferation, global financial governance, and climate change. This book argues that the strategic setting of a particular issue area has a strong influence on whether and how a rising power will contribute to global governance.

- Kavalski, Emilian (ed.), *China and the Global Politics of Regionalization* (Burlington, VT: Ashgate, 2009).

  A comprehensive and critical assessment of China's impact on the global politics of regionalization, the book investigates aspects of the Chinese practice of regionalization that set it apart, and demonstrates China's transformative potential in international life.

- Kennedy, Scott (ed.), *Global Governance and China: The Dragon's Learning Curve* (London: Routledge, 2017).

  A systematic analysis of China's growing engagement in global governance over the past three decades, the volume examines Chinese involvement in a wide range of regimes, including trade, finance, intellectual property rights, foreign aid, and climate change.

- Kornberg, Judith F. and Faust John R., *China in World Politics: Policies, Processes, Prospects* (Boulder, CO: Lynne Rienner, 2005).

  The book outlines the political, security, economic, and social issues China faces in the early 21st century. It familiarizes the reader with the Chinese framework for analyzing the issues in question. Alternate policy choices are suggested, along with supporting data for each course of action.

- Li, Mingjiang (ed.), *China Joins Global Governance: Cooperation and Contentions* (Lanham, MD: Lexington Books, 2012).

  The contributors cover a broad range of issues, including China's vision and strategy in global multilateralism; role in global economic/financial/trade governance, policy toward the global environment and international development; and approaches to various global security concerns, such as nuclear disarmament and non-proliferation.

- Li, Xing, *The International Political Economy of the BRICS* (Abingdon, UK: Routledge, 2019).

  The book focuses on the degree and consequence of BRICS' emergence and explores how important cooperation is to individual BRICS members' foreign policy strategies and potential relevance as leaders in regional and global governance.

- Medeiros, Evan S., *China's International Behavior: Activism, Opportunism, and Diversification* (Santa Monica, CA: RAND, 2009).

  The work analyzes how China defines its international objectives, how it is pursuing them, and what this means for U.S. economic and security interests.

- Wang, Yiwei, (王义桅). *世界是通的: 一带一路的逻辑* (*The World Is Connected: The Logic of One Belt One Road*) 商务印书馆 (Beijing: The Commercial Press, 2016).

  In the globalized world, how can China contribute to the formation of a community with a shared future through promoting connectivity and inclusiveness? The Belt and Road Initiative may be the answer.

- Zeng, Ka and Wei Liang, (eds.), *China and Global Trade Governance: China's First Decade in the World Trade Organization* (Abingdon, UK: Routledge, 2013).

  Through a thorough examination of China's World Trade Organization (WTO) compliance record and experience in multilateral trade negotiations, this volume seeks to better understand the sources of constraints on China's behavior in the multilateral trade institution as well as the country's influence on the efficacy of the WTO.

Part II
Selected Essays on Chinese Foreign Policy (2008–2018)

Chapter

3

U.S.–China Relations

Trump Offered Kim His Hand, but Asia Will Do the Heavy Lifting

The Globe and Mail, June 12, 2018

By all indications, the Trump–Kim meeting in Singapore on June 12, 2018 went very well, with President Donald Trump claiming it the start of an "excellent relationship."

But the celebration will be short-lived; what lies ahead will be more challenging. Very soon, it will become clear once again that without cooperation from others — particularly China and South Korea — the United States cannot achieve denuclearization of North Korea alone.

Global attention before and after the summit has focused on whether the meeting itself is a success or failure, with little understanding of its significance and the grave challenges ahead. The handshakes alone will remain historic, but this is just the first step in the long march toward lasting peace and prosperity on the Korean

74 A Critical Decade: China's Foreign Policy (2008–2018)

Peninsula — one must learn to walk before running. Mr. Trump has narrowly focused on North Korea's promised denuclearization, without much interest in what takes place next. Empty rhetoric such as "great things will happen to North Korea" does nothing to help the process. Does the United States have any specific plan to help a post-nuclear North Korea? The U.S. objective of complete, verifiable, irreversible denuclearization (CVID) should be replaced by co-operative, verifiable, irreversible demilitarization and development (CVIDD) of the Korean Peninsula.

Recent developments on the Korean Peninsula suggest that international cooperation will be the key to solving the North Korea problem. Supreme Leader Kim Jong-un started 2018 with a very modest hope in his New Year's address that North Korea could participate in the Pyeongchang Winter Olympics in the South. South Korean President Moon Jae-in immediately embraced the idea. North Korea not only participated in the Olympics, but its ice hockey players also joined their South Korean counterparts and competed as a unified Korean team. Both Mr. Kim and Mr. Moon must be commended for restarting the reconciliation process and reigniting the hope of a peaceful and unified Korean Peninsula.

Before the Trump–Kim summit, Mr. Moon and Mr. Kim met twice at Panmunjom, outlining plans to move forward. Mr. Kim also visited China twice, repairing the strained relationship with Chinese leaders and winning President Xi Jinping's backing before heading to Singapore. The Singapore government graciously agreed to host the summit and chip in to cover Kim's travel expenses while China provided air transportation for Mr. Kim. The Singapore summit would not have taken place without the months-long preparatory work that involved multiple countries.

In Kim's view, he went to the Singapore meeting from a position of strength, since North Korea is already a nuclear state, and Mr. Trump's agreement to meet is a tacit acceptance of its nuclear status. It will be important to help North Korea denuclearize gracefully and in a respectful manner. Security guarantees must be provided to North Korea, preferably by China, given the deep distrust between

U.S.–China Relations 75

the United States and North Korea, and America's overwhelming military advantage over North Korea.

Different from his father and grandfather, Mr. Kim has focused on both military development and economic growth since gaining power in 2011. His *byungjin* policy is quietly and slowly changing North Korea. Both peace and development are needed on the Korean Peninsula and, as the denuclearization process begins, relevant countries must be prepared to work together to help integrate North Korea into East Asia's dynamic economic development.

China has begun to normalize relations with North Korea which deteriorated in the past few years. After a hiatus of more than 6 months, China's flag carrier Air China resumed direct flights between Beijing and Pyongyang before the Trump–Kim meeting. As Mr. Trump's America retreats from global leadership, China can play a positive role by incorporating North Korea into its Belt and Road Initiative (BRI) and by welcoming North Korea into the Asian Infrastructure Investment Bank (AIIB). Other regional groups and trade clubs such as Shanghai Cooperation Organization (SCO) and Regional Comprehensive Economic Partnership (RCEP) should also open their doors to North Korea.

Right before the Trump–Kim summit, two other major gatherings of world leaders took place in China and Canada, respectively. The SCO and Group of 7 summits presented a sharp contrast of the roles of China and the United States in today's world. As the host of this year's SCO summit in Qingdao, Mr. Xi hammered home the themes of cooperation and a community with shared future. In Quebec, Mr. Trump had a tense and confrontational meeting with his G7 counterparts, skipping discussions on climate change and insulting his allies. China and the United States are clearly not on the same wavelength in their approaches to foreign policy. Perhaps it is time for Mr. Trump, Mr. Xi, and other leaders in the region to sit down and map out a viable plan for East Asia's future together.

See: https://www.theglobeandmail.com/opinion/article-trump-offered-kim-his-hand-but-asia-will-do-the-heavy-lifting/.

76 A Critical Decade: China's Foreign Policy (2008–2018)

US and Allies' Plan to Counter the BRI is their Response to China's Rise

Interview with *Sputnik*, February 22, 2018

The U.S., Australia, India, and Japan have reportedly been negotiating the establishment of a joint regional infrastructure plan to counter China's multi-billion-dollar Belt and Road Initiative (BRI). *Sputnik* discussed the issue with Zhiqun Zhu, Professor of Political Science and International Relations at Bucknell University.

Sputnik: How realistic is this plan by the United States and its allies to establish a joint project that can compete with China?

Zhiqun Zhu: It's too early to tell because this idea is still at the discussion stage. (Australian) Prime Minister Malcolm Turnbull and President Donald Trump will discuss this when Turnbull visits the United States later this week, so at this stage, we don't exactly know the scale of this proposed project and its objectives, and most importantly, we don't know how this is going to be funded and implemented, so I don't think that right now this means much to China.

Sputnik: So what impact can this announcement have on China's Belt and Road Initiative?

Zhiqun Zhu: I don't think this is a challenge to the BRI. I think the BRI is open and inclusive and China would actually welcome it. Competition is going to be welcomed by everybody including China; for those countries in different regions, I think they would appreciate different choices. Let's say China wants to build a road through a region with civil wars or terrorist activities, obviously if other countries are involved with a greater international presence, you're likely to see more security.

Sputnik: What's your take on the fact that some experts have said that it remains unclear whether the countries will have enough liquidity and money to invest in the project?

Zhiqun Zhu: Funding will be a big problem here. We all know that President Trump has the "America First" policy, but where does the money come from? Japan's Prime Minister Shinzo Abe has this Abenomics economic policy, and it has achieved some positive results, but it has not succeeded in all aspects. India sometimes exaggerates its power. Australia trades extensively with China, and China has been Australia's largest trading partner in the past decade or so. I don't think these countries will really disrupt their fruitful relations with China, and particularly, I doubt they will come up with any money to fund this massive project.

On the other hand, I don't think this is purely an economic project. I tend to think that this is more of a political, strategic, and diplomatic project, because at the basic level you see the rise of China, you see the Belt and Road from China — such an ambitious, extensive project. I think the United States, Japan, and India feel challenged and even threatened so they have to do something. I consider this idea, this new proposed project from these countries part of their efforts to counter China's growing influence globally. I don't worry about whether they have money or not; I am more concerned about how this is going to lead to strategic competition and rivalry.

Sputnik: Some analysts have said that the nations could use this project to exert pressure on Beijing on issues like the South China Sea disputes, is this likely to be true?

Zhiqun Zhu: To some extent yes, because a part of the Belt and Road Initiative includes the maritime Silk Road that extends from southern China to the South China Sea and all the way to South Asia and Africa. So, yes, if these four countries build their own program, it will be a rival to China's maritime Silk Road since the South China Sea is exactly located in that area, and there will be some pressure on China. However, I really don't think this proposed program is aimed at the South China Sea. I think it is part of a broader and multilateral response to China's rise. At the fundamental level, these countries don't know what to do about the rising power of China, so they're initiating all these different kinds of programs as a way to deal with the ongoing power shift in the Asia-Pacific.

78   A Critical Decade: China's Foreign Policy (2008–2018)

The views and opinions expressed by Zhiqun Zhu do not necessarily reflect those of Sputnik.

See:https://sputniknews.com/analysis/201802221061890122-us-china-silk-road/.

Xi and the North Korea Challenge in the Trump Era

e-International Relations, March 26, 2017

The vicious cycle of North Korea's missile/nuclear test followed by international sanctions that keeps repeating is a clear sign that the international community has failed to curb North Korea's nuclear ambitions. As President Donald Trump revamps America's Asia policy and Xi Jinping prepares to enter his second 5-year term as the CCP General Secretary, it is an opportunity to rethink the North Korea challenge.

North Korea's masterful diplomatic skills have ensured its successful maneuvering among major powers, like the proverbial shrimp among whales. It has proved repetitively that it often emerges as a winner in a messy situation in Northeast Asia. While others disagree over their strategies, North Korea has been working to improve its missile and nuclear technologies. It is extremely abnormal to let North Korea dictate the agenda of Northeast Asian politics.

Since Trump took office on January 20, 2017, North Korea has provoked the international community recurrently with missile launches and the assassination of Kim Jong-un's brother, Kim Jong-nam, in Kuala Lumpur with a VX nerve agent, a banned weapon of mass destruction (WMD). As a result, the United States canceled a prearranged meeting in New York between North Korean diplomats and a group of former U.S. officials in February.

Since 1992, when China and South Korea established diplomatic relations, China has been one of the very few countries that maintained close ties with both Koreas. After Kim Jong-un succeeded his father in December 2011, China–North Korea relations began to deteriorate. Meanwhile, China–South Korea relations quickly warmed up, with extensive economic and cultural exchanges and regular high-level talks. The relationship reached its apex in 2015 when President Park Geun-hye, defying pressure from the United States, attended the military parade in Beijing to mark the 70th anniversary of the end of World War II. However, after the U.S.–ROK decision in July 2016 to deploy the THAAD anti-ballistic missile system in South Korea, China–South Korea relations plummeted. By the time President Park was forced out of office in March 2017, the bilateral equation had reached its lowest point in decades.

China's leverage over North Korea is sometimes exaggerated. After decades of following the Juche policy, North Korea has become highly self-reliant. Trade with China, though important to North Korea, is not quite the lifeline of its economy. Locked in a strategic rivalry with the United States, China is unwilling to abandon North Korea now. Through continued interactions, it hopes Pyongyang will focus on growth instead of guns. Such a strategy has proved to be wishful thinking and is hurting Beijing's international image and national interests.

Kim Jong-nam's assassination was an additional blow to China, after Kim Jong-un executed his uncle Jang Song-thaek, who admired China's economic prowess. Kim Jong-nam, though seemingly disinterested in politics, could have possibly led a more liberal, China-friendly North Korean government. With him gone, China–North Korea relations are likely to worsen in the short term.

North Korea is not just an ungrateful "white-eyed wolf," as many Chinese commentators would call it, but has become a direct security threat. China stopped importing coal from North Korea for the rest of 2017, but no one is certain how this will be strictly implemented and whether it will be enough to compel Kim Jong-un to change his mind. The United States is still waiting for "positive actions" from North Korea before appearing willing to deal with North Korea directly. In Washington's policy corridors, many believe that the United States should avoid talking with North Korea to reciprocate its conduct. Such an arrogant and short-sighted

80 A Critical Decade: China's Foreign Policy (2008–2018)

approach, however, is not just counterproductive, but shirks moral responsibility.

Trump must abandon the mistaken assumption that China alone can solve the North Korea problem. It is merely a cliché that China is the sole ally of North Korea and holds the key to the Pyongyang puzzle. The reality is that few Chinese still consider North Korea an ally. The 1961 Sino-North Korea Treaty of Friendship sits covered in dust. North Korea, too, on the other hand, shows signs of dislike for China. Recently, for instance, North Korea's Central News Agency publicly slammed Beijing for "dancing to the tune of the U.S."

Beijing has been flummoxed by Seoul's turnabout in its THAAD decision. It does not seem to fully understand the rationale behind the THAAD's installation or the priority of the U.S.–South Korea alliance for Seoul. The THAAD is supposed to be a shield against North Korean missiles, but China views it as a regional security threat. The anti-ballistic system is, consequently, likely to deepen the distrust between the United States and China. However, the future of the THAAD is uncertain, as South Koreans shall elect a new president in May.

There exist, as generally accepted, three options to deal with North Korea: continued sanctions, a pre-emptive military strike, or a creative and constructive approach. Sanctions have failed and the military option is too risky, especially considering South Korea's interests. With tensions remaining high on the Korean Peninsula, all parties must resist the temptation to use force so that peace can prevail. A constructive way forward could be that China and the United States switch their approaches, as China takes more resolute measures against Pyongyang while the United States holds out carrots. With the prospect of no support from China and some security guarantee from the United States, North Korea is more likely to return to the negotiation table. Is there such a possibility?

Trump said during the presidential campaign that he was willing to invite Kim Jong-un to the United States for a meeting over a hamburger. While a historic Trump–Kim meeting in Washington or

Pyongyang is unthinkable for most, it might be something needed now to achieve denuclearization of the Korean Peninsula.

Meanwhile, U.S.–China relations have showed some positive developments after the roller-coaster ride since Trump's election. A recent video showing Kim Jong-nam's son Kim Han-sol thanking both China and the United States for helping him, his mother, and his sister in the aftermath of his father's assassination suggests that the Beijing and Washington have been working in convergence on North Korean matters in the past few weeks.

Both Trump and Xi are leaders with a strong sense of mission. As they prepare to meet for the first time at Trump's Mar-a-Lago resort in April 2017, one hopes that they can grasp the opportunity to defuse tensions on the Korean Peninsula. The United States and China must jointly address the North Korea challenge urgently, based on the consensus that North Korea has become a common security threat and that a peaceful resolution of the issue is still possible. Missing such an opportunity and miscalculating the situation are likely to turn the cold war in Northeast Asia into a hot war once again.

See: https://www.e-ir.info/2017/03/26/xi-and-the-north-korea-challenge-in-the-trump-era/.

Raising U.S.–China Relations to a New Height

China Daily USA, September 23, 2015

Pessimism about U.S.–China relations seems to be permeating the air recently. Many observers on both sides have rung alarm bells about growing tension in the relationship, especially over cybersecurity, the South China Sea, and stock market turmoil. What has gone wrong? How can the two countries move this vital relationship forward?

In 1940, Kenneth Wherry, mayor of Pawnee City, Nebraska, said, "With God's help, we will lift Shanghai up and up, ever up, until it is just like Kansas City." If Wherry, who became a U.S. senator later, were still alive today, he would be surprised to learn that modern Shanghai remains different from Kansas City, but it is probably Kansas City that needs to be lifted up in terms of development now.

Americans have had a missionary impulse to change China, either by christianizing it in the 19th century or democratizing it in the 21st century. From the very beginning of interactions, the United States has been dealing with China from a position of strength; it is ill-prepared to live with a nation as big and almost as powerful as itself.

China's meteoric re-emergence as a global force in the early 21st century is truly stunning to Americans and to many Chinese. The U.S. economy suffered seriously in the 2008–2009 financial crisis, from which it is still recovering. Meanwhile, the Chinese economy has continued to charge forward, and after overtaking Japan as the world's second-largest economy in 2010, it is poised to take the top spot soon. The global power structure has changed fundamentally.

The American concern about China's rising power reflects Americans' lack of confidence in their competition with China. The reality is that China remains a developing country despite a large economy. According to Premier Li Keqiang, 200 million Chinese still live in poverty. China faces tremendous domestic challenges, including a widening income gap, an aging population, rampant corruption and a deteriorating environment. The United States remains far ahead of China, especially in technology and innovation.

The two economies and societies are complementary in many aspects. A recent study by the National Committee on United States–China Relations and the Rhodium Group reveals that from 2000 to 2014, Chinese firms spent nearly $46 billion on new establishments and acquisitions in the U.S. Chinese-affiliated companies directly employ more than 80,000 Americans. If the U.S. continues to welcome China's booming investment, it could receive between $100 billion to $200 billion from China by 2020, which would add between 200,000 and 400,000 full-time jobs in the U.S.

China is the largest trading partner of a growing number of countries, from Asia to Africa and from Latin America to the Middle East. A trade regime without China's participation is unlikely to succeed. China-led new initiatives such as the Asian Infrastructure Investment Bank (AIIB) complement the work of the World Bank and Asian Development Bank.

"Pivot" and "new type of great power relations" are attempts by the United States and China, respectively, to handle the complicated relationship, but they are poorly defined and largely misunderstood by the other side. Americans generally believe that China has become more assertive in foreign policy and intends to replace the U.S. in global affairs. Many Chinese genuinely think the United States is trying to block China's rise.

Lack of trust has been identified as the outstanding problem between the two countries. But how to build trust? Going forward, the two countries must first readjust their mentality. For China, the priority remains at home. Chinese leaders must resist the temptation to flex muscles abroad. It is not time to abandon Deng Xiaoping's dictum of lying low and focusing on growth. The United States, on the other hand, must be realistic and remove ideological lenses to overcome the "China fear." It must also rein in its smaller allies in Asia so as to avoid conflicts that will drag the U.S. and China into direct confrontation.

China and the United States are joined at the hip. There is no bad blood between them. They cannot afford to allow hardliners or protectionists to interfere with the generally cooperative relationship. Disagreement on certain issues and occasional quarrels are part of the normal life in a relationship. Mutual accommodation and appreciation will enhance personal relations as well as relations between nations.

See: http://usa.chinadaily.com.cn/epaper/2015-09/23/content_21959393.htm.

84　*A Critical Decade: China's Foreign Policy (2008–2018)*

Big Picture of China Lost in the Debates

CNN, October 29, 2012

The real issue is not over China's currency, but the power transition as its economy is expected to surpass the U.S.

Story highlights

- Obama and Romney mentioned China 53 times in the U.S. presidential debates
- Their discussions of China missed the big picture: China's rapid rise
- Biggest challenge is the power transition as China gallops ahead, writes Zhiqun Zhu

The Communist Party leaders inside the *Zhongnanhai* compound in Beijing may have found solace in the Obama-Romney debates: Though China was mentioned 53 times, both presidential candidates avoided harsh rhetoric toward China.

Despite Romney's repeated avowal to label China a "currency manipulator" and Obama's branding of China as "an adversary," both sounded moderate and called China a partner, which leaves the door open for building a good working relationship with China's new leaders. The candidates traded jabs on how they would deal with the trade and currency issue but skipped other major controversial topics such as human rights, Tibet and censorship. To Beijing's relief and to American conservatives' disappointment, the highly anticipated "China bashing" was absent from the debates.

Also missing was the big picture — America's relative decline, China's rapid rise and the ensuing power restructuring in the global system. Is the United States ready to cope with an increasingly powerful, confident and yet non-democratic China? The real issue is not whether China is a currency manipulator or not — after all, the *yuan* has appreciated more than 11% since 2010 and more than 30% since 2005.

Obama's and Romney's narrow focus on trade and currency when mentioning China, which is understandable due to America's lackluster recovery, and their dodging of other major problems between the two countries may be misinforming Americans who, as a result, do not fully understand the nature of this complex relationship.

This is a multifaceted relationship, strong but difficult at times. The biggest challenge the two countries face is the power transition between them, as China continues to gallop ahead and is expected to surpass the United States as the largest economy within a decade. Both countries are struggling to deal with the new power structure in the international system.

In fact, China is rising so rapidly that it has difficulty adjusting to its newfound power and sometimes behaves clumsily in international affairs as evidenced in China's perceived forcefulness in the Diaoyu/Senkaku dispute and South China Sea controversy.

U.S. politicians are used to speaking from a position of dominance. Both Obama and Romney claimed they would push China to "play by the rules." Such a condescending approach will not work with today's more assertive and nationalistic China.

The United States must play by the rules first. For example, Huawei was recently singled out by Congress as a company threatening U.S. national interests and was essentially declared unwelcome in the U.S. The telecoms giant has businesses globally, including a recent £1.3 billion investment in the United Kingdom which would create 500 jobs. In September, Obama issued a rare presidential order instructing Ralls Corp., whose owners are Chinese, to divest itself of four Oregon wind farm projects near a military base, citing a national security threat. But firms operated by other foreign owners in the same area are apparently conducting business as usual. Where is the level playing field?

The United States still maintains some Tiananmen-era sanctions against China, including the ban on exports of high-tech equipment and products to China. One wonders how the United States can narrow its trade deficit with China, if it only sells apples and oranges to China?

Is China friend or foe? This often-asked question misses the central point that the United States and China are so interdependent that they no longer have the luxury to make such a choice.

The two countries are separated by huge gaps in political systems and cultural values, which can be a major cause of conflict. The two governments still deeply distrust each other. Since the Obama administration's implementation of its "strategic rebalancing" toward Asia in 2010, the U.S. government has failed to convince China and many other countries in Asia that its purpose is not to counter China's growing power. America's deployment of more forces in the Asia-Pacific region and beefing up its alliances with China's neighbors smack of a policy of encircling China. Of course containment will not work in this day and age, and Asian countries do not want to be drawn into a great power conflict.

It has become politically incorrect to say anything good about China during America's elections. Candidates tend to compete over who is tougher on China. It has become an accepted norm to blame China for America's domestic woes. Such practices may help a candidate to win an election, but they are very harmful to U.S.–China relations in the long term. The United States is at the risk of creating a resentful China during the Asian power's transition to a more diverse and open society.

Nothing is wrong with focusing on economic issues now, but Americans should never lose sight of the big picture. As a global leader, the United States has the moral responsibility to help promote democracy, human rights and rule of law in the world. With China in transition, the United States has a great opportunity to help shape the future of a nation with which it will be politically and economically intertwined for generations to come.

See: https://www.cnn.com/2012/10/27/opinion/china-u-s-debates/index.html.

Cultural Gap Hinders U.S.–China Ties

The Taipei Times, January 27, 2011

Chinese President Hu Jintao's state visit to the U.S. ended without many surprises. After the pomp and circumstance, major issues of contention remain between the two sides. Though both governments have claimed the visit to be a success, one should not expect a smooth road ahead in U.S.–China relations. Taiwan, Tibet, and trade will continue to disturb Beijing and Washington, even as they cooperate on a wide range of other issues. However, the biggest obstacle to better relations is a deeply rooted cultural misunderstanding of the two societies.

A couple of events that occurred during Hu's visit show how big this cultural gap is.

"National Image" Campaign

Beijing launched an aggressive and expensive "national image" campaign in the U.S. to coincide with Hu's visit. It began to display a high-profile, 1-min advertisement on six huge screens in New York's Times Square. The ad is to be shown 300 times a day until the middle of this month, with images of a select group of happy, smart and wealthy urban Chinese elites, including actors, athletes, scientists, entrepreneurs, and astronauts. It aims to boost China's image abroad and present a modern and peaceful nation to the world. The ad also runs on CNN and other networks.

Most Americans are probably indifferent to this ad. Some of them might interpret it as China's implicit message to the U.S. that China can do well and beat the U.S. in every aspect, including the space program.

According to a recent Pew survey, 47 percent of people in the U.S. think China is now the biggest economic power, compared with 31 percent who believe the U.S. is still the top dog. Americans also consider China to be the greatest threat, ahead of North Korea and Iran. In this context, this ad may add to the fear among Americans

88 A Critical Decade: China's Foreign Policy (2008–2018)

that China is ambitious, fast-developing and will eventually defeat the U.S. economically and militarily. With some members of the U.S. Congress blaming China for the high unemployment rate, this ad could cause concern among Americans given the grim economic conditions.

Reach Out to Americans

Whoever advised the Chinese government on this ad does not seem to understand the U.S. society. Americans prefer straightforward conversations. It would be more effective for the Chinese government to reach out to Americans directly and explain in plain language how China's growth can contribute to the U.S. economy and benefit U.S. consumers.

Cultural misunderstanding is also obvious on the U.S. side. A lack of sensitivity to other cultures is a common problem in U.S. foreign relations. During the U.S.–China press conference at the White House, Ben Feller from *The Associated Press* was given the opportunity to ask the first question, and he asked a question about human rights.

"President Obama, you've covered the broad scope of this relationship, but I'd like to follow up specifically on your comments about human rights. Can you explain to the American people how the United States can be so allied with a country that is known for treating its people so poorly, for using censorship and force to repress its people? Do you have any confidence that as a result of this visit that will change? And, President Hu, I'd like to give you a chance to respond to this issue of human rights. How do you justify China's record, and do you think that's any of the business of the American people?" he asked.

Human Rights

Feller, like many in the U.S., is concerned about human rights conditions in China and he has every right to raise this important issue. Most Americans will not see any problem with this question and the way it was asked, but to many Chinese, this was an inappropriate question to begin the question-and-answer session with, and Feller's attitude was impolite, accusatory, if not outright rude. In the Confucian tradition, you'd begin with more pleasant remarks before shifting to any disagreements and you definitely do not "give" a senior leader or an elder "a chance to respond." That's very disrespectful.

Remarkably, both Obama and Hu handled the human rights question well. Noting the differences between the two countries in history, culture and political system, Obama emphasized the importance of continuing frank dialogues and discussions. At the same time he acknowledged the "incredible achievements of the Chinese people." Obama also pointed out that differences on human rights should not prevent the two countries from cooperating in other critical areas.

Hu did not answer the question initially due to translation problems, but when asked again by Hans Nichols from *Bloomberg*, he said "a lot still needs to be done in China in terms of human rights" after asserting that China recognizes and respects the universality of human rights, but one needs to take into account the different national circumstances in discussing human rights.

The two leaders seem to understand the importance of mutual understanding and have encouraged more people-to-people interactions, but there is a long way to go to narrow the gap since the two societies remain far apart in terms of political values and cultural traditions. More exchanges at the societal level will be pivotal to sustaining and developing this most important bilateral relationship. If this Obama–Hu summit is able to result in more mutual learning between the two peoples and bring the two societies closer, it will be remembered as a truly successful meeting of minds between the two leaders and the two nations.

See: https://www.bucknell.edu/x67112.xml.

China's Hu Can Rightly Ask Obama: What Have You Done for Me Lately?

Chinese President Hu and President Obama must work toward building mutual trust between the U.S. and China when they meet in Washington. But Obama must allay China's concerns on North Korea before the U.S. can press China for more.

The Christian Science Monitor, January 17, 2011

Chinese President Hu Jintao will begin his swan song visit to the United States on January 18, 2011 before he steps down in 2012. High on the agenda of this visit will be North Korea and East Asian security. President Obama is likely to urge his Chinese counterpart to put more pressure on North Korean leader Kim Jong-il, who created one crisis after another last year.

But China's major concerns about the aftermath of the North Korean regime's expected collapse have to be taken seriously before the United States can successfully persuade China to be more cooperative on North Korea and other issues. Simply pressuring China to do more without considering its legitimate concerns is not only condescending but also counterproductive.

At the beginning of the New Year, the two Koreas struck some conciliatory tones and were able to avoid a war that seemed so imminent just a few weeks ago. Western media cited China's quiet diplomacy as a major cause of the encouraging restraint on the Korean Peninsula now. Still, the United States has high expectations of China, hoping that China will become a more active and responsible player to help terminate North Korea's nuclear program and rein in its reckless dictator.

China Thinks the U.S. Doesn't Care

A key obstacle to further U.S.–China cooperation on North Korea is the lack of mutual trust between the two powers. U.S. expectations of China notwithstanding, China does not have strong incentives to cooperate, largely because it believes that the United States does not seem to care about China's interests and concerns.

China is obviously not proud of being regarded as an ally of the Kim Jong-il regime. Within China, scholars and officials have been debating over how to deal with a recalcitrant North Korea that often embarrasses China. There is a growing voice within Chinese academia and the government that China should dump North Korea, since continuing to support Pyongyang hurts China's international image and does not serve China's long-term interest.

The fact that China is still behind North Korea is puzzling to many. Yet, one has to realize China has its own considerations and priorities. A power transition is under way in Beijing, as Mr. Hu is expected to pass the baton to Vice President Xi Jinping next year. This explains why the Chinese government emphasizes stability and continuity of its policies.

The U.S. Must Allay China's Concerns

Before it will fully cooperate with the United States on North Korea, China's two major concerns have to be eased, both of which derive from the expected eventual collapse of the North Korean regime as a result of heavy international pressure. One is the potential massive wave of North Korean refugees to China. The other is the status of U.S. troops on what would become the unified Korean Peninsula. In addition to addressing these Chinese concerns, the United States must reach out to the next generation of Chinese leaders for lasting cooperation.

In the event of a sudden North Korean regime breakdown, many North Korean people will attempt to cross the demilitarized zone (DMZ) into South Korea, a scenario that the South is anticipating and preparing for now, with support from the United States. An equally likely scenario is that tens of thousands, and possibly even more, North Korean refugees will flood into China, which will create serious economic, social, and political challenges for northeast China.

Have the United States and other Western governments ever considered assisting China in dealing with this humanitarian nightmare? How can the United States and others share the burden with China?

The United States also has yet to explain what it will do with its forward deployment of some 28,500 troops on the Korean Peninsula after Korea's potential unification. Will the U.S. troops remain in the unified Korea, continue to stay south of today's DMZ, or withdraw completely from the Korean Peninsula? How about U.S. forces in Japan?

A Chance to Build Mutual Trust

The obstacles are clear. China is uncertain about North Korea's future and U.S. intentions in Asia. China and the United States do not trust each other, and the two militaries perceive one another as the main rival.

The Hu–Obama meeting in Washington will thus be a great opportunity for the two countries to alleviate Beijing's concerns, build mutual trust, reach consensus on North Korea and other key issues, and lay a solid foundation for jointly tackling common challenges in East Asia in the years ahead.

See: https://m.csmonitor.com/index.php/Commentary/Opinion/2011/0117/China-s-Hu-can-rightly-ask-Obama-What-have-you-done-for-me-lately.

North Korea Tests U.S.–China relations

The Korea Times, December 13, 2010

Since North Korea's recent artillery attack on South Korea's Yeonpyeong Island heightened tensions on the Korean Peninsula and brought strong condemnations from the international community, the global limelight has focused on China as Beijing is perceived to be the lifeline of the recalcitrant North Korean regime.

Yet, what is really tested are relations between China and the United States. That China has not publicly criticized North Korea should not be construed as Beijing's support for North Korea's maverick behaviors. To fully comprehend the situation, one needs to understand the complexity of the issue and the dilemma China faces.

China's Dilemma

China–North Korea relations are rooted in the Korean War, which has not officially ended since no peace treaty was signed when the fighting stopped in 1953. After Beijing improved relations with the West in the 1970s and 1980s, it began to adopt a "two Koreas" policy, which eventually led to the establishment of diplomatic relations between China and South Korea in 1992. Kim Il-sung reportedly howled at the Chinese emissary who delivered Beijing's decision to him. North Korea probably has never fully forgiven China's "betrayal."

South Korea has become a much more important economic partner for China. Trade between the two sides amounted to $141 billion in 2009, with China absorbing a quarter of South Korea's exports and South Korea being a major investor in China. The two countries plan to open free-trade talks in 2011 and increase their bilateral trade to $300 billion a year by 2015.

On the other hand, while some of China's northeast border regions benefit from trading with North Korea, the world's last Stalinist country is essentially a black hole sucking away China's resources. Politically and diplomatically, North Korea has become a liability for China. Yet, strategically, North Korea remains valuable to China as a buffer separating the U.S. and South Korean forces from China. Beijing has other concerns too. For example, if North Korea suddenly collapses as a result of international and Chinese pressure, millions of hungry and desperate North Korean people will flood into China, creating a humanitarian disaster and tremendous political, social, and economic burdens on China.

Gunboat Diplomacy

The North Korea conundrum epitomizes U.S.–China competition in East Asia. While the United States and its allies have resorted to "gunboat diplomacy" by sending warships to the region and staging massive military exercises near North Korea and China, Beijing prefers talks and negotiations and has called for restraint.

The U.S., Japan and South Korea rejected China's proposal for the resumption of the Six-Party Talks for the North's denuclearization, yet the foreign ministers of the three allies held their own exclusive meetings in Washington. Such uncoordinated efforts run the risk of reviving the Korean War-era division of East Asia into opposite camps, with the United States, Japan, and South Korea on one side, China, Russia, and North Korea on the other, which will only make matters worse.

The "gunboat diplomacy" is unlikely to solve the problem since it is built upon false assumptions: North Korea is scared now, and it will not be provocative again.

Although not directly criticizing North Korea's action, Chinese leaders expressed opposition to "any provocative military behavior" that escalates tensions on the Korean Peninsula, a statement that would also apply to the U.S.–South Korean joint naval exercises in the Yellow Sea and the even larger U.S.–Japan military exercises south of Japan.

Winston Churchill once said, to jaw–jaw is always better than to war–war. The United States and its allies have to decide what to do after the show of force. If they really want to solve the North Korea problem, they'd have to engage North Korea directly. To reject dialogue with North Korea as a punishment of its bad behavior is simply a poor decision.

Strengthening U.S.–China Relations

Few in China still consider North Korea an ally despite the 1961 friendship treaty between China and North Korea. Secret cables made open by WikiLeaks, if reliable, confirm that the Chinese leadership is ready to abandon North Korea. However, all things considered, it seems that maintaining the Korean Peninsula status quo is in the best interest of China, and arguably of all other parties involved.

After all, South Korean people are not enthusiastic about unification now, let alone sharing the hefty economic costs of taking over North Korea. A unified and pro-West Korea also means that it will be difficult for the United States to justify its forward troop deployment in Korea and Japan. Even Japan will have second thoughts about having a nuclear-equipped and historically anti-Japan neighbor with over 70 million people.

The United States and China are suspicious of each other's long-term intentions. The U.S. will continue to be a major Asian power in the years ahead and will maintain troops in the region as an insurance against a potentially aggressive China. Beijing is deeply concerned about a quick South Korean and U.S. takeover of North Korea with U.S. troops at China's doorsteps. Beijing and Washington seem to be sliding into a vicious cycle of mutual strategic mistrust. The deeper the mistrust, the more valuable North Korea is to China.

Clearly, the key to solving the North Korea problem lies in cooperative U.S.–China relations. Beijing and Washington must make sure that their long-term interests in Asia do not clash. A strong relationship between Beijing and Washington is crucial for untying the North Korea knot and achieving long-lasting peace in Asia.

See: http://www.koreatimes.co.kr/www/opinion/2018/03/198_77935.html#.

Clean Air Is Key in Talks between Hu and Obama

The Taipei Times, November 13, 2009

When U.S. President Barack Obama makes his first visit to China next week, human rights is likely to be one of the major issues in his talks with Chinese leaders. While it will be a great opportunity for him to express his concerns for human rights in China, he should address it with a different strategy and focus than past U.S. leaders. Instead of

96   *A Critical Decade: China's Foreign Policy (2008–2018)*

openly challenging the Chinese government on issues like political freedom and Tibet, which are bound to anger Chinese leaders and are not really helpful for improving human rights conditions in China, Obama should promote the idea of clean air as a human right.

One of the lingering disputes between China and the U.S. concerns differences on the meaning of human rights. While the U.S. and much of the Western world focus on political, religious and civil rights, China and many developing nations emphasize economic, social and cultural rights. Citing tremendous progress in improved living standards in China, the Chinese government and many Chinese citizens reject Western accusations of China's dismal human rights record. They ask: isn't lifting 500 million people out of poverty one of the greatest human rights successes in history? Instead of continuing to argue the meaning and scope of human rights, the U.S. and China should take a new approach and seek common ground for genuine cooperation to improve overall human rights in China.

With a narrow and misguided focus on the GDP growth rate, China's rapid modernization in the past 30 years has resulted in a nightmarish environment. Air and water are severely polluted in much of the country. Some studies even suggest that the top 10 most polluted cities in the world are all in China. Respiratory diseases have become the No. 1 cause of death in China.

Blind Eye to Achievements

All previous U.S. administrations criticized the Chinese government for its human rights violations, but all of them selectively focused on political and religious freedom in China. Many in China understand the importance of democracy and political freedom, but realize that these lofty goals must be obtained gradually. They feel that the U.S. government turns a blind eye to what China has achieved in the past three decades and fails to appreciate the daunting domestic challenges China faces today. Even critics of the Chinese government may not agree with the U.S. government when it openly confronts China with the human rights issue. What the U.S. has advocated seems so distant and detached from the lives of ordinary Chinese. If Obama continues to talk about human rights only through the lens of political and religious freedom during his visit, he is likely to alienate much of the Chinese public. Instead, he should raise China's environmental degradation as a human rights issue and offer the U.S.' strong support for a better environment in China. Clean air is a basic human right that all Chinese care about, but do not have.

Chinese President Hu Jintao announced his government's commitment to cutting greenhouse gases during the UN Climate Summit in September 2009. Both China and the U.S. hope that the Copenhagen Climate Conference in December 2009 will bring about an agreed framework for climate change. As the world's two biggest emitters of carbon dioxide, the U.S. and China should take the lead in specifying their goals and measures to address climate change.

The Obama–Hu meeting in Beijing will be a litmus test of how serious they are in curbing greenhouse gases. To a large extent, a successful Obama visit to China depends on whether the two countries will agree to cooperate on clean air in China and elsewhere.

See: https://www.bucknell.edu/x57087.xml.

Joined at the Hip

Sino-U.S. relations have deep regional and global implications for maintaining peace and ushering in prosperity in the 21st century.

Beijing Review, September 22, 2009

On October 1, 2009, the People's Republic of China will celebrate its 60th anniversary. Many people are wondering: Are China and the United States friends or enemies? What are the prospects for their bilateral relationship?

98 A Critical Decade: China's Foreign Policy (2008–2018)

U.S. Senator Kenneth Wherry of Nebraska expressed his hope in 1940 that "with God's help, we will lift Shanghai up and up, ever up, until it is just like Kansas City." Were he alive today, the senator would be surprised to learn that Shanghai, China's commercial and economic hub, has indeed been lifted up, and is actually much taller and more dynamic than Kansas City or any U.S. metropolis. But it is the United States, not God, which has contributed positively to China's fast growth in the past 30 years, especially through trade and investment, and through maintenance of peace and stability in East Asia.

Trade remains one of the thorniest issues between the two countries. Now China and the United States have become each other's second largest trading partners with bilateral trade volume surpassing $333 billion in 2008.

With foreign exchange reserves of over $2.1 trillion, China is in a position to invest in the United States and purchase money-losing U.S. companies. But America remains ambivalent about Chinese investment, often on grounds of national security, as in the case of Unocal a few years ago, when China was forced to abort its purchase of the California-based oil company.

Amid the current global economic crisis, China's stimulus packages have fueled domestic economic growth, which in turn, contributes to America's economic recovery. China is America's biggest creditor, with an estimated two thirds of its foreign exchange reserves in dollar assets, including more than $800 billion in U.S. Treasury bonds.

Many in the United States unfairly blame China for the huge trade deficit and loss of jobs, not knowing that U.S. exports to China grew by 20 percent annually in the past 5 years and that Washington continues to forbid the sale of high-tech products to China.

Realistically, Washington cannot expect its trade deficit with China to be significantly reduced if it maintains sanctions on China. The trade imbalance is also structural, since many of America's other key trading partners in Asia, such as Japan and South Korea, have moved their production facilities to China, and now export their products directly from China.

The two countries must work together to achieve a more balanced trade. However, in a clear violation of World Trade Organization rules, Washington recently imposed punitive tariffs on steel pipes and car and light truck tires from China.

Such protectionist measures, which have already triggered China's tit-for-tat responses, are counterproductive, and harmful to bilateral relations. Beijing is thus likely to have become a scapegoat for the current high unemployment rate in the United States.

Whether China and the United States are friends or enemies is a false debate. It misses the central point that the two countries are so interdependent today that they no longer have the luxury of making such a choice.

Even at the height of the Cold War, the two countries opted for cooperation. U.S. President Richard Nixon made history by traveling to China and meeting with Chinese leaders Mao Zedong and Zhou Enlai in 1972. Seven years later, President Jimmy Carter welcomed Deng Xiaoping to the White House when the two countries just established diplomatic ties. In addition, U.S. leaders encouraged Deng's reform initiatives. After 30 years of profound economic reforms, China is reemerging as a major player on the world stage.

Today, exchanges at all levels of society have greatly expanded across the Pacific. With monthly contacts among senior officials and regular strategic dialogues, Beijing and Washington are institutionalizing their interactions.

Unquestionably, summit diplomacy has maintained its momentum. Not long after National People's Congress Standing Committee Chairman Wu Bangguo visited the United States in early September, President Hu Jintao will be coming to attend UN meetings in New York and the G20 summit in Pittsburgh.

President Barack Obama, meanwhile, will go to China in November to seek more cooperation with the Chinese in dealing with the global economic recession, climate change, energy security, terrorism and other pressing issues. China and the United States are unlikely to see eye to eye on everything, but they are not engaged in a zero-sum game in international politics.

For the foreseeable future, the two powers will have to learn to live together. The most critical issue in their relations in the future will probably not be Taiwan or trade, but determining and abiding by

100 *A Critical Decade: China's Foreign Policy (2008–2018)*

their respective roles in international political economy. They must form a long-term vision for the future of their relations.

Sino-U.S. relations have deep regional and global implications. The era of Chimerica or G2 will not arrive any time soon — but good relations between the world's sole superpower and the largest rising power are vital for maintaining peace and promoting prosperity in the 21st century.

See: http://www.bjreview.com.cn/print/txt/2009-09/22/content_218080.htm.

Forget Bush's Wars and Work with Asia

Asia Times, October 24, 2008

John Hay, the 37th U.S. Secretary of State, said in 1889, "The Mediterranean is the ocean of the past, the Atlantic, the ocean of the present, and the Pacific, the ocean of the future."

The future is now. The "Asia-Pacific century" is not a prediction anymore; it's reality. Based on purchasing power parity, three of the four largest economies in the world are in Asia — China, Japan, and India. And if the United States is included, then all the top four economies are in the Asia-Pacific region.

The United States has longstanding interests in Asia. Two of the world's potentially most explosive places are located in East Asia: the Korean Peninsula and the Taiwan Strait, where the United States has significant economic, geopolitical, and strategic interests. Since the end of World War II, the U.S. has had extensive economic interactions with Asian nations. It played an instrumental role in Japan's post-war recovery and the economic takeoff of the four Asian "tigers" — South Korea, Hong Kong, Singapore, and Taiwan. Since the early 1980s, China has also benefited enormously from America's huge investment and its insatiable consumer market. It is not an exaggeration that East Asia is of critical importance to America's future.

One wonders whether the fact that Asia has not been a major foreign policy issue in the 2008 U.S. presidential election is good news or bad news. The new U.S. president must move beyond President George W Bush's preoccupation with the "war on terror" and pay more attention to Asia.

Mixed Legacy

On the positive side, U.S. alliances with Japan, South Korea, and Australia remain strong. In the past 8 years, Japan, South Korea, and Australia all had leadership changes, and in Japan's case there have been four different prime ministers. All these Asian leaders have firmly supported America's "war on terror." They have all visited Washington to show solidarity with Bush.

One of the rare bright spots in Bush's foreign policy is China. A stable and strong relationship between the United States and China is probably Bush's greatest foreign policy achievement. Bush and his family are now considered "friends" by the Chinese government and Bush's decision to attend the Summer Olympic Games in Beijing, though controversial at home, was welcomed by China where members of the Bush family were warmly received.

Prodded by the United States, the new Kuomintang (KMT) government in Taiwan headed by Ma Ying-jeou has abandoned the pro-independence policies of his predecessor Chen Shui-bian and has endeavored to improve cross-strait relations. As a result, military conflict in the Taiwan Strait is becoming much less likely now.

Opportunities

However, Bush has also failed miserably in East Asia overall, most notably with regard to the unresolved issue of North Korea's nuclear program. Opportunities to denuclearize North Korea have come and gone during the 8 years of the Bush administration.

102 A Critical Decade: China's Foreign Policy (2008–2018)

An agreed framework was reached between the US and North Korea in 1994. Denuclearization of the Korean Peninsula seemed to be within reach. President Bill Clinton sent Secretary of State Madeleine Albright to North Korea in October 2000 to talk to North Korean leader Kim Jong-il directly. Clinton was even prepared to visit North Korea himself to improve relations.

After Bush came to office in January 2001, he refused to honor the 1994 agreement and rejected direct talks with North Korea directly. After the September 11, 2001, bombings he labeled North Korea as part of the "axis of evil." North Korea was outraged and felt cornered; it hardened its position on the nuclear issue and decided to proceed with nuclear technology. Even many South Koreans felt offended: North Korea is poor, but it is not evil.

Six-Party Talks

Eventually China launched the Six-Party Talks in 2003. The U.S. accepted this multilateral forum for discussion but still refused to deal with North Korea directly. After tough negotiations, North Korea finally agreed, in February 2007, to shut down its main nuclear reactor in exchange for food and aid from the other five parties.

In June 2008, North Korea blew up the cooling tower of its Yongbyon nuclear reactor and handed over to the U.S. a declaration of its nuclear activities. However, by August, the U.S. had not removed North Korea from the state sponsors of terrorism list, as it had promised earlier, while insisting that it wanted independent verification of North Korea's nuclear disarmament. Accusing the U.S. of breaking its promise, North Korea then announced it had suspended disabling its nuclear facilities.

In a dramatic development, on October 11, 2008, Bush decided to remove North Korea from the list of states that sponsor terrorism. This was an encouraging step, but it may have come too late.

Serious Challenges

As a result of Bush's policies, the new U.S. president will face several serious challenges in East Asia. The immediate security challenge is a nuclear-capable North Korea. Recent reports about Kim Jong-il's poor health added complexity and uncertainty to the nuclear issue and security in East Asia.

For Washington, the shortest diplomatic route to Pyongyang may be through Beijing. China has a strong interest in preventing the nuclearization of the Korean Peninsula, in part because it does not want to give Japan an excuse to go nuclear.

North Korea has not accounted for dozens of Japanese citizens abducted by North Korean agents in the 1970s and 1980s, and the new U.S. president needs to explain to Tokyo that as important as the matter is, it should not be linked to North Korea's denuclearization. Japan can seek to resolve the abduction issue through other channels, preferably by engaging with North Korea directly. The United States must coordinate its policy closely with China and other nations in the region in order to break North Korea's nuclear stalemate.

Economic Integration

Asia also poses tough economic challenges to the new president. The U.S. must become actively involved in economic integration with Asian nations, otherwise it risks being marginalized in Asia. It cannot afford to continue to stand on the sidelines as the 10-member Association of Southeast Asian Nations and northeast Asian nations discus a regional free-trade zone.

The United States had been the dominant economic power in Asia, but now China has become the largest trading partner of almost every country in Asia and the U.S. is already playing second fiddle. Asian economies are some of the biggest holders of U.S. Treasury bonds with Japan and China together holding about half of all Treasury bonds sold abroad.

China has become America's third-largest export market after Canada and Mexico, and its foreign exchange reserve is quickly approaching US$2 trillion. The recent financial crisis in the U.S. makes it imperative for the new president to work more closely with East Asian nations. Shortly after the U.S. Congress passed the $700 billion financial rescue package in September, the People's Bank of

China reportedly expressed interest in purchasing $200 billion worth of U.S. Treasury bonds. Undoubtedly, East Asia will be part of the solution to the current financial problems in America.

The biggest challenge for the U.S. and its new president is China. The challenge from the re-emerging power of the Middle Kingdom is on all fronts. China's economy continues to gallop forward, despite the impact of the financial crisis. For many developing countries, China's development model, the so-called "Beijing Consensus" of economic liberalization under tight political control, offers an attractive alternative to the "Washington Consensus" of the U.S.

After Beijing passed the Olympics test with flying colors, and after Chinese astronauts successfully conducted their first spacewalk, the Chinese people have every reason to celebrate. As a result, nationalism has grown even stronger in China. Dealing with this increasingly powerful and proud nation of over 1.3 billion people is no easy task — and China–U.S. relations have become increasingly complex.

From issues ranging from trade imbalances to independence protests in Tibet, the two countries have many differences. The recent U.S. sale of $6.5 billion worth of weapons to Taiwan certainly does not bode well for bilateral ties. The rise of China — a nation that does not share core values with the United States — will be the most pressing foreign policy challenge for the next American president.

Bush preferred unilateralism in foreign policy, and in Asia he preferred strong bilateral alliances built upon historical ties with key allies. But this bilateral alliance structure is rooted in Cold War ideology and is outdated today. The new American president must go beyond unilateralism and bilateralism and move toward multilateralism on a wide range of issues.

In Asia, the new American president must be a uniter, not a divider. In addition to resolving North Korea's nuclear dilemma, fighting infectious diseases, piracy on the high seas, global warming, and financial crises all require multilateral cooperation between the United States and the nations of Asia and the world.

See: http://www.worldsecuritynetwork.com/Koreas/Zhu-Zhiqun/ Forget-Bushs-wars-and-work-with-Asia.

Chapter 4

The Korean Peninsula

China and the Prospect for North Korea's Denuclearization

Jeju Peace Institute, The Republic of Korea, July 24, 2018

China is surrounded by more nuclear powers and nuclear-capable states than any other country in the world. A nuclearized North Korea does not serve China's interests. If North Korea decides to denuclearize, its relations with China will immediately improve, as evidenced by the fact that shortly after President Donald Trump and Chairman Kim Jong-un agreed to meet face-to-face, Kim was welcomed to Beijing and met with President Xi Jinping in March 2018. Xi even accepted Kim's invitation to visit North Korea at a convenient time. Kim subsequently paid two additional visits to China in May and June 2018. Some thought that the Kim–Trump meeting in Singapore might marginalize China. Kim's visits to China not only bolstered his bargaining position *vis-à-vis* Trump, but also reaffirmed China's central role in Korean affairs.

China's position on the North Korean nuclear issue has been consistent. China has three main objectives: peace and stability in Northeast Asia, denuclearization of the Korean Peninsula, and peaceful reunification of Korea. It has recently proposed the "dual suspension" plan: North Korea suspends nuclear and missile tests in exchange for suspension of joint U.S.–South Korea military exercises. On this basis, North Korea's denuclearization can be achieved step by step.

Successive US administrations have preferred to use sanctions, backed by joint U.S.–ROK military drills, to bring North Korea to its knees. Some people believe that China holds the key to the North Korea problem while the Chinese government argues that the United States and North Korea are the principal actors and must talk to each other directly to resolve the issue.

In theory, North Korea and China are still "allies" even though China follows the "non-alignment" foreign policy; in reality, the relationship is ambiguous. The Chinese generally look down upon the Pyongyang regime and feel sympathetic for the North Korean people. The North Koreans reportedly despise the Chinese who, in their views, betrayed North Korea in 1992 when Beijing established diplomatic ties with Seoul. China–DPRK relations deteriorated after Kim Jong-il died in 2011. Despite the deep freeze in the relationship between 2011 and early 2018, Sino-DPRK relations seem durable, especially when international situations change.

Even before Kim Jong-un's surprise March 2018 visit to China that repaired bilateral relations, Beijing's *Global Times* asserted in an editorial that friendly Sino-DPRK relationship should not be disrupted by other countries. It suggested that North Korea was a country to be respected since it "has high degree of independence and autonomy," which is very rare in Northeast Asia now. The editorial also argued that maintaining friendly relations was in the interest of both countries.

After the Trump–Kim meeting in Singapore, expectations have grown regarding North Korea's denuclearization. However, with rising tensions between China and the United States on trade and other issues, China is likely to maintain good relations with North Korea in the near future, which will make North Korea's denuclearization more complex. As North Korea's relations with China, Russia and South Korea improve, it will be more difficult to keep sanctions on North Korea.

What can be done about North Korea's denuclearization from China's perspective? Most importantly, denuclearization must be achieved peacefully and gradually. Dialogue at the bilateral and multilateral levels must be promoted. The United States, China, and other stakeholders must seriously address the North Korea issue from the broad context of East Asian security and political economy. There is no simple or immediate solution, and a package of agreements and frameworks will likely be the outcome of such serious discussions. Denuclearization is an objective, not a precondition, of peaceful talks. Without security guarantees, it may be wishful thinking to expect North Korea to voluntarily denuclearize.

Sanctions have proved ineffective, and military actions are too risky. The only viable option is to return to the negotiation table. Demanding North Korea to abandon its nuclear program before negotiations can start between the United States and North Korea is like putting the cart before the horse. Without incentives or compensations, why would North Korea denuclearize? China's "dual suspension" proposal is a realistic and pragmatic way to get the ball rolling.

Some people in Washington do not support U.S. engagement with North Korea since they believe talking to a rogue regime is to reward its bad behavior. Such a condescending attitude is not conducive to peaceful resolution to any disputes. Diplomacy is an art of reaching a mutually acceptable solution to a dispute without war. Negotiators do not have to like each other, but they share the common goal of peaceful resolution.

Possessing nuclear weapons does not necessarily make North Korea more dangerous; it's the intention to use them that does. As Kim Jong-un's 2018 New Year's Day message reveals, North Korean leaders are not irrational or suicidal; they are unlikely to use nuclear weapons without provocation. With political and economic incentives North Korea is more likely to join the international community. Developments in 2018 including the Kim–Trump meeting,

108 A Critical Decade: China's Foreign Policy (2008–2018)

reconciliation between the two Koreas, and improvement of Sino-DPRK relations are promising. The United States and its allies used to pay more attention to restrictions on North Korea than addressing its security concerns. The Trump administration's reaching out to North Korea is a positive step in the right direction. Moving forward, all relevant parties, particularly China and the United States, must work together to encourage North Korea to denuclearize and welcome it into the international community.

See: http://jpi.or.kr/kor/regular/policy_view.sky?code=archive&id=5653.

Beijing will Be the Silent Partner at a Trump–Kim Meeting

The Globe and Mail, May 23, 2018

Developments around the North Korean nuclear issue since the beginning of 2018 have been so rapid and dramatic that most observers feel as if they are on a roller-coaster ride. Expectations remain high for the historic meeting between Donald Trump and Kim Jong-un despite recent doubts. With North Korea threatening to pull out of the Singapore summit, both South Korea and China appealed to Washington and Pyongyang to stay on course. Amid the uncertainty there were several significant developments.

First of all, the shortest line between Washington and Pyongyang may run through Beijing. Twice, in late March and early May, Mr. Kim traveled to China to meet with President Xi Jinping in an effort to seek China's support ahead of his meeting with Mr. Trump. The TV footage showing a smiling Mr. Xi walking alongside a relaxed Mr. Kim sent a powerful message of a united front. This is a U-turn in the tense relationship between the two leaders, and between the two countries, since they took office in 2012 and 2011, respectively. Notably, North Korea appeared to have hardened its stance toward the United States after the second Xi-Kim meeting.

When Mr. Kim first announced his plans to meet with South Korean president Moon Jae-in and Mr. Trump, some suggested that China might be sidelined in this new round of diplomacy. Indeed, it would be a public breakup of the China–North Korea relationship if Mr. Kim went ahead and met with Mr. Moon and Mr. Trump before meeting with Mr. Xi. As it turned out, Mr. Kim went to China before his scheduled meeting in April with Mr. Moon. From then on, it has become clear that China remains an indispensable player on the Korean Peninsula. It is no coincidence that Mr. Trump got on the phone with Mr. Xi shortly after both Xi–Kim meetings. It is more than just a courtesy when Mr. Trump calls Mr. Xi his "friend" and praises him for helping with the nuclear issue.

Second, despite North Korea's dismal record in keeping its denuclearization promises in the past, this time around Mr. Kim seems serious. He has already frozen missile and nuclear tests, and dismantled a nuclear test site. He also released three Korean–Americans held by the North. Such gestures are symbolic and were not possible just a few months ago. Mr. Kim has taken important initial steps and is waiting for reciprocity from Mr. Trump.

Some in the U.S. administration think that by agreeing to meet with Mr. Kim, Mr. Trump has made a huge concession, since a meeting with a U.S. president has long been "craved" by North Korean leaders. Such a haughty view does not augur well for U.S.–North Korean relations. Mr. Kim's position is secure at home, and the closer ties between him and Mr. Xi will only consolidate his power. A meeting with Mr. Trump will not add much to what he already enjoys. Indeed, Mr. Trump wants the meeting as much as Mr. Kim does since it fits his personality of talking and doing big things, and a successful meeting will possibly also help his Republican Party in the U.S. mid-term elections later this year (2018).

Third, Mr. Xi's remark that China and North Korea are socialist countries and their relationship has major strategic significance

110 *A Critical Decade: China's Foreign Policy (2008–2018)*

indicates that he intends to revitalize the special friendship between the two traditional allies, though it may not be a return to the golden days when the relationship was as close as "lips and teeth."

China and North Korea do need each other now. Mr. Kim needs China's backing and reassurance as he enters talks with the unpredictable Mr. Trump, and China will definitely not abandon North Korea in the complex strategic rivalry in Northeast Asia, especially when the Trump administration has flirted with playing the trade and Taiwan cards.

Mr. Xi's support for North Korea's shift to economic development suggests that China will likely ease sanctions against North Korea soon, despite Mr. Trump's claim that he and Mr. Xi agreed to keep the sanctions on until North Korea denuclearizes.

Finally, is Mr. Trump ready for a serious deal that will require change in his approach toward North Korea? If Mr. Trump could just walk away from the Paris Agreement on Climate Change and the Iran nuclear deal, one wonders whether he will keep any agreement he reaches with Mr. Kim. The Trump administration should know that while it is demanding a "permanent, verifiable, and irreversible" destruction of North Korea's nuclear programs, its own credibility is in question.

Mr. Kim's promise to denuclearize comes with preconditions. In his view, if "relevant parties" abolish their hostile policies and remove security threats against North Korea, there is no need for North Korea to be a nuclear state. Will the United States ditch those "hostile policies" such as joint military exercises, continued sanctions, reluctance to sign a peace treaty to end the Korean War, etc.?

North Korea stated that it would not be interested in a meeting with one-sided demand for denuclearization. Is Mr. Trump willing to meet Mr. Kim half way and reciprocate Mr. Kim's initial goodwill with tangible incentives? There have been murmurs about Mr. Trump being a strong contender for the Nobel Peace Prize. Can Mr. Trump really bring peace to the Korean Peninsula?

See: https://www.theglobeandmail.com/opinion/article-beijing-will-be-the-silent-partner-at-a-trump-kim-meeting/.

Dennis Rodman May Be Our Only Hope

Don't dismiss the former NBA star's "basketball diplomacy" with North Korea.
U.S. News & World Report, December 29, 2017.

Tensions on the Korean Peninsula are dangerously high as a defiant North Korea keeps testing and improving nuclear weapons, while a frustrated United States sends stealth fighter jets and B-1 bombers to the region. People agree on the severity of the situation, but nobody seems to know exactly how to defuse tensions and avoid a potential war.

Maybe Dennis Rodman is the answer. The colorful former basketball star has visited North Korea five times in the past few years and cultivated a special friendship with North Korean leader Kim Jong-un. It may be time for the Trump administration to embrace his peacekeeping efforts.

Jeffrey Feltman, the United Nations under-secretary-general for political affairs, recently returned from a rare visit to North Korea. In a statement to journalists, he said there's an "urgent need to prevent miscalculations and open channels to reduce the risks of conflict." Obviously, lack of direct communications between the United States and North Korea has been extremely unfortunate and worrisome. Under the current circumstances, any move that may facilitate communications between the two sides should be welcome.

It is encouraging that U.S. Secretary of State Rex Tillerson just announced that the U.S. government is ready to talk to North Korea without any preconditions, reversing Washington's long-standing policy of demanding Pyongyang abandon its nuclear program first. It is indeed unrealistic to ask North Korea to give up its nuclear program before entering any meaningful talks.

Meanwhile, Rodman is planning to visit North Korea again. The Obama administration categorically distanced itself from Rodman's previous trips, but President Donald Trump once praised Rodman's trips as "smart." Knowing both Kim and Trump, Rodman believes he can broker a peace deal between the United States and North Korea. He thinks the two leaders have something in common: they both love control.

In this self-claimed humanitarian trip, Rodman visited Guam, Japan, and China, but has been unable to proceed to North Korea under the new U.S. policy that prohibits American passport holders to travel to the North. Rodman planned to use a "special pass" to enter North Korea, where he will make a documentary and write a book about his unique relationship with Kim.

Rodman also proposed a basketball game between a North Korean team and a team from the U.S. territory of Guam, which Kim threatened to attack and sink with missiles. U.S. officials and many analysts do not take Rodman seriously. Most media reported Rodman's proposed "basketball diplomacy" dismissively, considering the famous "bad boy" an attention-hungry outcast.

It is unclear how North Korea will respond to the proposal, but China seems lukewarm. When asked during a regular news briefing whether China supports the proposal, the foreign ministry spokesperson said he was unaware of the situation. However, E.J. Calvo, the head of Guam's national basketball team, told journalists that "this possible game would be a great opportunity."

Kim is known for being a fervent basketball fan since he was a teenager at an international school in Switzerland. Love of basketball helped form the special bond between him and Rodman, who is one of the few Americans having met Kim in person multiple times.

The United States and all other powers in the region are still committed to the peaceful resolution of the North Korea crisis, but peace will not come automatically. Conscientious efforts by the governments and the publics are needed at this difficult time. Private citizens can help bring the two sides closer through informal diplomacy such as cultural, educational and sports exchanges.

In the early 1970s, "Ping Pong diplomacy" helped pave the way for President Richard Nixon's historic visit to China and the subsequent normalization of relations between the United States and the People's Republic of China. Though many may argue there is little analogy here, few can dispute that people-to-people interactions form the foundation of diplomatic relations between two countries.

In the absence of diplomatic ties and official contacts, Rodman's efforts should be praised and encouraged. Shall we just brush off

Rodman's initiative as a fantasy? Let's not make hasty judgements about Rodman or his intentions. Self-righteousness is the last thing we need now in dealing with North Korea. Engagement both at the official and unofficial levels and diplomacy stand the best chance for securing and maintaining peace on the Korean Peninsula.

See: https://www.usnews.com/opinion/world-report/articles/2017-12-29/dennis-rodman-may-be-the-only-hope-for-peace-with-north-korea.

A Peaceful Approach to North Korea

The Korea Times, November 16, 2017

After U.S. President Donald Trump's first Asia trip in November 2017, one hopes that he will have a clear understanding of how to deal with the North Korea challenge properly and develop a rational, realistic and feasible Asia policy.

Broadly speaking, there are three approaches to address North Korea's nuclear issue: continuation of the sanction-based policy; military action; and returning to negotiations. The U.S.-preferred sanction-based policy has obviously failed to curb North Korea's nuclear ambitions. It's had its chance to succeed but only driven North Korea closer to an effective nuclear weapon.

Worse, any military action on the Korean Peninsula will have unbearable consequences for all parties, especially the Korean people. With a quick glance at how prosperous South Korea is and some historical knowledge of how South Koreans built the economic miracle after the Korean War, it's obvious why South Koreans strongly oppose war and why President Moon Jae-in has insisted that no U.S.-led war on the Korean peninsula will be allowed without South Korea's consent. No one in South Korea is willing to sacrifice what they have

114 A Critical Decade: China's Foreign Policy (2008–2018)

earned through diligent work, and many South Koreans feel disgusted by President Trump's threat of "fire and fury" over North Korea.

But conditions are not right for an immediate return to the negotiation table. Even China who sponsored the Six-Party Talks between 2003 and 2009 realizes that distrust between the United States and North Korea is a gap too far to bridge. The United States has insisted that North Korea must abandon its nuclear program before any meaningful talks can be held, but North Korean will not abandon the nuclear program as they think the U.S. threat is clear and present. In their minds, it's leverage they can't afford to cede.

A blind spot in the current debate about North Korea is a fundamental question that is not often asked: why does North Korea want to develop and maintain nuclear weapons? If the international community can create conditions under which North Koreans feel it unnecessary to develop nuclear weapons, then this problem will automatically disappear. This holds the best hope for a peaceful resolution of the stalemate.

Denuclearization is an objective, not a precondition for peaceful talks. Without security guarantees from the U.S., it's wishful thinking to expect North Korea to voluntarily denuclearize. A softer approach toward the North has the potential to achieve this ultimate objective.

Promoting cultural exchanges and welcoming North Korea into the international community should be an integral part of such an approach. Public diplomacy can be an effective way to break diplomatic stalemates. In 2008, the New York Philharmonic Orchestra paid a historic visit to Pyongyang, where it performed to a polite and enthusiastic audience. When the Star Spangled Banner was played, the fascinated North Korean audience reportedly all stood up and showed respect to America.

Former NBA player Dennis Rodman traveled to North Korea several times in recent years, but each time the U.S. State Department quickly distanced itself from the famous "bad boy," turning away opportunities to generate goodwill between the North Korean people and Americans through such people-to-people exchanges. Kenneth Bae, a Korean–American who was released in November 2014 after being sentenced to 15 years of hard labor in North Korea, said he thought Rodman increased public awareness of his imprisonment leading to his release.

Former U.S. President Jimmy Carter, at age 93, admirably offered to travel to Pyongyang again to help defuse tensions, but the Trump administration has rejected the proposal. Carter has been to North Korea at least three times in a non-official capacity to help negotiation deals with North Korea and seek the return of American citizens held by North Korea.

Effecting positive changes inside North Korea through extensive interactions with North Korean people remains the best approach for a peaceful resolution of the North Korea dilemma. The 2018 Winter Olympics, the 2020 Summer Olympics, and the 2022 Winter Olympics will be held in PyeongChang, Tokyo, and Beijing, respectively. These are great opportunities to welcome North Korea to be part of the international community.

"War made the state, and the state made war," asserted sociologist and political scientist Charles Tilly. By the same token, states make peace, and peace can make a new state out of North Korea. With concerted efforts by all relevant parties, peace is within reach and sustainable on the Korean peninsula.

See: https://www.koreatimes.co.kr/www/opinion/2018/07/162_ 239397.html#.

China Can't Fix North Korea

It's a myth that China holds the key to the North Korean problem. *U.S. News & World Report*, August 1, 2017.

After North Korea's second intercontinental ballistic missile test at the end of July 2017, President Donald Trump tweeted his frustration and disappointment. China "could easily solve" the North

Korea problem, he said, a view shared by many in his administration. Up to now, the Trump administration, much like the previous administration, has outsourced North Korea's denuclearization to China.

One wonders how much longer it will take for Trump and similar-minded people to wake up to the cold reality: It's a myth that China holds the key to the North Korea problem. As veteran journalist and author Mike Chinoy pointed out, many high-level North Koreans "resent the hell out of the Chinese." Though it has applied unprecedented sanctions such as stopping coal imports from North Korea, China simply cannot force its way with North Korea's leadership.

China does not want North Korea to collapse because a chaotic North Korea is likely to open a Pandora's box, including humanitarian, economic, security and political challenges that are too daunting for China to absorb. Furthermore, a failed North Korea will lead to reunification of the peninsula under the leadership of a pro-U.S. government in the South, with U.S. troops remaining in Korea. So long as the U.S. and Chinese militaries view each other as the potential enemy — and the U.S. government does not address China's concerns, including its trepidation over the terminal high altitude area defense system (THAAD) — it is unrealistic to expect China's full cooperation to rein in North Korea.

The United States tends to dismiss or ignore what its opponent thinks. North Korea behaves in its unique way. Its nuclear and missile tests bizarrely serve as an invitation for talks. North Korean leader Kim Jong-un undoubtedly worries about regime survival, but he, like his father and grandfather, persistently wants two things from the United States: a peace treaty to formally end the unfinished Korean War, and diplomatic recognition to normalize relations. The United States has rejected such demands but has been unable to offer a convincing justification.

Trump also ripped China for doing "NOTHING" to help the United States on North Korea, which is certainly untrue. China's position has been consistent: The United States and North Korea are the two

The Korean Peninsula 117

principal parties to the tensions on the Korean Peninsula. They should work toward deescalating tensions simultaneously. Threatening the use of force, just like nuclear tests themselves, is only adding fuel to the fire.

"The time for talk is over," declared U.S. Ambassador to the United Nations Nikki Haley following North Korea's recent ICBM test. But the Trump administration never seriously planned to talk to North Korea. Vice President Mike Pence said "all options are on the table" now, as the U.S. sent two B-1 bombers from Guam over the Korean Peninsula. However, Secretary of Defense James Mattis warned earlier that war with North Korea would be "tragic on an unbelievable scale."

In his first few months in office, Trump already slapped sanctions on Russia, Iran, North Korea, Venezuela, among others, and is now contemplating sanctions on China for its inability to control North Korea. In international politics, sanctions have a poor record of success. What makes Trump and his advisers think that China will act in the way Washington desires when Washington cannot even change North Korea's behavior?

Like it or not, North Korea is already a nuclear state. The ostrich policy must be changed. Keep your friends close and your enemies closer. Communicating to Kim directly — not necessarily negotiating with him or making concessions to him — so that he understands the dire consequences of any adventurism might be the best way forward.

In an interview with *Bloomberg News* earlier this year, Trump remarked that he would be "honored" to meet with Kim to defuse tensions on the Korean Peninsula "under the right circumstances." Indeed, creative and bold thinking is needed in dealing with North Korea as the United States runs out of options and time. This could be a "Nixon goes to China" moment. Is Trump game enough to travel to Pyongyang or invite Kim to Washington now?

See: https://www.usnews.com/opinion/world-report/articles/2017-08-01/why-donald-trump-is-wrong-about-china-being-the-key-to-stopping-north-korea.

Talk to North Korea

Understanding what the North Koreans want is key to preventing conflict.

U.S. News & World Report, May 4, 2017

North Korea's nuclear and missile programs have become a clear and present danger to international security. Recently, President Donald Trump made headlines by saying that he'd be "honored" to meet with North Korea's Kim Jong-un "under the right circumstances." He's since received tremendous backlash for even considering talking to the North Korean leader.

But as the international community weighs options for resolving the North Korea crisis, one important factor has been missing in the consideration: What does North Korea want? A sit down with the leader might finally remove that blind spot from the discussion.

The international community has been deliberating on what it can do to curb North Korea's aggressive behaviors, but it has completely ignored the other side of the coin. Without understanding North Korea's concerns and wants, it will be difficult to solve the problem.

Most analysts believe that the Kim regime only cares about its survival. This might be true, but what are specific steps to achieve this objective? For years, North Korea has been consistent in what it wants: to sign a peace treaty with the United States to officially end hostility stemming from the unfinished Korean War, normalize diplomatic relations with the United States and Japan, and develop its backwater economy. Such a wish-list is not unreasonable. In particular, North Korea takes offense at the joint U.S.–South Korean military exercises that occur routinely on its doorstep.

Since the Six-Party Talks broke down in 2009, the United States has basically rejected directly and publicly talking to North Korea. In the view of many U.S. officials and policy analysts, the United States will not talk to North Korea because "we cannot reward its bad behavior." Such an arrogant and misinformed attitude is counterproductive and completely disregards the role of diplomacy in international affairs. Diplomacy, simply put, is the art and practice of conducting negotiations between nations in an attempt to reach a mutually acceptable outcome. It is not a form of rewarding or punishing other countries.

The international community has become accustomed to purely relying on "sticks" to force North Korea to abandon its nuclear program. The question is: Why will North Korea comply if it does not receive any "carrots" in return? From North Korea's perspective, the outside demand for its de-nuclearization is completely unacceptable and unfair. North Korea has proved resilient enough to resist sanction after sanction. It is time that the international community changed its approach now.

Despite the fact that the United States has assembled a large military force, including the USS Carl Vinson, near the Korean Peninsula, and that U.S. officials have repeatedly warned that a military strike against North Korea is on the table, Trump seems to prefer a diplomatic solution. He has praised Chinese President Xi Jinping's efforts to put more pressure on North Korea and expressed hope that de-nuclearization of North Korea can be achieved peacefully. The Trump administration has declared the end of the "strategic patience" policy toward North Korea practiced by President Barack Obama, but a new policy has yet to be officially announced.

Meanwhile, Chinese Foreign Minister Wang Yi reiterated China's intolerance to any disturbances near its border. Japanese Prime Minister Shinzo Abe and Russian President Vladimir Putin agreed during their recent meeting that the North Korea crisis must be resolved peacefully. South Korea, with Seoul only 30 mi away from the demilitarized zone, is most firmly opposed to war with North Korea.

It is not a coincidence that North Korea recently detained a Korean–American professor who was about to leave Pyongyang after teaching there for a few weeks. Though this is a nightmare for the professor and his family, it signals that North Korea is ready to talk and will likely use this as a bargaining chip. Kim is ruthless but not crazy. He is defiant but calculating. His *byungjin* policy of developing nuclear weapons and the economy simultaneously seems to have achieved some success. It is useless for outsiders to condemn North Korea without trying to understand the rationale behind its behavior. A compromised outcome is far better than a calamitous war.

The current development surrounding the Korean peninsula offers a rare and fleeting opportunity for all parties to cool down and resume diplomatic negotiations. No one really wants war now, and there is a glimmer of hope for peace. To entice North Korea to the negotiating table, the other parties, especially the United States, will need to offer some "carrots," sooner rather than later. Is Trump ready?

See: https://www.usnews.com/opinion/world-report/articles/2017-05-04/president-donald-trump-should-talk-to-north-korea.

Some Lessons from the North Korea Crisis

The recent North Korea crisis offers lessons about great power relations and East Asian security.
The Diplomat, February 22, 2016

Realists in international relations believe that small players have little room to maneuver in a world dominated by big powers, yet the North Korean tail has been wagging the big power dog for decades. The recent North Korea crisis offers several lessons about great power relations and East Asian security.

First of all, with the deterioration of security environment in Northeast Asia, no one emerges as the winner from the crisis, but China and the United States are the biggest losers.

In the eyes of many observers, Beijing has failed to play its expected role as a responsible power, putting its own interest above the global interest of nuclear non-proliferation. It is understood that if China tightens the screw on North Korea, the Pyongyang regime will quickly collapse, triggering a massive refugee stampede into China and leading to Korean reunification under U.S. influence.

This is why China has balked at crippling the North Korean economy.

But Beijing will pay a price for its continued shielding of North Korea. If the THAAD anti-missile system is deployed in South Korea, the PRC–ROK honeymoon will be over. Japanese Prime Minster Shinzo Abe conveniently seized the opportunity to promote constitutional change and a more assertive defense policy, with China probably as the real target. In a short span of time, China has found itself facing moral, diplomatic and strategic challenges.

North Korea's nuclear advances also mark a failure of U.S. foreign policy. The Obama administration has outsourced de-nuclearizing North Korea to China. Believing China holds the key to the North Korea problem, Washington shifted all responsibility to China while waiting for North Korea to collapse or repent. As the global leader, the U.S. should have paid more attention to such a critical security issue; it is irresponsible to expect China to solve the problem without considering its concerns. Hawks in Washington may be secretly celebrating since the crisis provides additional justification for the controversial "pivot" to Asia policy. But whatever the United States gains there is offset by the growing suspicion and tension between the United States and China.

Second, there should be no doubt that China and North Korea are not allies. Western observers and journalists routinely portray China as North Korea's "only ally." The fact is North Korea is not China's client state and it does not care what China thinks. Chinese disdain for North Korea is growing. Many consider North Korea China's burden and an annoying neighbor instead of an old friend. Veteran diplomat Wu Dawei's last minute efforts to persuade North Korea to halt the satellite launch failed. North Koreans hate being lectured to by the Chinese. Pyongyang defied the international community, but particularly China, and launched the satellite on Chinese New Year's Eve. The rift between China and North Korea will only grow larger.

In a recent interview with the *New York Times*, Yan Xuetong of Tsinghua University suggests that China and North Korea are not allies. Yan notes that since at least 2013 China has treated China–North Korea relations as normal state-to-state relations. Yan is not the first to make that claim. In fact, no Chinese officials or diplomats in recent memory have called North Korea an ally. To acknowledge the fact that China and North Korea do not even like each other helps us understand why China's leverage over North Korea is limited.

Third, this is not so much a North Korea problem as it is a U.S.–China problem. Though the United States and China share the objective of a nuclear-free Korean peninsula, their approaches to achieving it are vastly different, and their visions for East Asia's future do not converge. From North Korea to Taiwan, from the East China Sea to South China Sea, the two powers have been unable or unwilling to compromise their positions. At the core of the latest crisis is a lack of strategic trust between the United States and China. The two powers have lost another opportunity to strike a grand deal to build trust and promote peace in East Asia.

Finally, Kim Jong-un's ability has been underestimated. Few expected the inexperienced young dictator to stay in power for long. Yet, more than 4 years after he succeeded his father, Kim appears to have consolidated his position. Fully aware of the U.S.–China division, the capricious Kim is very calculating and has pushed forward North Korea's nuclear program. While U.S. President Barack Obama is exercising "strategic patience" and Chinese President Xi Jinping is emphasizing "stability" in Northeast Asia, Kim has advanced North Korea's nuclear technology and boosted his stature at home. A more benign view is that with the successful nuclear test and satellite launch, Kim may now be able to turn his attention to the economy. The implementation of his *byungjin* policy (parallel development of the economy and nuclear program) may soon be in full swing. But there is no way we can tell what is on Kim's mind. The only thing that is predictable about North Korea is its unpredictability.

The North Korea crisis reveals deep-rooted problems in the region. As the international community plans to impose new sanctions of questionable efficacy, all players involved must take the moment to somberly rethink these fundamental problems and redouble their efforts to bolster regional security.

See: https://thediplomat.com/2016/02/some-lessons-from-the-north-korea-crisis/.

Ms Park Goes to Beijing, but Will Xi Cooperate on North Korea?

East Asia Forum, August 29, 2015

South Korean President Park Geun-hye will visit China from September 2–4, 2015 to attend Beijing's official activities to mark the 70th anniversary of the end of World War II, including a military parade on September 3. Her visit comes fresh off the heels of inter-Korean tensions triggered by a North Korean landmine which maimed two South Korean soldiers. Though the situation is calming, North Korea remains a security challenge for both China and South Korea and is likely to dominate talks between Park and Chinese President Xi Jinping. But achieving a long-lasting peace on the Korean peninsula will require nothing short of joint efforts by all major players in Northeast Asia, especially China and the United States.

President Park's planned visit speaks volumes of how far the Sino-ROK relationship has come since the two countries normalized relations in 1992. For China, South Korea is a good neighbor and reliable friend. Park's visit demonstrates the warm relationship between the two countries as well as the close personal ties between her and Xi. This is in contrast to relations with North Korea, which while traditionally described as close as "lips and teeth," have deteriorated in recent years given North Korea's nuclear testing and the execution of Kim Jong-un's uncle and China point-man Jang Song-thaek.

The China visit makes economic and political sense for South Korea. China has been South Korea's largest trading partner for over a decade. South Korea trades more with China than with the U.S. and Japan combined. Both South Korea and China are critical of what they see as Japanese historical revisionism: in particular, they are disappointed with Prime Minster Shinzo Abe's August 14 statement. Their common interest is in peacebuilding in East Asia, a peace built on truthful reflection on the painful past.

For China, Park's visit also shows that South Korean foreign policy, in contrast to Japan's, is more independent from Washington.

124 A Critical Decade: China's Foreign Policy (2008–2018)

The Japanese media reported that the United States had pressured Park to cancel her upcoming trip to Beijing. Despite denying this, the U.S. government's concerns are understandable. First of all, the United States does not want to send a signal in favor of China's saber-rattling military parade in Beijing. It wants its allies to follow its lead and not attend the parade. And it does not want to encourage China's potential military adventurism, especially when China is embroiled in territorial disputes in the South China Sea and East China Sea.

Washington is especially concerned about the timing of the parade. The Chinese government has stated that the military parade, part of the 70th anniversary celebration, is not aimed at any particular country. Yet, given the delicate state of Sino-Japanese relations today, it may unnecessarily raise tensions in the region. The United States does not have any problem with South Korea developing robust economic and even political relations with China. But it feels deeply uncomfortable when South Korea moves closer to China while Japan–South Korea relations remain frosty. The United States "rebalance" toward Asia is significantly complicated if two of its key allies there are not getting along.

During the upcoming Park–Xi summit, President Park is likely to urge China to play a more active role in persuading North Korea to return to the Six-Party Talks. But China–DPRK relations have been weakening and Pyongyang does not take Beijing's advice seriously these days. Kim Jong-un will not go to Beijing for the commemoration event, either because he did not receive the invitation from China or because he rejected it. In the midst of the current tensions, North Korea has reportedly claimed that it will not heed Beijing's call for restraint since such a strategy does not work anymore.

South Korea needs to be realistic and patient. As many have argued, China's leverage over North Korea may have been overrated. It really will take concerted efforts by all major players, including efforts to revive the China–Japan–South Korea trilateral summit later this year as well as strong U.S.–China cooperation, to resolve the deadlock on the Korean peninsula. Unfortunately, Beijing and Washington seem to have outsourced their responsibilities to each other regarding the North Korea issue. They seem powerless or uninterested in dealing with North Korea and its young leader now.

Two events in 2015 have both raised hopes and created frustrations for observers of the Korean Peninsula. The first was the international agreement reached by the United States, China and other major powers with Iran over the latter's nuclear program; the other was the resumption of diplomatic ties between the United States and Cuba after decades of hostility. When can a solution to the North Korea problem be found? The latest tensions on the peninsula highlight the urgency of this issue.

With the presidential election season gearing up in the United States, North Korea is unlikely to become a priority issue for the departing Obama administration. China, on the other hand, is suffering from a deteriorating relationship with North Korea and its influence over Pyongyang has drastically declined. In this regard, President Park's diplomatic activism comes at a critical time and hopefully will lead to positive results on the Korean Peninsula in the years ahead.

See: http://www.eastasiaforum.org/2015/08/29/ms-park-goes-to-beijing-but-will-xi-cooperate-on-north-korea/.

The West Must Try a "Third Way" to Change North Korea

South Korea's carrots and America's sticks have both failed to tame North Korea. There is another way. With a new regime and small, but positive changes stirring in North Korea, the international community should seize the chance and begin cultural exchanges with the North. *The Christian Science Monitor,* June 12, 2012.

The international community has tried two dominant approaches to deal with North Korea in the past two decades: South Korea's generous incentives and America's punitive sanctions. So far, both have failed.

126 A Critical Decade: China's Foreign Policy (2008–2018)

Since its failed satellite launch in April 2012, North Korea has reportedly been preparing for a third nuclear test. The dire situation on the Korean Peninsula calls for an alternative and more effective approach by the international community. With a new regime and small, but positive changes stirring in North Korea, the international community should seize the chance to influence real changes in Pyongyang's policies.

Ten years of engagement by South Korea (1998–2008) through the "Sunshine Policy" of President Kim Dae-jung and the "Peace and Prosperity" policy of his successor Roh Moo-hyun did not create a cooperative and peaceful North Korea. Instead, a frustrated South Korea and the world witnessed North Korea's enhanced efforts to develop weapons, including two nuclear tests, one in 2006 and one in 2009.

North Korea also initiated major provocations by allegedly sinking the South Korean warship *Cheonan* and shelling Yeonpyeong Island in 2010, killing a total of 50 South Koreans. For the South, enough was enough. President Lee Myung-bak came to office in 2008 and scrapped the soft approach toward the North. He was criticized for being too hawkish on North Korea, but his policy was based on a realistic assessment of the failed engagement approach.

On the other hand, sanctions and punishment have dominated America's approach toward North Korea since the 1994 Agreed Framework broke down, although the United States has maintained communication channels with North Korea. But sanctions have barely hurt the ruling elites in Pyongyang and have not changed regime behaviors. It is the poor North Korean people who have been suffering from these punitive measures. The West's current approach to North Korea not only lacks creativity, it is morally deficient.

There is another way — the third way. The international community should initiate a new strategy with one primary objective: the peaceful evolution of the North Korean regime.

This new strategy must include comprehensive contact with North Korea's people, not just its government. Such full-scale contact would involve more than just providing food and fuel to North Korea as outlined in the now broken Leap Day agreement between the

The Korean Peninsula 127

United States and North Korea. And this third way would take a far more specific and encompassing outreach approach than South Korea's "sunshine policy." As a pillar of this approach, exchanges at the societal level must be promoted.

For example, the United States and other Western nations can establish scholarships to invite North Korean students to study abroad. North Korean cultural, educational, and sports teams should be we comed to participate in more international events. Even military-to-military contact between North Korea and the West, while inconceivable now, should be explored. Full engagement does not mean endorsement of the North Korean regime but aims at positive changes within North Korea.

While the North Korean leadership appears united, different views exist among top leaders. The West can apply a "divide and conquer" strategy to isolate hardliners and encourage potential reformers. Such a strategy has a better chance to influence long-term developments in North Korea than punitive sanctions.

This is not a quixotic idea, but a policy based on reality. Interestingly, North Korea also seems ready to try something new. After the young Kim Jong-un succeeded his father who suddenly died last December, most observers think that life will go on as usual in North Korea. Few have paid attention to recent positive changes inside the Hermit Kingdom.

While Western nations continue to drum up sanctions against North Korea, the isolated country is reaching out to other nations to explore ways to break up ostracism and develop its economy. Kim Yong-nam, president of the presidium of North Korea's parliament, recently concluded a visit to Singapore and Indonesia, in an apparent attempt to draw foreign investment and expand trade. Mr. Kim is North Korea's ceremonial head of state; his visit to Southeast Asia is significant and adds to a recent spate of positive developments in North Korea. In January, *the Associated Press* became the first Western media outlet to open a full-time, all-format news bureau in Pyongyang. In May, North Korea and Indonesia signed an agreement to share news stories, photos, TV and video footage, and eventually swap journalists.

128 A Critical Decade: China's Foreign Policy (2008–2018)

The late Kim Jong-il visited China several times, touring boom-towns like Shanghai and Shenzhen. Many wondered why he did not introduce Chinese-style reforms to North Korea. For North Korea, the experiences of smaller Southeast Asian nations are perhaps more relevant.

North Korea considers Singapore a model for growth and attracting foreign direct investment. Singapore became North Korea's 6th largest trade partner in 2010, according to the Korea Trade-Investment Promotion Agency in Seoul. By firming up trade relations with other countries, North Korea also appears to be trying to avoid over-dependence on China.

The leadership style in Pyongyang has changed too. One may be surprised to notice that an official portrait of Kim Jong-un released by the North Korean government shows the young leader wearing a Western-style suit and tie. Mr. Kim is also often depicted in photos with thrilled and emotional North Korean citizens who hug and embrace him. Such intimate physical contact between the supreme leader and ordinary citizens was very rare in the past.

And on a smaller, but no less significant note: Previously, visitors to North Korea were not allowed to take photos or use cell phones. Recently such restrictions have been eased in Pyongyang. The signs of encouraging changes in North Korea are unmistakable. The international community should heed them and act.

The possession of nuclear weapons alone does not make North Korea more dangerous. If North Korea's security is guaranteed, it will be unlikely to use those weapons. For the new diplomatic approach to succeed, it is essential that the U.S. and China cooperate and provide joint security for North Korea. In exchange for the security assistance, the two powers could pressure North Korea to carry out immediate and meaningful economic reforms.

China's cooperation in this new initiative is vital, but it is also unrealistic to place all the burdens for changing North Korean behaviors on China. China's help to prop up the Kim regime in the past cannot be equated with supporting North Korea's repulsive behaviors. In fact, the voice is growing louder inside China to abandon and even punish the North Korean regime, which was recently involved in the kidnapping of 28 Chinese fishermen.

Kim Jong-un is very young, and the future of North Korea under his leadership is uncertain. The international community should grab the inherent opportunity to influence shifts in Pyongyang. A new policy of comprehensive contact together with security assurance has a better chance than sanctions to prod North Korea to open up and join the international community. With the failure of previous policies and emergence of positive, albeit small, changes within North Korea, the "third way" approach is at least worth trying.

See: https://www.csmonitor.com/Commentary/Opinion/2012/0612/West-must-try-a-third-way-to-change-North-Korea.

The Korea Crisis and China's Policy

e-International Relations, June 2, 2010

China's mild response to the March 2010 sinking of South Korean navy warship *Cheonan* has frustrated many people. Since the publication of a report by a team of international investigators on 20 May 2010 implicating North Korea as the perpetrator, killing 46 South Korean sailors, China has not joined the United States, Japan, and South Korea in openly condemning Pyongyang and threatening punitive measures. Meanwhile, Chinese leaders have expressed condolences to the South Korean government and South Korean families affected by the tragedy. What explains China's fence-sitting on this issue? What are China's interests on the Korean Peninsula?

There are many misperceptions of China's policy toward the Korean Peninsula. Some people believe that North Korea provides a friendly buffer zone between China and democratic South Korea where some 28,000 U.S. troops are based. Others assume that China needs to prop up the Kim Jong-il regime for fear of a massive influx of hungry and desperate North Korean refugees to China triggered by the sudden collapse of the Kim government. Western media routinely portray China

130   *A Critical Decade: China's Foreign Policy (2008–2018)*

as the major ally of the North Korean government and hint that China will always support Pyongyang in a conflict between the two Koreas.

These observations, though not completely wrong, do not reflect the full picture and complexity of China's Korea policy. The fact is since August 1992 when Beijing established diplomatic relations with the Republic of Korea (South Korea), China has adopted a "two Koreas" policy and has not stood by North Korea indiscriminately. For example, China condemned North Korea's missile tests in May 2009 and supported the UN resolution against North Korea.

On the other hand, very few bilateral relations have grown more rapidly than those between China and South Korea in less than 20 years. China's bilateral trade with South Korea reached $156 billion in 2009 while its trade with the North was less than $3 billion. China and South Korea are negotiating a free trade agreement to further boost trade to $300 billion by 2015. They have also established the so-called strategic partnership in 2008, a close relationship that China has formed with less than a dozen countries. China has become the largest trade partner, the biggest export market and the largest source of imports of South Korea, while South Korea is the fourth largest trade partner of China. The two societies are also getting closer. The two countries have established more than 120 pairs of sister cities. Every week over 830 flights and 100,000 people travel between the two countries. South Korean movie and music stars boast millions of feverish fans in China, and vice versa.

China–North Korea relations are rooted in the past, while China–South Korea relations are oriented toward the future. China–North Korea relations used to be as close as "lips and teeth" during the Korean War. But China has grown increasingly unhappy with North Korea in recent years, and one can argue that North Korea has become a liability for China.

Economically, North Korea has become a burden for China. North Korea is like a black hole, endlessly absorbing China's supply of food and fuel. What China gets in return is a recalcitrant North Korea that frequently challenges the international system and embarrasses China. Diplomatically, North Korea, a small nation of less than 23 million people, has consumed way too many resources of China.

A large part of China's diplomacy today revolves around North Korea, constraining China's ability to conduct diplomacy in other countries and regions. Politically and strategically, the perceived China–North Korea alliance deeply hurts China's international image. China has its own national interests such as maintaining good relations with its neighbors. However, offering continuous support for a repressive regime and sometimes tacitly condoning its reckless behavior are not commensurate with China's claim as a responsible great power.

Even within China, there have been calls for delinking with the Kim Jong-il regime. Then why hasn't China abandoned North Korea yet? The short answer is that China is in a dilemma on the Korean Peninsula. China is ambivalent about and unprepared for the future of Korea. It is afraid that a united, pro-West Korea may pose a more serious challenge to China. The two Koreas already have historical and territorial disputes with China now. A unified Korea is likely to be emboldened to officially claim part of northeast China as its own. A unified Korea may also deny China potential access to rich minerals in the North.

It is in the best interest of China, and arguably of other countries in the region, to keep the status quo on the Korean Peninsula. The United States is obviously not prepared to start another war now to help achieve Korean reunification. Japan, despite its anti-North Korea position, will be very concerned about having a unified, nuclear-capable neighbor of over 75 million people when Japan itself is not allowed to go nuclear.

China's priority remains stability at home and in the neighborhood so as to concentrate on economic development. Any harsh reaction toward North Korea risks triggering a conflict on the Korean Peninsula. China will oppose actions and measures by any party that will escalate tensions in the region.

China's policy toward the Korean Peninsula is based on its own national interest, not its endorsement of North Korean adventurism. The North Korea–China Treaty of Friendship, Cooperation, and Mutual Assistance was signed in July 1961 and remains valid unless one side agrees to a revision or abolishment. A clause guarantees

132   *A Critical Decade: China's Foreign Policy (2008–2018)*

automatic intervention if one of the signatories is attacked by a country or allied countries. However, China has downplayed this treaty and is trying hard to avoid the outbreak of conflict on the Korean Peninsula.

North Korea is a country under siege. Its leadership succession is inconclusive. Kim Jong-il's youngest son, the 27-year-old Kim Jong-un, is mysterious and untested and does not seem to enjoy widespread support within the government and the military. Kim Jong-il may be a much hated person, but he is very calculated, and he often stirs up something like firing a missile or attacking a warship in order to attract international attention, rally the nation and the military around him and his family and extract more aid from the international community.

The Korea crisis poses serious challenges to East Asian security. China's peaceful policy toward the Korean Peninsula is not likely to satisfy everyone, especially during a crisis, but under the current circumstances it serves the best interests of every party involved. The future of North Korea is far from clear, but one thing is certain: China will do its best to continue to promote peace and stability on the Korean Peninsula.

See: https://www.e-ir.info/2010/06/02/the-korea-crisis-and-china%e2%80%99s-policy/.

Should Obama Sign a Peace Treaty with North Korea?

It's too late to rid the country of nukes, but we can keep its program under control.
The Christian Science Monitor, July 28, 2009

A rare opportunity has emerged for the United States and North Korea to directly engage in diplomatic dialogue. The Obama administration should quickly and firmly grab it.

North Korea's Foreign Ministry issued a statement on July 27, 2009 saying that "there is a specific and reserved form of dialogue" with the U.S. that can address the nuclear situation. The statement followed remarks over the weekend by Sin Son-ho, North Korea's ambassador to the United Nations, who said his government was "not against a dialogue" with Washington. These statements are apparently in response to U.S. Secretary of State Hillary Rodham Clinton's call for North Korea to return to the negotiating table.

Secretary Clinton said last week in Thailand that if North Korea agreed to irreversible de-nuclearization, the U.S. would move forward on a package of incentives, including normalizing relations with Pyongyang. Clinton later said on NBC's "Meet the Press" that North Korea wouldn't be "rewarded for half-measures" toward ending its nuclear weapons program.

The willingness on both sides to resume talks is encouraging, but there are major hurdles ahead. Frankly, it is unrealistic for the U.S. to ask North Korea to give up its nuclear technology. The reason is simple: The nuclear card is the only one North Korea has; it will not easily give it away. The ostrich policy of refusing to accept North Korea as a nuclear state has to be ditched. A solution to the North Korea conundrum must begin with recognizing the fact that North Korea has the ability to produce nuclear weapons and will remain nuclear-capable.

The Cold War has not ended on the Korean Peninsula. Regime survival is a top priority for Pyongyang. Depicted as being belligerent and menacing to its neighbors and the U.S., North Korea retorts that it is the U.S. that has been hostile and provocative.

The impoverished North needs the nuclear program as a bargaining chip. It is also in dire need of energy, which nuclear technology can provide. It is highly unlikely that Pyongyang will actually use nuclear weapons against its neighbors or the U.S.–North Korean leaders are fully aware that it would be suicidal.

In the 1990s, President Bill Clinton took a soft-line policy toward North Korea. He promised millions of dollars in aid, food, oil, and even two nuclear reactors in exchange for denuclearization. President Clinton also sent Secretary of State Madeleine Albright

134 *A Critical Decade: China's Foreign Policy (2008–2018)*

to Pyongyang to meet with Kim Jong-il. But U.S. Congress never approved the budget for the construction of the two nuclear reactors, there was evidence that North Korea was violating its end of the bargain, and Clinton left office, unable to solve the problem.

Then George W. Bush put North Korea on the "axis of evil" list and took a hardline approach, which also backfired. More sanctions will not affect the lives of North Korean rulers and will only cause more suffering for the common people. Heated rhetoric does not help solve the problem, either.

But that doesn't mean there's no way forward. Kim Jong-il is now apparently picking his successor. Kim Jong-un, his youngest and favored son, has been rumored to be the next leader of North Korea. If this is true, there might be some hope for North Korea.

The younger Kim was educated in the International School of Berne in Switzerland. He is reported to have been introverted but friendly to his classmates. Unlike his father and grandfather, he has first-hand experience in a Western society.

It would be a mistake to dismiss the possibility that Kim Jong-un may introduce political and economic reforms to North Korea after he consolidates his power. Consider China: Mao Zedong, who only spent a few months in Moscow and never ventured to the West, kept China in isolation and constant conflict with foreign powers while Deng Xiaoping, who studied and lived in France as a teenager, brought sea changes to post-Mao China.

When Deng emerged as China's leader after the Cultural Revolution, the U.S. and other Western countries welcomed him. President Jimmy Carter invited him to Washington and praised his bold economic reform initiatives.

Nearly two decades after Russia and China established diplomatic relations with South Korea, neither the U.S. nor Japan has taken steps to recognize North Korea. Why doesn't President Obama reach out to Kim Jong-un and establish a working relationship with him as early as possible?

North Korea is predictably unpredictable, but one thing is clear now: It is determined to keep nuclear technology and strengthen its nuclear weapons. Yet, what North Korea needs most is not the two

The Korean Peninsula 135

light water reactors promised to it under the collapsed 1994 Agreed Framework; it needs security guarantees and diplomatic recognition.

Acquiring nuclear technology does not make North Korea more dangerous; it is how the regime uses this technology that matters. Since North Korea is already nuclear-capable, the U.S. should keep this traditional enemy close by signing a nuclear cooperation deal with it and co-managing its nuclear program. Both South Korea and China are also supportive of a less confrontational approach to North Korea.

Ultimately, the U.S.–North Korea dialogue should aim at establishing diplomatic relations and signing a peace treaty, which may be the best way to keep North Korea's nuclear program and technology under control.

See: https://www.csmonitor.com/Commentary/Opinion/2009/0728/p09s02-coop.html.

Chapter

5

China's Relations with India and Japan

Raising China–India Relations to a New Height

Eurasia Review, September 1, 2018

Relations between China and India — two emerging great powers — will undoubtedly shape the future of our world. The multi-dimensional bilateral relationship has been complex, sometimes difficult, in recent history. The 70-plus day tense standoff in Doklam/Donglang in summer 2017 brought the two sides dangerously close to the first large-scale military clash since the 1962 border war.

Fortunately, cooler heads prevailed on both sides and the high tension was defused. The Doklam/Donglang incident served as a wake-up call for both sides: distrust still runs deep in the relationship and they must work hard to manage the relations prudently. The incident also made the two countries realize once again the importance of cooperation and the risks of confrontation.

2018 will be remembered as a year when the two governments worked conscientiously to open a new chapter in bilateral relations. The "informal" meeting between Indian Prime Minister Narendra Modi and Chinese President Xi Jinping in Wuhan, China in April is significant in the history of the relationship. It does not matter which side initiated the Wuhan meeting; the fact the two leaders had a candid, thorough, and respectful dialogue alone is worth commending. During the meeting the two sides reportedly identified over 100 areas — both new and old — for potential cooperation. The two leaders also pushed for closer economic ties, with the target of raising bilateral trade to $100 billion by 2020. Shortly after the Wuhan meeting, Xi and Modi met again in June and July during the Shanghai Cooperation Organization (SCO) Qingdao Summit and the BRICS Summit in Johannesburg, South Africa, respectively, with both leaders reiterating the theme of close cooperation. Notably Chinese defense minister Wei Fenghe visited India in late August to enhance military interactions.

However, the picture is not always so rosy. In addition to long-standing territorial disputes, India–China relations face serious challenges, particularly in strategic and economic spheres.

Strategically, India views China's rise with concerns while China worries about India's siding with the United States in the latter's effort to counter China's rise. For example, India considers the China–Pakistan Economic Corridor (CPEC) a violation of its sovereignty since the CPEC passes through the controversial Kashmir region, which India claims to be its territory. India is also deeply concerned about Chinese investment in smaller South Asian countries, which India fears China is using to encircle India. China has invested in many infrastructure projects in South Asia, such as the Hambantota Port in Sri Lanka, which India fears China may use for military and intelligence-collecting purposes. With China's growing clout in South Asia, India feels uncomfortable and fears losing its traditional sphere of influence. In implementing the Belt and Road Initiative (BRI), China needs to be more sensitive to concerns by countries along the routes.

China's Relations with India and Japan   139

Nevertheless, officially and publicly India does not consider China's rise as a threat. For example, India has been lukewarm to the much-touted term "Indo-Pacific" that is increasingly being used by the United States to replace the traditional "Asia-Pacific." A reason America changed the geographical term as well as its military command in Asia from Pacific Command (USPACOM) to Indo-Pacific Command (USINDOPACOM) is to highlight India's potential role in America's effort to counter China's growing power and influence. However, India, following the traditional non-alignment spirit, has kept some distance from the quadrilateral group of the United States, Japan, Australia, and India. Both India and China maintain independent foreign policies and promote a multipolar system in which all nations live equally and peacefully.

Economically, though there is a huge potential for close cooperation, right now India has a considerable trade deficit with China. In 2017, China–India trade hit $84.44 billion, and India's trade deficit with China reached $52 billion. If not fixed, the trade imbalance will become a thorny issue in the bilateral relationship. The good news is China has promised to buy more from India, including rice, sugar, and pharmaceutical products and services.

To raise the relationship to a new height, both sides must also overcome another imbalance in the relationship. Presently the relationship is a little skewed, with India fixated on China while China is not paying sufficient attention to India. According to a recent study by the Inter-American Dialogue, a Washington, DC-based think tank, China now boasts nearly 60 research centers on the Latin American region. China probably has more such centers focused on the United States or Japan. It is unclear how many South Asia studies centers China has, let alone India studies centers, but Chinese scholars estimate the number of South Asia/India focused centers in China is much smaller. While many India's China scholars are fluent in Chinese or are learning the language, very few Chinese scholars understand Hindi or other non-English Indian languages. On the other hand, China has hosted thousands of Indian scholars in recent years, but few Chinese scholars have been invited to visit India.

140 *A Critical Decade: China's Foreign Policy (2008–2018)*

Frequent meetings between Xi and Modi in 2018 have mapped out a promising future for the India–China relationship. The real challenge now is to turn that vision into reality.

See: https://www.eurasiareview.com/01092018-raising-china-india-relations-to-a-new-height-oped/.

Is Indo-Pacific the "New" Pivot?

It is unclear exactly what the Indo-Pacific concept entails — especially regarding the future relations between New Delhi and Beijing.
The National Interest, November 23, 2017

Government officials and scholars around the world have quickly switched their label for Asia from "Asia Pacific" to "Indo-Pacific" after President Donald Trump popularized the latter during his first Asia trip in November 2017.

"Indo-Pacific" as a geopolitical concept first appeared in European publications in the 1920s. For example, it was mentioned in retired German general Karl Ernst Haushofer's *Geopolitics of the Pacific Ocean*. In recent years, however, several countries, including the United States, Japan, Australia and India, have rekindled their interest in this concept, with some people suggesting that the four countries should form a democratic quadrangle in the region. In fact, the four countries held the first quadrilateral meeting at the ministerial level on the sidelines of the 2017 ASEAN Summit in Manila recently. While all four members have denied any connection of the quadrilateral to China, there is absolutely no doubt that the rise of China has led them to balance that rise and perhaps contest the new hegemon.

U.S. Secretary of State Rex Tillerson first promoted a "free and open Indo-Pacific" in his speech at CSIS on October 18, 2017, boosting India's stature in America's Asia policy, and President Trump mentioned "Indo-Pacific" several times during his Asia trip the following month. However, it is unclear exactly what this concept entails — especially regarding the future relations between India and China. It may be tempting to group democracies in the region as a natural camp against the rise of a non-democratic China, but such a division will have unsettling consequences for a largely peaceful and stable region.

India is a leader in the Non-Aligned Movement and has maintained an independent foreign policy since 1947. Unlike the United States and Japan, the Indian government has not showed much enthusiasm and has wisely taken a restrained approach toward the "Indo-Pacific" concept, mindful of China's sensitivities. For India, such a concept is neither new nor particularly exciting since India's "Look East" and "Act East" policies already treat India an integral part of the dynamic Asia. If India joins a potentially anti-China camp as some might have hoped, then India's relations with its largest trading partner will undoubtedly deteriorate and Asia will become more unstable.

Both India and China follow the "Five Principles of Peaceful Coexistence," known as the Panchsheel Treaty, which was developed by Prime Ministers Jawaharlal Nehru and Zhou Enlai, so external nomenclatures such as "rebalance" to Asia or "Indo-Pacific" are unlikely to disrupt India–China relations. The India–China standoff at Doklam/Donglang that ended diplomatically in August 2017 is quite telling of the relationship: it's full of challenges, but the two powers have the wisdom and will to resolve their problems peacefully.

Due to long-standing border disputes, power rivalry, and strategic distrust, India and China have their work cut out for them to improve their complex relations in the years ahead.

First of all, this relationship is asymmetric. While China does not take India very seriously, India is super-sensitive to every move China makes. The Chinese tend to ignore India and even deride its "backwardness" while Indians are fixated on China, determined to beat the giant neighbor in every aspect. Those Chinese who have briefly visited

India with some superficial knowledge of the country often report that India is dirty and messy and is decades behind China in infrastructure.

India aims to catch and surpass China, much like China's focus on the United States. Indian students studying in China have increased steadily in the past decade. A record 18,717 Indian students were enrolled at Chinese colleges in 2016. In contrast, only about two thousand Chinese students were studying in India. In the past two decades, China invested tens of billions of U.S. dollars in Africa and Latin America, but its share of total foreign direct investment in India is only 0.5 percent, despite being India's largest trading partner, according to India's Department of Industrial Policy & Promotion. Going forward, China will need to pay more attention to India and India must work harder to entice more investment and young people from China.

Second, the 1962 war casts a long shadow on relations today. Prime Ministers Nehru and Zhou formed close personal bond in the early 1950s as they worked together to push for South-South cooperation. Yet, the border war broke out in October 1962, setting back the relationship, and Indians still feel deeply humiliated.

If there is another war, India is determined to take revenge. Statements such as "The India of 2017 is different from what it was in 1962" by India's defense minister Arun Jaitley reveal such sentiment. Meanwhile, China continues to fume over India's hosting of the Tibetan government in exile and allowing the Dalai Lama to visit the disputed Tawang area. One should not forget history, but it is unwise to let historical disputes dictate relations today.

Third, and most significantly, India and China are engaged in a strategic rivalry, particularly in South Asia and the Indian Ocean. The two countries have cooperated well in BRICS and Asian Infrastructure Investment Bank (AIIB), and recently India, together with Pakistan, joined the Shanghai Cooperation Organization (SCO). But India remains frustrated by China's "all-weather friendship" with arch-enemy Pakistan, its apparent opposition to India's bid in the Nuclear Suppliers Group and its tepid support for India's ambition to become a permanent member of the UN Security Council. China, on the other hand, is irritated by India's strengthening of strategic ties with the United States and Japan and growing voice in the South China Sea brawl.

China opened its first military base overseas in Djibouti in 2016. Djibouti's position on the northwestern edge of the Indian Ocean has fueled worry in New Delhi that China is encircling India with a string of partnerships that include Sri Lanka, Bangladesh, Myanmar and Nepal. China's Belt and Road Initiative (BRI) has generated widespread interest. So far India has not publicly supported it and dislikes the China–Pakistan Economic Corridor (CPEC) that passes through the controversial territory of Kashmir.

Frankly speaking, it will not be easy to overcome key hurdles in Sino-Indian relations. To allay mutual security concerns, India and China could work together to implement the proposed Bangladesh–China–India–Myanmar Corridor, and interlink it with the CPEC and thus create a grand South Asian Economic Corridor, as suggested by an aide to India's former Prime Minister Atal Bihari Vajpayee. China should also help India to become a full member of the Asia Pacific Economic Cooperation (APEC).

A free, open, prosperous and inclusive Indo-Pacific serves the long-term interests of all countries in the region. But if this concept turns out to be a divisive vision for Asia, both India and China must oppose it since it will destabilize the region and add fuel to the fire in the delicate bilateral relationship. As two large emerging powers, India and China have huge stakes in Asia's future. Obviously, they will benefit from a cooperative, not a confrontational, relationship.

See: https://nationalinterest.org/feature/indo-pacific-the-new-pivot-23321.

The East Asian Dispute the World Isn't Talking about

The Hill, July 14, 2017

While much attention has rightly been placed on North Korea and its test launch of an intercontinental ballistic missile, which came on Independence Day of all days, another potential conflict between major Asian powers continues to fester. Japanese and Chinese relations have suffered in recent years due to disputes over history and territory, as well as power rivalry in Asia.

A potential military conflict between the two powers in the East China Sea is no longer unimaginable. In order to move forward, the two sides must face reality and change their mentalities.

From the early 1970s, when diplomatic relations were established, to the early 1990s, when the Chinese economy began to take off, the Chinese viewed their smaller neighbor with admiration, hoping to emulate and catch up with Japan. More Chinese students studied in Japan than in America or Europe during the period. The Japanese, meanwhile, viewed China with mixed feelings — both a sense of superiority and a willingness to help China, which suffered from Japan's past militarism. China was a top destination of Japanese investment and the Official Development Assistance (ODA) program.

From the 1990s on, the mentality on both sides completely changed. After joining the World Trade Organization (WTO) in 2001, China's economic rise expedited. By 2010, China's total GDP had surpassed that of Japan, trailing only the United States. Some Chinese developed a bloated sense of nationalism, belittling Japan; while the Japanese developed a conflictual attitude toward China — marveling at its rapid growth but sneering at its society that is still backward in many aspects.

Rightists in Japan tend to exaggerate the threat from China and use it as a pretext to revise the peace constitution and transform Japan into a normal country with a regular military. Many Chinese believe Japan is not truly remorseful for its war past, while many Japanese feel China is ungrateful for Japan's support for China's modernization.

China's Relations with India and Japan 145

A new vicious cycle has emerged in the bilateral relationship: The public's favorability in each nation of its counterpart has sharply plummeted, and each nation blames the other whenever problems arise in the relationship.

In much of the history of bilateral interaction, China was the stronger party. Japan rose to the top through Meiji Restoration, a rapid industrialization program that began in 1868, leading to victory over imperial China in the 1894–1995 Sino-Japanese War, which marked the beginning of Japan's dominance in East Asia. China remained poor and weak during most of the 20th century. Post-Mao economic reforms fundamentally changed China and the East-Asian power structure. For the first time in history, both China and Japan are strong today — a situation that both have difficulty adjusting to, echoing a Chinese saying: "One mountain cannot accommodate two tigers."

It is not in the interests of either nation to have a prolonged frosty relationship. Japan occupies a significant position in China's foreign policy since it is where China's "big power diplomacy" and "good neighbor diplomacy" merge. Without a healthy and friendly relationship with Japan, China cannot claim to have successful diplomacy.

China has become the leading economy in Asia. When other U.S. allies, such as Australia and South Korea, are balancing their relations with the United States and China and jump on the wagon of China's fast growth, Japan must ditch its "ostrich policy" toward China. It is encouraging that Japan recently reversed its cold reaction to China's ambitious Belt and Road Initiative and expressed willingness to participate in the China-led Asian Infrastructure Investment Bank (AIIB). Japan is also eager to host the Japan–China–South Korea summit scheduled for late 2017 or early 2018, when Chinese Premier Li Keqiang is expected to attend, resuming official exchange of visits at the highest level.

Japan remains a shining example of a traditional society that is highly modernized with an exceptionally clean environment. China must be humble, treat Japan with respect and continue to learn from it. Japan, on the other hand, must overcome its Sinophobia and consider China as an opportunity and partner. It takes two to tango. To move the relationship forward, it's imperative for both countries to face the reality and adjust their mentality so as to work together to build a better future for the people in both countries and beyond.

See: http://thehill.com/blogs/pundits-blog/international-affairs/342007-the-east-asian-dispute-the-world-isnt-talking-about.

Reflecting on India's Nuclear Suppliers Group Bid

e-International Relations, July 14, 2016

India's bid to enter the Nuclear Suppliers Group (NSG), the exclusive club that controls global nuclear commerce, was foiled during its plenary session in Seoul at the end of June 2016, as China and a few other members — including fellow BRICS member, Brazil — reportedly insisted on India signing the nuclear Non-Proliferation Treaty (NPT) before gaining admission.

When the news reached India, many of its citizens were enraged at China, as dozens either protested outside the Chinese embassy in New Delhi or resorted to the social media vent. The story continues to make headlines in the Indian media. However, it must be noted that India's official response has been restrained, with Prime Minister Narendra Modi saying that India and China may differ on several issues, but they will continue to talk "in a straight-forward manner."

The incident has been overblown by the media, which provided inaccurate or incomplete accounts of what happened at Seoul. Some Indian media outlets unnecessarily raised expectations before the NSG meeting, assuming that with the U.S. support, India's NSG membership was guaranteed. Since the plenary session was held behind closed doors, such reports were only based on speculation. India's Minister of State for External Affairs, General V.K. Singh expressed surprise over reports that Beijing had blocked India's bid. "The speculation doing the rounds in media regarding China's protest over NSG membership to India is not true," he said.

Prime Minister Modi also claimed that the criticism in the media about the failure at Seoul was a result of heightened hype due to his successful U.S. visit prior to the NSG's plenary session. "Had it [the visit and the speech before the U.S. Congress] not been hyped so much, there would not have been so much criticism on the NSG issue. [The Indian] government is being criticized not for any mishandling of the NSG issue, but because we were so successful over there [in the U.S.]," said Modi.

Regrettable as it may be for India, the NSG issue is unlikely to precipitate anything more serious in India–China relations. The bilateral relationship is indeed multifaceted, complex, and sometimes difficult, but is also resilient and much stronger than it appears on surface.

Recent examples of close India–China cooperation can be found at the recently launched Asian Infrastructure Investment Bank and the new BRICS Development Bank. High-level contacts have been frequent, including President Xi Jinping and Prime Minister Modi's recent meeting during the Shanghai Cooperation Organization (SCO) summit in Tashkent, and Indian President Pranab Mukherjee's visit to China in May. When Xi and Modi paid state visits to India and China in 2014 and 2015, respectively, they traveled to each other's hometown as a special sign of goodwill. As for entry to pinnacle multilateral clubs, China has consistently supported India's SCO membership. It has also publicly supported India's bid for a permanent seat at the UN Security Council. In contrast, China vehemently opposes Japan's bid.

While they share several international concerns such as curbing poverty and climate change, India and China may not always see eye to eye. In case of the NSG, the Chinese view is that the group itself needs to first agree on the criteria for the entry of countries that are not parties to the NPT. Hence, the recent developments were never a bilateral matter between India and China. As India's External Affairs Minister, Sushma Swaraj remarked, China was not opposing India's NSG bid, but only talking about the criteria and procedures to be adopted for membership to the elite club. China's stance was reportedly backed by nearly ten other countries. There was no consensus on the matter among all NSG members.

With a long history of mutual learning and fruitful interactions, India and China are friends as well as competitors today. The 1962 Sino-India War cast a long shadow on the relationship and their border dispute has remained unresolved since. The relationship has, nonetheless, improved much since the 1990s, with trade and cultural exchanges expanding amidst the post-Cold War transitions. A strong indicator of this relationship's maturity is the fact that, today, India's largest trading partner is China.

With that said, more certainly needs to be done to develop this important relationship of the 21st century at both the official and societal levels. According to a 2014 *BBC World Service* poll, 33 percent of Indians view China positively, with 35 percent expressing a negative view; whereas 27 percent of Chinese view India positively, with 35 percent expressing a negative view.

In 2013, India and China signed the Border Defense Cooperation Agreement during a visit by India's then Prime Minister Manmohan Singh to Beijing, establishing a formal mechanism to improve security along the Line of Actual Control in Kashmir. However, the agreement has yet to be translated into real structural formulations on the ground. In November 2015, General Fan Changlong, the Vice-Chairman of China's Central Military Commission (the chairman of which is President Xi), led a 26-member delegation to India and held talks with the Indian side, headed by Defense Minister Manohar Parrikar. This was the highest level of a Chinese defense delegation's visit to India in recent years, which signals enhanced defense exchanges. Yet, the meeting achieved no significant progress on the border dispute, as local border-level skirmishes continue to occur sporadically even today.

In this context, India's nuclear program is a sensitive issue in India–China relations. One may recall that in 1998, as India conducted its nuclear tests, its Defense Minister, George Fernandes, called China "India's potential enemy number one." Though one may not hear such hostile public comments by senior officials from either side any more, the strategic suspicion runs deep.

China has a strong desire to maintain balance of power in the region, especially when tensions remain high in the South China Sea. It is deeply concerned that India has established close strategic and military ties with the United States and Japan recently. China is unlikely to support India's NSG membership without inviting Pakistan to join the group alongside, given the "all-weather friendship" between China and Pakistan, which allegedly lobbied intensively against India's entry.

One can also argue that the Indian case at the NSG is a glaring contradiction, and an indication toward the double-standards of U.S. policies, rather than simply being a result of China playing politics. The U.S. advocated India's entry on the basis of an exclusive India-specific approach, owing largely to commercial and strategic motivations. It argued that India was like-minded *vis-à-vis* the NSG states with respect to its non-proliferation commitments. As a Pakistani scholar pointed out, this tailor-made India-specific approach was contrary to the criteria-based approach followed by opposing states, which emphasized equal consideration to all NSG aspirants having similar nuclear credentials.

For India, participation in international organizations is highly symbolic of its growing clout, and the NSG membership is such a pathway to great-power status. Some Chinese continue to view India as an inferior rival and do not take its pursuits seriously. Such chauvinistic mentality must be ditched in China's India policy. China is not in a position to antagonize an important neighbor like India, given the many challenges China faces in its foreign relations.

There is no need to panic about India–China relations due to India's recent NSG setback, since the relationship remains robust. Yet, China needs to reassure India that it supports India's desire to play a bigger role in international affairs. India, for its part, must continue to resist wooing from conservative forces in the U.S. and Japan toward an anti-China alliance.

Moving forward and taking different interests into account, the current NSG members could perhaps reach a deal on both India's and Pakistan's memberships. They can support India's membership in the near future on the condition that India will not block Pakistan's membership when it's ready. With adequate patience and wisdom, India's NSG ambition will be realized and India–China ties strengthened.

See: https://www.e-ir.info/2016/07/14/reflecting-on-indias-nuclear-suppliers-group-bid/.

Don't Blame Abe ... Help Him!

Asia Research Institute, University of Nottingham, April 9, 2015

Japanese Prime Minister Shinzo Abe has been portrayed as a staunch nationalist bent on revising Japan's pacifist Constitution. From visiting the Yasukuni Shrine to his claim that "invasion" is not clearly defined internationally, from pressuring McGraw-Hill to revise a history textbook, to beefing up Japan's military power, Abe has repeatedly demonstrated his revisionist view of history and his stance of being unafraid of going against the international community.

Except for his awkward hand-shake with Xi Jinping during the November 2014 APEC summit in Beijing, Japan's relations with China and South Korea have deteriorated considerably since Abe assumed office in December 2012. Despite initial signs of improvement in relations in recent weeks, political tensions between Japan and its two neighbors are likely to remain high for some time. It is tempting, but simplistic, to attribute all the diplomatic problems in Northeast Asia to Abe. The truth is both international and domestic environments provide an inviting setting for Abe to carry out his conservative foreign policy agenda.

The international environment has significantly changed since the beginning of the 21st century. Global terrorism continues unabated and even re-energized with the rise of ISIS. The United States is experiencing relative decline while China continues to expand its power and influence. Terrorism and China's rise will be the two largest security challenges for the United States for many years to come. In both challenges, the United States has found the most reliable and perhaps indispensable ally in Japan.

Japan has become an ardent supporter for the U.S.-led global campaign against terror and America's "pivot" to Asia. While domestic debate over whether and how it should become a normal country is inconclusive, Japan, nominally still a pacifist nation based on its Constitution, has charged onto the forefront of international affairs, in coordination with the United States. The recent hostage tragedy in which two Japanese citizens were killed by ISIS terrorists highlights the depth of Japan's involvement in international affairs. The true intentions of America's "pivot" strategy remain elusive, but it is at least partially designed to counter China's growing power. Japan has welcomed America's strategic rebalancing and taken actions to assist it, such as working to permit the Self-Defense Forces (SDF) to exercise the so-called "right of collective self-defense" — a step further to turning the SDF into a regular military.

Japan's potential remilitarization used to be alarming to everyone. The United States and many other countries were once concerned about letting the "genie out of the bottle" should Japan remilitarize. Allowing Japan to rearm "is like giving chocolate liqueur to an alcoholic," commented the late former Singaporean Prime Minister Lee Kuan Yew. Today, it seems only China and South Korea firmly oppose Japan's move to the right. During her visit to Japan in March 2015, German Chancellor Angela Merkel urged Japanese leaders to face history "openly and squarely" while also nudging Japan's neighbors to be more generous. Unfortunately, other world leaders have not spoken out unambiguously against Japanese leaders' revisionism and denial of history. The United States, the most influential country in Japan's foreign affairs, expects and even encourages its ally to become more militarily involved in international affairs. A victim of Japan's past militarism, the United States has not come out strongly criticizing some Japanese politicians' attempt to rewrite history.

Admiral Robert Thomas, Commander of the Seventh Fleet and the top U.S. naval officer in Asia, said in an interview with *Reuters*, the United States would welcome help from Japanese air patrols to monitor the territorial dispute in the South China Sea. Though Thomas' comments are in line with broader U.S. support for Japan's military playing a more global role, they are essentially elbowing Japan to get involved in the territorial dispute despite the fact that Japan had not publicly expressed such an interest itself and Japan is not a claimant to the South China Sea islands. Other U.S. defense officials have also encouraged Japan to be more involved in the region. U.S. Under Secretary of State Wendy Sherman's remarks that "Nationalist feelings can still be exploited, and it's not hard for a political leader anywhere to earn cheap applause by vilifying a former enemy" may not be

152 A Critical Decade: China's Foreign Policy (2008–2018)

just a slip of tongue but are a revelation of America's siding with Japan in the current imbroglio between Japan and its neighbors.

Typically, Japanese leaders who get the support of the United States are more likely to stay in power for longer. Prime Minister Yukio Hatoyama, from the Democratic Party of Japan, wanted to shift Japan's focus from an America-centric foreign policy to a more Asia-focused policy. He worked to deepen economic integration with the East Asian region. Under his leadership, Japan's relations with both China and South Korea greatly improved. He ended an 8-year SDF refueling mission in Afghanistan, displeasing the United States. His foreign and domestic policies backfired, and his tenure lasted just 9 months.

In the past three decades, only two Japanese prime ministers had stayed in office for as long as 5 years: Yasuhiro Nakasone and Junichiro Koizumi. Nakasone was prime minister for 5 years from 1982 to 1987. A nationalist who twice visited the Yasukuni Shrine, Nakasone was best known for his close relationship with President Ronald Reagan, popularly called the "Ron–Yasu" friendship.

Junichiro Koizumi was prime minister from April 2001 to September 2006. He was criticized for actions such as visiting the Yasukuni Shrine annually which allegedly ran contrary to his expression of remorse on the 60th anniversary of WWII's end. He focused on closer relations with the United States and went further to pursue supporting US policies in the War on Terrorism. He deployed the SDF to Iraq — the first mission in active foreign war zones since the end of WWII. He developed a close personal friendship with President George W. Bush. An avid Elvis Presley fan, Koizumi traveled to Graceland during his final visit to the United States in June 2006, personally accompanied by President Bush.

Prime Minister Abe has developed a close relationship with President Barack Obama. Although U.S. officials privately urged Abe not to visit the Yasukuni Shrine, he still went in December 2013, and the harshest reaction he received from the United States was a mere expression of "disappointment." Abe will visit the United States in late April and become the first Japanese prime minister to speak at a joint sessions of U.S. Congress. The United States is offering unconditional support to Abe without knowing what he will say about Japan's past on the 70th anniversary of the end of WWII.

With strong support from the United States and little opposition from the international community, the Abe administration is forcing forward its assertive and revisionist foreign policy, and the United States is only happy to have such a royal, cooperative, and pliant deputy sheriff in its global strategy.

Ichiro Ozawa's 1993 book *Blueprint for a New Japan* generated heated debate over the future of Japanese foreign policy and constitutional amendment. Constitutional revision used to be a taboo topic in Japan, but support for amending the Constitution, especially its war-renouncing Article 9, steadily increased in the 1990s and early 2000s. Japanese public opinion favoring constitutional amendment rose to over 50 percent by the early 2000s before declining in the following years.

A recent survey by *Yomiuri Shimbun* shows that on the thorny issue of Abe's hope to revise the Constitution's Article 96, which will potentially pave the way for him to try and garner enough support to amend Article 9, 51 percent said they oppose the idea, compared with 35 percent who support it. The hurdle for constitutional change remains high.

Yet, Abe's overall approval rating is strong, with over 50 percent supporting him, even though a sales tax increase in April 2014 and lacklustre performance of Abenomics led to a decline in his public support. After the ISIS hostage crisis, *Yomiuri Shimbun* found that support for Abe's government had risen to 58 percent. Abe does not have the mandate for constitutional revision, yet he remains a strong and popular leader, and Japan's rightward drift becomes speedier under his leadership. Through introducing national security bills to bypass the constitutional constraints, the Abe cabinet is building momentum to inch toward eventually revising the Constitution.

Buoyed by the results of the December 2014 elections and a modest growth of Japan's economy now, Abe is poised to push forward constitutional revision as a major policy objective. Meanwhile, there is little domestic pressure for him to improve relations with China and South Korea. His November 2014 meeting with Xi Jinping and December 2013 Yasukuni Shrine visit did not noticeably affect his domestic support one way or the other.

Though the Komeito serves as a break on Abe's aggressive agenda in the coalition government, and the Japanese Communist Party fights hard against his policies, overall, opposition in and outside the Diet is not stiff enough to compel Abe to change his revisionist mind. Japan's peace groups seem to have failed to restrain him either. With a more "recalcitrant" North Korea, a more "aggressive" China and a more "nationalistic" South Korea, Abe is winning growing support at home to expand the role of the SDF and to amend the Constitution. With sporadic and feeble domestic resistance, Abe has been able to selectively frame security issues to justify his desired policy changes.

Few would oppose Japan's more active political, economic, and cultural involvement in international affairs. But due to its war history and Abe's lack of sincerity in reflecting upon the past, Japan's growing military role abroad and constitutional amendment will create unnecessary tensions in its foreign relations. Japan may have come to terms with the imperial war domestically, but it is not perceived so by the outside world. Abe's revisionist views have become a stumbling block in Japan's relations with China and South Korea. Unless the international community, especially the United States, becomes more forceful in resisting Abe's historical denialism and unless Japan's peace movement is revitalized, little will prevent Abe from attempting to translate his ultra-nationalist outlook into policy.

Emotionally, some Japanese feel that the Constitution was imposed by the United States during the occupation period. For Japan to become a "normal" country, it needs an authentic Japanese-drafted Constitution. So revising the Constitution will get some support — sometimes even over 50 percent of the public. However, the pacifist Constitution served Japan well in the past 70 years. Revising the Constitution and building a stronger military will not improve Japan's international standing or ensure safety of Japanese citizens abroad. A *Kyodo News* poll after the ISIS hostage crisis in February 2015 showed 57.9 percent of the respondents said Japan's support for war against terror should be non-military. Prime Minster Abe should heed what the Japanese people say and defend Japan's status as a global civilian power.

If Abe succeeds in amending Japan's Constitution, the global image of Japan as a peace-loving nation may fundamentally change. And if Abe does not fully and sincerely address the wartime history on the 70th anniversary of the end of WWII, he will be considered a leader without integrity and courage, and Japan may find itself facing an increasingly suspicious and hostile international environment. Instead of blaming Abe, the international community and Japanese public should help him make wise choices now.

See:http://theasiadialogue.com/2015/04/09/dont-blame-abehelp-him/.

People-to-People Diplomacy in China–Japan Relations

With frosty relations at the highest levels, citizen exchange becomes all the more important.
The Diplomat, March 17, 2015

International relations are traditionally conducted by national leaders, government officials, and diplomats. The power of citizen exchanges, or "people-to-people diplomacy," is often underestimated. People-to-people diplomacy, as part of public diplomacy, complements traditional and formal diplomacy. It has a significant impact on relations between nations since bilateral relations are not sustainable without solid public support.

It is well-known that the "Ping-Pong diplomacy" of 1971 helped pave the way for President Richard Nixon's historic visit to China the following year. Less talked about is the indirect role Japan played in the process. Both Chinese and American Ping-Pong players were attending the 31st World Table Tennis Championship in Nagoya, Japan at the time. When American player Glenn Cowan missed him team's bus, he was invited to ride with the Chinese players. His

156   *A Critical Decade: China's Foreign Policy (2008–2018)*

conversation and gift exchanges with Chinese player Zhuang Zedong are today household stories. The Ping-Pong diplomacy that began in Japan led to the normalization of U.S.–China relations.

Amidst the tense political relations between Japan and China today, attention has focused on national leaders and how they help or hinder relations. Many blame either Prime Minister Shinzo Abe's revisionist views and hardline policies or President Xi Jinping's tough style and assertive diplomacy for the deterioration of bilateral relations. They assume that only national leaders and politicians matter in international relations. Such perspectives overlook the power of people-to-people diplomacy and are therefore detrimental to improving relations.

Japan and China established diplomatic ties in 1972. In the 1970s and 1980s, the Japanese had extremely favorable views of China. China was a top destination for Japanese tourists and numerous Japanese companies set up businesses in China. From 1978 to 1988, 70 to 80 percent of Japanese surveyed viewed China favorably. The good feelings were mutual. Ken Takakura's *Kimi Yo Fundo No Kawa O Watare* (中文: 追捕) and *The Yellow Handkerchief* were among the first foreign movies to be screened in post-Mao China. His passing in November 2014 generated fond memories of him and Japan among many Chinese in their 40s and 50s. In the 1980s, more Chinese chose to study in Japan than in any other country.

Japanese manga and anime are popular around the world. But even before this new wave of Japanese soft power, the Chinese had long enjoyed Japan's popular culture. *Ikkyū-san* (聪明的一休) and *Astro Boy* (铁臂阿童木) were some of the earlier popular Japanese anime and their theme songs were among Chinese children's favorites in the 1980s and 1990s. The mutual affection between the two societies clearly played a positive role in maintaining a friendly political relationship.

CCP General Secretary Hu Yaobang and Japanese Prime Minister Yasuhiro Nakasone exchanged visits in 1983 and 1984. Understanding the power of people-to-people diplomacy, Hu invited 3,000 Japanese youths to visit China, including Nakasone's son. Hu reportedly dispatched his daughter to personally accompany Nakasone's son. Notably, Nakasone was involved in setting up a "comfort station" during Japan's imperial war and he visited the Yasukuni Shrine as prime minister, but Hu's pragmatism and foresight, aided by friendship between the two societies, overcame the difficulties and led to healthy growth in bilateral relations in the 1980s and early 1990s. After the Tiananmen Square tragedy, Japan was the first power to lift sanctions against China, and Japanese businesses continued to invest in China. In 1992, Emperor Akihito and Empress Michiko visited China.

As political and economic frictions grew in the second half of the 1990s, Japanese public opinion favoring China steadily dropped, but still about 50 percent of Japanese claimed feelings of friendship for China throughout the 1990s. According to a 2014 *BBC World Service* Poll, however, only 3 percent of Japanese viewed China's influence positively, with 73 percent expressing negative views, the most negative perception of China in the world. In return, only 5 percent of Chinese viewed Japan's influence positively, with 90 percent expressing negative views, the most negative perception of Japan in the world. This appalling level of mutual dislike is extremely disturbing and must be reversed. Political leaders must be cautious in their words and deeds since they affect public opinion. The public, on the other hand, can exercise their power to influence national policies.

Japan and China have different systems. And hawkish politicians, media, and military personnel on both sides are drumming up nationalism and creating tensions in the relationship. But ordinary people have much in common. A distinction needs to be made between fervent nationalists and ordinary citizens, especially when political relations are sour.

I spoke to a group of Japanese college students in Kyoto recently. In exploring the Japan–China relationship, the students seemed very rational, asking what both Japan and China could do to improve the relationship — in sharp contrast to the positions of the two governments, each blaming the other for the problem.

Despite political tensions, Chinese tourists continue to flock to Japan. In 2014, 2.4 million mainland Chinese visited Japan, slightly fewer than the 2.8 million from Taiwan and 2.7 million from South Korea, but mainland Chinese spent more than their counterparts from any other place. With Japan's relaxation of visas for Chinese visitors, a weaker yen, and tax exemptions for foreign tourists, mainland Chinese could easily become the largest source of foreign visitors to Japan in 2015. During the 2015 Chinese New Year break, busloads of Chinese thronged major malls in Tokyo. Many Japanese businesses have hired Mandarin-speaking staff to better meet the needs of Chinese travelers. At Osaka's top tourist sites such as Umeda, the Osaka Castle, and Dotonbori, one will not fail to see groups of Chinese tourists, often with their hands full of shopping bags. The Chinese love high-quality Japanese products. Electric rice-cookers, air filters, and multi-functional toilet seats are reportedly favorites. Most Chinese leave with a very positive impression of Japan and the Japanese. Some Japanese may be stunned by Chinese tourists' purchasing power or disapprove of occasional bad behavior, such as talking loudly and smoking in public, but most welcome Chinese tourists and appreciate their contributions to Japan's economy. "If there is an increase in the number of Chinese who visit Japan and observe Japan as it is, there might be a gradual deepening of understanding between the peoples of the two nations," a high-ranking Japanese Foreign Ministry official said, highlighting the power of such people-to-people exchanges.

Recognizing the importance of enhancing people-to-people understanding, especially among the young, the two governments are beginning to act. For example, the Japanese embassy in Beijing has co-sponsored Japanese speaking and writing contests in China in recent years and recently invited 2000 young Chinese to visit Japan. Meanwhile, the Chinese embassy in Tokyo co-sponsored the 2014 all-Japan Youth Writing Contest on Japan–China relations and invited prize winners to visit China for a week.

At the Kyoto International Community House, paintings of artists from Kyoto's sister cities, including Xi'an, were on display earlier this year. More such cultural activities at the local level are needed in the current political atmosphere. Indeed, there is ample scope for citizen exchanges to grow between China and Japan. For example, in 2014, 6.13 million Chinese visited South Korea, constituting 43.1 percent of all foreign visitors to South Korea. According to Japan National Tourism

Organization, about 2.88 million Japanese tourists visited China and 2.75 million went to South Korea in 2013. Both figures are down about 10 percent from 2009, largely because of the weaker yen and the worsening image held by Japanese toward China and South Korea.

The power of people-to-people diplomacy is woefully underutilized in Japan–China relations. When political relations at the top remain lukewarm at best, citizen exchanges at the grassroots become all the more important. After all, it is ordinary people that form the foundation of a strong and durable bilateral relationship.

See: https://thediplomat.com/2015/03/people-to-people-diplomacy-in-china-japan-relations/.

Will Xi and Abe Meet at APEC in Beijing?

It is time for both leaders to begin repairing the battered relationship.
The Diplomat, August 1, 2014

At an international conference in Honolulu recently, a Japanese scholar asked me: Will President Xi Jinping and Prime Minister Shinzo Abe meet in Beijing during the upcoming APEC summit? "Maybe," I said. Since this is a very serious question, I think it deserves a more careful answer.

Sino-Japanese relations have taken a nosedive since 2012. Since then, the two countries' top leaders have been busy traveling around the world — sometimes on each other's heels, as evidenced by Xi's and Abe's most recent visits to Latin America where they were only separated by a couple of days — yet they have not visited each other nor met bilaterally. The only place they could meet now is in a multilateral setting, yet even there a bilateral meeting is not guaranteed during the APEC summit to be held in Beijing in November 2014.

The Japanese side, including Abe himself, has expressed a strong desire for a bilateral meeting in order to mend the seriously damaged relationship. Recently, Xiong Bo, a deputy director general of the Asian Affairs Department of the Chinese foreign ministry, met a senior official from the Asian and Oceanian Affairs Bureau of the Japanese foreign ministry and discussed the potential of a Xi–Abe meeting at APEC. Xiong expressed China's concern about Abe's visits to Yasukuni Shrine and his position on the disputed Diaoyu/Senkaku Islands, and questioned Japan's sincerity.

After this initial meeting, Chief Cabinet Secretary Yoshihide Suga issued a statement on July 9 saying that the Senkaku islands, as Japan's inherent territory, should not be an obstacle for Chinese and Japanese leaders to meet at APEC. As for the visit to Yasukuni Shrine, Suga wrote it off as more spiritual than political. Qin Gang, spokesperson for China's foreign ministry, immediately criticized Suga's statement and pointed out that there would be no foundation for China and Japan to talk if Tokyo was not willing to change its attitude regarding the two sensitive issues. If Japan is insincere about improving its relationship with China, then talk is futile, said Qin.

As the host of the APEC summit, Xi probably should seize the opportunity to have a serious dialogue with Abe, but he faces considerable domestic pressure to be tough. These are two proud nations and two strong leaders, with two adamant but opposing positions. What can be done to pave the way for a meaningful Xi–Abe meeting? Political wisdom and courage are required on both sides to correct the current diplomatic stalemate. In the weeks leading up to the APEC summit, both sides need to take steps to create an atmosphere conducive to the bilateral meeting. An initial step for Abe to take would be to make a public statement that he will not visit Yasukuni Shrine again for the sake of improving relations between Japan and its neighbors. In return, China should consider scaling back its air and maritime patrols of the disputed islands. The two countries should basically attempt to return to the pre-2012 status quo.

Abe's actions — from visiting the Yasukuni Shrine to pushing for Japan's collective self-defense — have added fuel to the fire and further antagonized China. Most believe his foreign policy is intended to

China's Relations with India and Japan   161

satisfy the right-wing element within Japan, and some argue that the Prime Minister is right-wing himself. However, the so-called right-wing is only a small minority of the Japanese population. Japan remains a pacifist nation with the majority of its people being rational and peace-loving. It is high time that Abe demonstrated some political wisdom. If he pledges not to visit Yasukuni Shrine again as prime minister, he may be pleasantly surprised to find his domestic approval rating rising, because the majority of the public will think that he is prudent and has the courage to improve Japan's relations with China and South Korea. He will not be perceived as weak; instead his already strong leadership will be further boosted at home.

On the other hand, rather than rebuffing positive gestures from Japan, the Chinese side should not continue to snub Abe. Xi should publicly reiterate that China values its long-standing relationship with Japan and is prepared to work with Japan to improve relations soon. To help Abe save face, China can convey its concerns about his rightist leanings privately.

Meanwhile, the two sides should downplay the collective self-defense and air defense identification zone (ADIZ) issues. Various polls suggest that the majority in Japan still oppose the constitutional change to Japan's right to exercise collective self-defense. Though he has the backing of the U.S., Abe faces tremendous legislative and societal hurdles to fully execute this right. For Japan, China's November 2013 demarcation of its ADIZ is obviously offensive. China can keep its ADIZ but does not have to strictly or seriously implement it. Most of all, China's air and maritime patrols must be decreased proportionally in order to avoid accidental clashes with the Japanese in the disputed areas. Pushing these issues off center stage will help put the relationship on the right track again. Let's hope that wisdom will prevail on both sides, and that Abe will be courageous enough to take the first step in the next few weeks, and that Xi will quickly reciprocate so that the Abe–Xi meeting can take place in Beijing soon, leading to a significant improvement in bilateral relations.

See: https://thediplomat.com/2014/08/will-xi-and-abe-meet-at-apec-in-beijing/.

The Japan–China Relationship as a Structural Conflict

e-International Relations, December 31, 2013

Much has been said about China's Air Defense Identification Zone (ADIZ) in the East China Sea and Japanese Prime Minister Shinzo Abe's recent visit to the controversial Yasukuni Shrine, which escalated tensions between Japan and China. But few realize that the Japan–China conflict is structural in nature.

Historians will remember 2010 as a turning point in East Asia's international relations. In that year, China overtook Japan as the second largest economy in the world, a position Japan had held for nearly 40 years. After a couple of decades of economic stagnation, Japan's heyday as an economic superpower seems to be over. As a result, China and Japan are now facing each other as powers of relatively equal strength for the first time in their long history of interactions. Also in that year, a Chinese fishing boat rammed a Japanese Coast Guard vessel in the disputed East China Sea area, triggering Japan's arrest of the Chinese captain and its reluctant release of him a few weeks later under heavy Chinese pressure.

The already troubled bilateral relationship rapidly deteriorated after the Japanese government attempted to nationalize several disputed Senkaku/Diaoyu islands in 2012. In a classic security dilemma, Japan's efforts to respond to China's perceived assertiveness, such as by enlarging its military budget and beefing up its alliance with the United States, have been met with China's balancing actions, which include increased air and naval patrols of the disputed area and the designation of ADIZ in the East China Sea. China's ADIZ covers the disputed islands and overlaps with that of Japan, which has had its own ADIZ since 1969.

China's move to set up the ADIZ and Abe's visit to the Yasukuni Shrine were viewed by many as destabilizing and provocative. China's growing confidence *vis-à-vis* Japan's declining willingness to compromise ensures a potentially risky relationship between the two Asian powers. Unresolved historical and territorial disputes add fuel to the fire as a power transition takes place in East Asia. The United States, itself

China's Relations with India and Japan   163

engaged in a long-term and larger-scale power transition with China, strongly defends Japan as an ally. The regional competition between Japan and China coincides with the global competition between China and the United States. America's public support for Japan, including flying B-52s to the disputed East China Sea area despite its repeated avowal of neutrality in the Japan–China disputes, sends confusing messages and can only contribute to the spiral of regional tensions. If managed imprudently, such inherent structural conflicts may spin out of control and lead to actual military clashes in Asia.

Examining the Japan–China Power Transition

According to the power transition theory in International Relations, when an emerging power and an existing power achieve power parity and one of them is dissatisfied, the power transition will lead to conflict and even war. What makes the Japan–China power transition extremely difficult and dangerous to manage is that both Japan and China are unhappy with the status quo. Japan worries that an increasingly powerful China is challenging the status quo (a state of affairs that Japan prefers). Japan's power has been compromised, but it is not ready to yield to China in Asia's power rivalry. On the other hand, China is displeased because Japan does not recognize China's legitimate interests and refuses to reconcile historical issues.

Adding to the difficulties is Japan's identity crisis; it has yet to come to terms with the fact that the ghost of its militarist past is still haunting relations with its neighbors. While Japan has difficulty adjusting to its weakened power status and seriously reflecting upon history, China seems unclear about how to use its growing power to its greatest benefit.

Japan is an extremely proud nation and deservedly so. In history, Japan borrowed and learned a lot from China, whose culture left a permanent mark on Japanese way of life. What is unique about Japan, however, is that it did not just copy; it reinvented and outperformed its master. With its swift victories over China and Russia in the 1894–1895 Sino-Japanese War and 1904–1905 Russo-Japanese War and its successful industrialization beginning from the second half of the

19th century, Japan quickly propelled to the top rank of powers by the early 20th century. After its surrender at the end of World War II, Japan rapidly regrouped and recovered like a mythical phoenix coming back to life, creating Asia's first economic miracle. In success Japan trusts. However, it seems very difficult for Japan to accept the fact that many Asian countries, including the "four tigers" (Hong Kong, Singapore, South Korea, and Taiwan) and China, have quickly caught up in development.

Since Richard Nixon's historic visit to China, every American president has stated that a successful and prosperous China is in the interests of America and American people. Japan, like the United States, has helped China's economic modernization since the late 1970s and it was the first Western power to have lifted economic and trade sanctions against Beijing following the Tiananmen Square tragedy. But Japan has now become less enthusiastic to see a powerful neighbor emerging in Asia. One barely hears Japanese leaders make encouraging public remarks about China's positive developments.

In addition, Japanese politics has become more nationalistic and conservative in recent years. For example, in a very undiplomatic fashion, Prime Minister Shinzo Abe reportedly slammed China recently by calling China an "absurd" country and South Korea a "foolish" country. Most controversially, Abe visited the war-glorifying Yasukuni Shrine on December 26, 2013, in open defiance of China, South Korea, and even the United States. Such a sharp political turn makes it hard for those in China to champion improving relations with Japan. Indeed, given the increasing hostility and inflexibility of the Japanese government toward China, a small group of Chinese scholars who used to argue that China should move beyond history and treat Japan as a "normal" country and friendly neighbor may need to reconsider their position.

The Japan–China dispute goes beyond contentious issues such as the territorial dispute over the Senkaku/Diaoyu Islands, the visit to the Yasukuni Shrine, comfort women or the Rape of Nanking; it is about power rivalry and the future power arrangement in East Asia. Since the inherent structural conflict between Japan and China is unlikely to disappear, what can be done to manage the crisis in East Asia?

Improving Japan–China Relations

The improvement of Japan–China relations requires prudent leadership on both sides. Shinzo Abe and Xi Jinping are strong leaders who are increasingly constrained by growing nationalism at home. Both are apparently attempting to externalize domestic dissatisfaction. As a first step to cool tensions, they must refrain from making provocative remarks about the already tense relationship and encourage their ministers and generals to also remain cool-headed. All parties concerned, including the United States, must agree that diplomacy, not the use or display of force, should be the preferred method to resolve disputes. Neither side should take further unilateral or confrontational actions.

The two countries should focus on common interests, not long-standing disputes. It was such pragmatic policies from both sides that led to the normalization of relations in the early 1970s. Regardless of whether or not Prime Minister Kakuei Tanaka and Premier Zhou Enlai agreed to shelve the Senkaku/Diaoyu disputes in 1972 (although apparently today many in Japan believe they did not), the fact of the matter is that probably only the Japanese government thinks there is currently no territorial dispute between Japan and China. China's air and naval patrol of the area surrounding the islands as well as China's designation of an ADIZ represent its stepped-up efforts to challenge Japan's claimed exclusive control of those islands and are designed to compel Japan to return to the negotiation table. Japanese leaders must abandon the ostrich policy that pretends that no dispute exists in the East China Sea. They must also avoid provoking China (and South Korea), by desisting from revisiting the Yasukuni Shrine, for example.

Both Japan and China need to take a step back gracefully in order to maintain a stable and friendly relationship. China should clearly reiterate that the establishment of their ADIZ will not impact upon the freedom of navigation and safety of international commercial flights in the disputed area. China should refrain from increasing their military presence in the disputed area. Furthermore, China must be sensitive to Japan's feelings as the power transition (apparently in

China's favor) takes place. Japan's GDP has been eclipsed by China's, but Japan remains a major economic power. In many aspects, especially innovation, Japan is still significantly ahead of China. A cooperative relationship with Japan can only benefit China as it continues to modernize. China should therefore remain humble and not punch above its weight.

The two countries should also develop new thinking in dealing with each other. The Western concept of sovereignty is still held dear by both China and Japan. However, we are now living in an interdependent global village. The principle of sovereignty has faced a number of challenges throughout history. Japan and China should have the wisdom to move beyond the sovereignty dispute and develop some mechanism so that both countries will benefit from the resources near the Senkaku/Diaoyu Islands through joint explorations. Both nations should be forward-looking and work together to cooperate and bring this dispute to a resolution.

Concluding Thoughts

Without cooperation from the United States, neither China nor Japan can achieve their diplomatic objectives. Both China and Japan should welcome the United States to play a more active and constructive role in Asia. The shortest route between Beijing and Tokyo is sometimes via Washington. The United States must balance its interests between a longtime loyal ally and an increasingly interdependent economic partner. It is not in America's interest to contain China; it is equally detrimental to stability in Asia if America's "pivot" toward Asia emboldens Japan to pursue a more hawkish foreign policy. A strong and cooperative relationship between Beijing and Washington holds the key to peace and prosperity in Asia, including the East China Sea.

See: https://www.e-ir.info/2013/12/31/the-japan-china-relationship-as-a-structural-conflict/.

Chapter

6

The Taiwan Issue

Is America Preparing for Conflict with China?

A lack of public debate on China may lead to a short-sighted policy that will hurt American interests in the long term.
The National Interest, January 23, 2018

The delicate U.S.–China relationship survived President Donald Trump's first year in office without too many surprises. However, at the start of his second year in the White House, some dark clouds are hovering over the relationship.

Recent developments in Washington make one wonder whether some people in the U.S. government are actively seeking confrontation with the People's Republic of China. On January 9, 2018, the House of Representatives passed the Taiwan Travel Act, indicating that it wants the U.S. government to "encourage" visits between U.S. and Taiwanese officials "at all levels" — including officials from the State Department and Defense Department. If the Senate were to pass a similar act, and if President Trump were to sign it into law, then the unofficial U.S.–Taiwan relationship would be upgraded to an

167

official level, which would surely send U.S.–China relations into a tailspin. The Taiwan Travel Act arguably violates the 1979 Taiwan Relations Act, a U.S. law which set up the American Institute in Taiwan as a "nongovernmental entity" to promote "commercial, cultural and other relations" between the United States and Taiwan.

The House passed the Taiwan Travel Act on the heels of President Trump's signing of the 2018 National Defense Authorization Act in December 2017. The Defense Act contains some important items related to Taiwan. For example, it suggests that the United States "should" invite Taiwan to joint military exercises with the U.S. military and consider the advisability and feasibility of reestablishing port of call exchanges between the U.S. and Taiwanese navies. This undoubtedly raises a big red flag in U.S.–China relations.

Taiwan is not the only issue which the United States is using to irritate China now. While complaining about unfair Chinese trade practices and threatening a trade war with China, the Trump administration ignores the fact that the U.S. market is not completely open to China. Before Trump took office, he met in New York with Alibaba's Jack Ma, who agreed to help Trump create jobs. However, earlier this month Alibaba-affiliated Ant Financial was forced to withdraw its offer to buy money-transfer company MoneyGram. Ma reportedly lobbied Trump officials for months for this merger, pledging to create jobs in the United States, but some members of Congress expressed concerns that the Chinese government had a 15 percent stake in Ant, a claim that Ant denies. Consequently the Committee on Foreign Investment in the United States blocked the bid on national security grounds. Last year, Congress advised the Committee to further scrutinize acquisitions of U.S. assets by China's state-owned businesses or firms with ties to the Chinese government.

Other Chinese businesses such as Huawei and ZTE also hit the wall recently in their plan to expand business in the U.S. Huawei is a multinational telecommunications company but has had difficulty entering the U.S. market because its founder Ren Zhengfei was a former People's Liberation Army (PLA) soldier. No convincing evidence has been produced to show that Huawei has transferred technologies to the Chinese military.

Deep trouble is also spilling to the strategic field. The new National Defense Strategy that was released recently identifies China and Russia as America's biggest threats, replacing terrorism for the first time since 9/11. The document points to China's military actions in the South China Sea as evidence of Beijing's aggressiveness. But China and other claimants in the region have been working to lower tensions, and most notably relations between China and the Philippines have greatly improved over the past couple of years.

In the Washington policy and think-tank circles, there used to be two camps regarding U.S. approach toward China: the "panda-huggers" who promote engagement and friendly relations between the two powers, and the "dragon-slayers," who advocate tough handling of China through deterrence, sanctions, and military confrontation. The existence of the two camps and their rational debate have been healthy and helpful for U.S. policymaking. Today "dragon slayers" are sharpening their knives while "panda-huggers" seem to have either been sidelined or gone hiding.

There is an urgent need to return to a sensible and pragmatic approach to China based on common interests that has guided U.S. policy since President Nixon's visit to China in 1972. The rise of China and President Xi Jinping's strong leadership certainly present a serious challenge for the United States. But is poking China in the eye on issues like Taiwan and trade the best way to deal with China? Lack of public debate on China may lead to a short-sighted policy that will hurt American interests in the long term.

Amidst the turbulences, Trump and Xi spoke on the phone recently, suggesting that the two leaders are still committed to maintaining a stable relationship and settling the disputes through dialogue. Is the rapport between Trump and Xi strong enough to smooth bilateral ties? Prudence must prevail when conducting this most important bilateral relationship because the stakes are too high for the two countries as well as the international community.

See: https://nationalinterest.org/print/feature/america-preparing-conflict-china-24191.

170 A Critical Decade: China's Foreign Policy (2008–2018)

Book Review: Syaru Shirley Lin, *Taiwan's China Dilemma: Contested Identities and Multiple Interests in Taiwan's Cross-Strait Economic Policy.* Stanford: Stanford University Press, 2016, 304p. $81.80 Hardcover; $26.95 Paperback.

Journal of Chinese Political Science, 2017, Vol. 22, No. 3, pp. 495–497.

This book examines the puzzle of why Taiwan's economic policy toward China changes frequently and often appears "irrational." Using national identity as the key explanatory variable, Syaru Shirley Lin meticulously traces Taiwan's economic policy from Lee Teng-hui's administration to Ma Ying-jeou's presidency, and attempts to analyze what has caused the oscillation between enthusiastically embracing the Mainland market and erecting political barriers to doing business in China, or between extensive liberalization and extensive restriction.

In the existing literature, international structure and domestic politics are often used to explain trade policies. However, Lin argues that they cannot fully account for the inconsistent economic policies of Taiwan. She contends that national identity provides the missing key to understanding the inconsistencies in Taiwan's cross-Strait economic policy (p. 4). She argues that a full understanding of Taiwan's cross-Strait economic policy must "integrate the distributive effects of trade and investment with China and consolidation of Taiwanese identity as influences on policy" (p. 13).

The author selects four episodes since the early 1990s to analyze policy fluctuations based on identity changes. After his victory in the Republic of China's first presidential election in 1996, the independence-leaning Lee Teng-hui initially introduced the "Go South" policy to divert investments away from China, followed by the "No Haste, Be Patient" policy to restrict and forbid certain Taiwanese investments in mainland China. In 2001, President Chen Shui-bian, from the Democratic Progressive Party (DPP), changed his predecessor's policy to the more liberal "Active Opening, Effective Management" as a way to appeal to Taiwanese business people who had huge stakes in China and who did not vote for him. Toward the end of his second term, President Chen reversed the policy to the more restrictive "Active Management, Effective Opening" to curtail economic activities across the Taiwan Strait as a way to consolidate his DPP support base. After securing the presidency in 2008, Ma Ying-jeou, from the Chinese Nationalist Party or KMT, took a China-friendly approach under the slogan "Prosper Again" and expanded exchanges across the Strait. In 2010, the two sides signed the historic Economic Cooperation Framework Agreement (ECFA) that would gradually normalize trade and investment relations between the two sides.

This clearly written and carefully researched book is supported by primary sources including direct interviews in Taiwan and survey data from Taiwanese opinion polls. It provides a good starting point to examine relations between politics and economics, and serves as a useful reference for the study of Taiwan's economic development and cross-Strait relations over the past two decades.

While identifying national identity as the key factor behind Taiwan's changing economic policies toward China, the author raises some important questions that should have been explored in more depth. First, the relationship between Taiwan and China should have been more objectively defined. Throughout the book, the author views Taiwan–China relations as those between a small country and a hostile giant neighbor; but this is hardly an ordinary asymmetric relationship. Stating that "China and Taiwan share one of the world's most complex international relationships" understates the unique ties between the two sides and may challenge one's ability to observe and analyze economic issues effectively and objectively. Although the author notes Taiwan's unique history several times, she does not elaborate on it. In fact, one could argue that Taiwan's unique ties to China overshadow other factors in analyzing Taiwanese politics. Thus, accurately portraying cross-Strait relations must be the first step toward clearly understanding Taiwan's economic policies toward the Mainland. For example, this is a relationship *sui generis* that cannot be construed as one between two separate nations. In other words, this is not an international relationship. The author states that Taiwan's China dilemma is that overdependence on China will inevitably give

172 *A Critical Decade: China's Foreign Policy (2008–2018)*

China greater leverage and reduce Taiwan's political autonomy (p. 10), and asserts that Taiwan is not the first example of a society coping with this dilemma, and will not be the last (p. XX). How many other countries face such a difficult situation, where the two sides have become so interdependent while their constitutions still claim that the two belong to the same country?

Indeed, the unique historical and political ties between Taiwan and China should have been analyzed in order to arrive at a more comprehensive understanding of the complex dilemma. Taiwan seems to treat its economic relations with China like a faucet, turning trade on and off freely, vacillating between the two policies, which raises the question of why China would allow or tolerate this vacillating trade relationship. One important question would be: does China have this kind of relationship with any other partners? Although the book's focus is on Taiwan's policies, since China has the biggest external influence on how Taiwanese identity is formed and evolves, it would be helpful to add analysis of mainland Chinese views. Lin's research is supported by extensive interviews with Taiwanese politicians, scholars, journalists, and businesspeople only, so adding interviews with mainland policy-makers and scholars may facilitate a more complete analysis.

Second, the distinction between national identity and ideology is not very clearly presented. To what extent is Taiwan's national identity simply a manifestation of political ideology that has been sharply divided between pro-unification and pro-independence? What is the role of such bifurcated political ideology in the formation of Taiwan's identities and its China policy? Since the 1990s, Taiwan has become a highly dynamic democracy, but also an increasingly divided society. Arguably, Taiwan's China policy is driven by fluctuations in its identity, split by the government's and the public's attitudes toward China. As the author correctly notes, "cross-Strait economic policy strongly depends on which party is in power" (pp. 41–42). After the DPP's Tsai Ing-wen came to office in 2016, her administration immediately implemented the "New Southbound" policy to reduce economic reliance on China and to encourage investment in Southeast and South Asia. Was this in response to some quick change in Taiwan's identity from the previous year? Or is the DPP's political ideology the

The Taiwan Issue 173

main influence in this policy shift? Lin may have overemphasized the role of identity in Taiwan's economic policymaking toward China. In fact, the process of how identity leads to policy is not linear, which is quite different from what the author suggests (p. 22).

Sigmund Freud held that behaviors that seem accidental or irrational actually make sense once we understand the underlying subconscious forces that shape them. Do other factors equally contribute to identity change in Taiwan, such as democratization and the national ideology represented in the education system? In the 1990s, national identity in Taiwan was highly contested with more people preferring unification to independence; however, by the 2000s, it had reversed with pro-independence sentiment skyrocketing. Was China more threatening and hostile to Taiwan in the 2000s than in the 1990s, as the author reveals that China's missile tests before the 1996 presidential election "led to significant changes in national identity in Taiwan and to more restrictive cross-Strait economic policies" (p. 54)? Why has Taiwan's national identity become exclusively Taiwanese and not Chinese anymore? Does the DPP represent the growing pro-independence public sentiment in Taiwan? Or is public opinion shaped or even manipulated by the DPP government's cultural and educational policies? It is important to explore why the attitude among the younger generation in Taiwan is no longer anti-Chinese but just "non-Chinese" or not exclusively Chinese. Democratization, pro-independence education, and the unfinished Chinese civil war have contributed to split ideologies and identities in the Taiwanese public. Thus, Taiwan's struggle to rid itself of the special ties to China and its pursuit for *de jure* independence are the root causes of its China dilemma.

Overall Lin does a fine job in analyzing what she argues is the most important factor — Taiwan's national identity — in Taiwan's economic decision-making toward China. The book takes a considerable step toward tackling Taiwan's China dilemma, but it leaves some key questions unanswered. A more comprehensive understanding of the dilemma is obviously needed.

See: https://link.springer.com/article/10.1007/s11366-017-9505-8.

The Trump Challenge in U.S.–China Relations

IPP Review, December 14, 2016

Before the 2016 U.S. presidential election, many Chinese stated that they preferred Donald Trump to Hillary Clinton since she would be tough on human rights and security issues, and they believed Trump was a pragmatic businessman whom one could deal with. They may be missing Clinton now as Trump becomes the next U.S. president.

Observers and pundits have speculated on what Trump's China policy would be like. If Trump's unexpected phone call with Taiwan's leader Tsai Ing-wen on December 2, 2016 is any indication, the U.S.–China relationship will enter a period of uncertainty and instability. Indeed, Trump's ensuing tweets swiping at China's currency policy and military buildup in the South China Sea and his December 11 interview with *Fox News* suggesting he might tear up the "one China" policy hit some of the most sensitive issues in U.S.–China relations and could accidently throw the relationship into a tailspin before he even takes office.

Experts initially were divided on whether Trump's handling of Tsai's call was a diplomatic gaffe or a calculated move. Multiple sources later confirmed that the call was pre-arranged, involving weeks of coordination between Trump's team and the Taiwanese government. Notably, Trump did not consult with the White House or the State Department before the call, ignoring established practice. Trump might be unaware of the intensive preparatory work between his team members and Taiwanese authorities since he heard about the call "probably an hour or two before." Whether his forceful approach on this issue reflects his own thinking or that of his advisers is hard to know.

Will Trump Move Away From the "One China" Policy?

It's too early to determine whether Trump will stick to the "one China" policy that has underpinned U.S.–China relations for decades. The fact that his comments on China during the presidential campaign were limited to economic issues suggests that he may not fully understand the complexity of the bilateral relationship. Trump is surrounded by advisors who are staunch Taiwan supporters and China critics such as John Bolton, Stephen Yates, and Edwin Feulner. Bolton, a coarse former U.S. ambassador to the UN, has long advocated recognizing Taiwan. The most dreadful thing about Trump is that he does not know what he thinks he knows, which may be taken advantage of by those around him who are eager to influence his policies.

There is a good reason why all U.S. presidents since Richard Nixon, both Republican and Democrat, have avoided direct official contact with Taiwanese leaders. So far, no one from Trump's transition team has explicitly stated that the new administration will follow the "one China" policy. Instead, Trump seemed to think that he did not have to stick to "one China" unless he could strike a deal with China on other things, including trade, as he told *Fox News.* Trump's lack of historical awareness, political preparation, and diplomatic sensitivity makes him vulnerable to and easily shaped and even manipulated by his close advisers and lobbyists.

Taiwan has decades-long extensive lobbying activities in the U.S., often hiring former U.S. officials, among whom Bob Dole is perhaps the most senior and well-known. A lobbying disclosure document filed with the U.S. Justice Department reveals Dole's hand in making the 2016 Republican platform the most pro-Taiwan it has ever been. The new edition added language affirming the "Six Assurances" that President Ronald Reagan made to Taiwan's security in 1982. Unsurprisingly, Dole's lobbying firm has received money from the Taiwanese government.

To regain China's trust and to establish a good working relationship with Chinese leaders, Trump will need to reassure Beijing, privately or publicly, that the long-standing U.S. policy toward China will not change and U.S.–Taiwan relations will remain unofficial.

Why Has China Responded Mildly?

China's response to the Trump–Tsai phone call and Trump's provocative comments on China has been measured but principled,

176 *A Critical Decade: China's Foreign Policy (2008–2018)*

impressing many people including Henry Kissinger, who recently returned to the U.S. from a meeting with President Xi Jinping in Beijing, and who was consulted by Trump after the election. There may be several reasons for China's muted response.

First, China was giving Trump the benefit of the doubt since he said it was just "a courtesy call" from Tsai. When Foreign Minister Wang Yi labeled the call as a "small trick" played by Taiwan, he was giving Trump a ladder to step down while blaming Taipei for initiating the call. That Trump is the president-elect and not yet the president leaves Beijing some room to maneuver. By tweeting that Tsai "CALLED ME," Trump seemed to be backtracking a little, perhaps realizing this was not a simple issue. During the *Fox News* interview, he continued to emphasize the call was put to him by Taipei. After he hinted that he might ditch the "one China" policy, the Chinese foreign ministry only expressed "serious concern" without lashing out at him strongly. The foreign ministry spokesperson urged Trump and the new U.S. government to understand the seriousness of the Taiwan issue and to continue to stick to the "one-China policy," which suggests that the Chinese government is still taking a "wait and see" attitude toward Trump before the inauguration.

Second, the call caught both Chinese and American officials off guard. Chinese foreign ministry officials are probably still scratching their heads and asking themselves how this could have happened. The internal debate may have delayed a stronger response. In addition, the U.S. foreign policy establishment's immediate and almost unanimous attack on Trump's trashing of diplomatic protocol regarding "one China" makes it less urgent for Beijing to respond strongly. It is wise for Beijing to clearly state its principle and position but leave room for improving relations with Trump as he learns to be the president who has to deal with all complicated domestic and international affairs.

Third, China lodged a complaint with the "relevant party on the U.S. side" in Beijing and in Washington, but apparently the complaint went to the Obama administration, prompting the White House and the State Department to reaffirm America's "one China" policy. A senior foreign ministry official also met with U.S. ambassador Max Baucus in Beijing to lodge an objection. When pressed by journalists at the news briefing on December 5, the foreign ministry spokesman was unwilling to confirm unambiguously whether the representations were addressed to Trump's transition team directly, which points to the possibility that there might be no direct or smooth communication channel between the Chinese government and Trump's transition team, which is based in New York.

Yes, Trump and Xi Jinping spoke with each other over the phone earlier, but that was a pre-scheduled courtesy call, and China has been coy about what direct contacts it has with the Trump team. State Councillor Yang Jiechi's December 9 meeting with Trump's pick for national security adviser, retired Army Lieutenant General Michael Flynn, during a transit in New York, was the first and only report of such direct contact.

What Lies Ahead for U.S.–China Relations?

It is encouraging that Trump intends to improve relations with China by nominating Iowa Governor Terry Branstad, a longtime friend of Xi Jinping, to be the new U.S. ambassador to Beijing. Branstad and Xi met when Xi made his first trip to Iowa in 1985 during a sister-state/province exchange. At the time Xi was a young county official from Zhengding in Hebei province. The Chinese foreign ministry quickly embraced the appointment and called Branstad an "old friend of the Chinese people." An envoy with the ears of both Xi and Trump will likely help smooth the relationship.

However, Trump's inner circle currently does not include an individual who is well-versed about Asia and China. Trump tends to not play by the rules. He is not interested in daily security briefings by intelligence officials. His combative style decides that he will continue to shoot from the hip.

It is very likely that the Trump administration will strengthen relations with Taiwan, especially in elevating official contacts at the ministerial level. Taiwan has unfortunately resumed its role as a bargaining chip in U.S.–China relations. The big question is whether he can do so within the "one China" boundary. Beijing will resist any upgrading of Taiwan–U.S. relations particularly during a DPP

178 *A Critical Decade: China's Foreign Policy (2008–2018)*

administration. From Beijing's perspective, Tsai Ing-wen has refused to accept the one-China "1992 consensus." Friendly gestures like high-level contacts or weapons sales from Washington may embolden the DPP government to continue to defy Beijing.

The Taiwanese government's and public's desire for more respect and dignity in international affairs is legitimate and understandable. But Taipei needs to consider how to achieve this objective without stoking tensions between the U.S. and China and without worsening relations across the Taiwan Strait. Taipei will soon realize the risk of relying on Trump to achieve a diplomatic breakthrough since he tends to look at complicated political issues from a business perspective and may sell out Taiwan for economic gains. Taiwan wants to improve relations with the U.S., but not at the cost of being potentially betrayed by the U.S.

Can China and the U.S. work together during the Trump administration? Trump's campaign promises include bringing jobs back to America, labeling China a currency manipulator, and slapping 45 percent tariffs on Chinese imports. One will not fail to notice a huge gap between campaign rhetoric and reality. He has a great ambition "to make America great again." Before long he will realize that America's future is firmly tied to China's, and without China's cooperation, many of his domestic and foreign policy objectives — from job creation to international security — will be hard to achieve.

China is a rival but also a partner that can contribute to America's economic rebound. In 2015, Chinese investment in the U.S. surpassed U.S. investment in China for the first time. According to the Rhodium Group and the National Committee on U.S.–China Relations, over 90,000 jobs have been created in the U.S. by Chinese investment in the past few years. As Chinese businesses go global, more Chinese investment will come to America and help America to recover, for example, by fixing its dilapidated infrastructure.

Trump's victory in the 2016 presidential election exacerbated political divisions in the U.S., which will take a long time to heal. Likewise, his abrasive, eccentric, and unpredictable approach will create a lot of tensions in America's foreign relations. U.S.–China relations are both cooperative and competitive. Given Trump's style and inexperience, U.S.–China relations will face some serious and unprecedented challenges when Trump enters the White House. However, the bond between the two societies is solid, and the relationship is resilient. One does not need to be too pessimistic about the future of U.S.–China relations.

See: https://ippreview.com/index.php/Blog/single/id/307.html.

Trump's Bad Call

The President-Elect's Call with Taiwan Shows He Has a Lot to Learn about U.S.–China Relations.
U.S. News & World Report, December 5, 2016

Donald Trump's surprise and controversial December 2, 2016 phone call with Taiwan leader Tsai Ing-wen suggests that he will have a steep learning curve in foreign affairs. The ramifications of the call could accidently throw U.S.–China relations into a tailspin before Trump even takes office.

A constructive U.S.–China relationship begins with the understanding that certain issues, such as Taiwan and Tibet, must be handled with extreme caution. Sooner or later, Trump will realize that America's future is firmly tied to China's, and it would behoove him to learn it sooner. Without China's cooperation, many of his domestic and foreign policy objectives, from job creation to North Korea, cannot be realized.

Trump's comments on China during the campaign were limited to simplistic economic issues that illustrated a huge gap between campaign rhetoric and reality. Before taking office, Trump needs to devote serious thought to handle the rise of China — an issue that will affect the future of America and the world. China presents a challenge not just on an economic front, but politically and geostrategically. What should Trump's China policy look like?

For starters, understand that China has a different culture and political system and will not change overnight. The United States must stand firm on its key principles of democracy and freedom; however, it should jettison its habitual reliance on hard power to uphold those ideals. Principled engagement through soft power is a better way to advance these ideals. Feel good rhetoric cannot replace prudent diplomacy. For a long time, Americans have harbored a missionary urge to make China "more like us." China's authoritarian system works at the moment and there is no force in China to topple the regime. Xi Jinping is a tough but popular leader. Trump should establish a working relationship with him as soon as possible to implement America's policy agendas. Poking China in the eye on sensitive issues such as Taiwan runs the risk of creating a revengeful and uncooperative China.

China is a rival, but it's also a partner that can contribute to America's economic recovery. Chinese investment has created tens of thousands of jobs in the United States. The United States should grasp the opportunity to welcome Chinese participation in revitalizing the American economy. A mutually beneficial bilateral investment treaty must be signed without further delay. Such an agreement can not only regulate Chinese investment but also help combat illegal commercial espionage from China.

Trump's nomination of Elaine Chao as transportation secretary is encouraging. Though this appointment has little to do with China, Chao's rich experience will be a valuable source of inspiration for Trump's China policy. Her ties to China could be useful to bringing in Chinese investment to help achieve Trump's goal of revamping America's decrepit infrastructure in the next few years.

Today, China is projecting itself as a vanguard of globalization. America's retreat on the global stage will not serve its interest and has created grave concerns in the world. Even China prefers strong U.S. leadership in global affairs, since China is not prepared for such a role itself and there are concerns that the security environment in Asia will deteriorate without a robust U.S. presence. The U.S. must maintain its long-standing commitment to Asia. China's aggressiveness in maritime disputes must be countered, just like Japan's or Taiwan's adventurism must be resisted.

Like elsewhere, Trump's election generated confusion, anxiety, uncertainty, and even amusement in China. However, many in China believe and hope that Trump, as a shrewd and pragmatic businessman, will soon grasp the importance of diplomacy and the complex nature of U.S.–China relations.

While a physical wall was the campaign rallying cry, let's hope that Trump will instead focus his energy on building a symbolic bridge with China for the good of America, China and the world.

See: https://www.usnews.com/opinion/world-report/articles/2016-12-05/trumps-taiwan-call-shows-he-has-a-lot-to-learn-about-china.

Building Bridges, or a Bridge Too Far?

The meeting between Ma Ying-jeou and Xi Jinping built a bridge to reconciliation, but will future Taiwanese leaders be willing to cross it? *Policy Forum*, Australia National University, November 26, 2015

The November 2015 summit between Taiwan's leader, Ma Ying-jeou, and Mainland China's Xi Jinping sparked great international interest, even though nothing dramatic resulted from it.

The international media covered the carefully choreographed event in a largely positive light. That coverage wasn't surprising as the meeting was a great leap forward in cross-Taiwan Strait relations, despite a small but loud voice of opposition in Taiwan. Polls show even some pro-independence Democratic Progressive Party (DPP) supporters believe the meeting will contribute to improving cross-strait relations. A new bridge to reconciliation and peace has been

182 *A Critical Decade: China's Foreign Policy (2008–2018)*

built, although it is uncertain whether future leaders, especially from Taiwan, are willing to cross it.

Many Taiwanese worry that the island is becoming increasingly close to the Mainland economically, which might lead to eventual political reunion. They fear this over-dependence on the Mainland will deny Taiwanese options for the future, including independence.

As DPP presidential candidate Tsai Ing-wen said, Taiwan's young generation considers independence a natural part of life. Taiwanese students staged the high-profile Sunflower Movement in Taipei and occupied the Legislative Yuan in Spring 2014 to protest against Taiwan's closer economic ties with the Mainland, which was expedited during Ma's second term without much public debate. Beijing seems powerless in the face of the growing trend among Taiwanese to identify themselves as Taiwanese only, not Chinese.

The DPP and its supporters' knee-jerk opposition to the Xi-Ma meeting and to the Chinese government reflects their deep-rooted angst about Taiwan's future being determined by Beijing. It is Beijing's job to allay such worries and narrow the gap between the two sides. After the historic Singapore summit, many wonder what might happen next.

The Mainland can take several concrete steps to soften its image among the Taiwanese. First of all, Beijing should consider removing or reducing missiles deployed in Fujian Province facing Taiwan. This will not affect the People's Liberation Army's overall strategy but will be a tremendous sign of goodwill to the Taiwanese. Ma already expressed dissatisfaction with Xi's claim during the meeting that the missiles were not targeted at Taiwan. A friendly gesture like this from Beijing is worth thousands of words and is more powerful than the missiles themselves.

Second, the Mainland should map out specific plans about how to help Taiwan enjoy more international space and participate in international organizations in a meaningful way acceptable to both sides. This includes Taiwan's participation in the regional integration process such as the Trans-Pacific Partnership (TPP) and Regional Comprehensive Economic Partnership (RCEP). Beijing should also welcome Taiwan's membership in the Asian Infrastructure Investment Bank (AIIB).

The Taiwanese society must achieve a consensus on what is in Taiwan's best interest. When neither unification nor independence is feasible, pragmatism must prevail. The Xi–Ma summit is significant for cross-strait relations and peace and stability in the Asia-Pacific. It has opened a new chapter in Taipei–Beijing relations. The DPP must have the wisdom and courage to seize the opportunity before it slips by. If the "1992 consensus" is objectionable to the DPP, what can it propose that will be agreeable to both Beijing and Washington?

Finally, the United States remains a crucial external player affecting the future of cross-strait relations. How the U.S. will react to the 2016 Taiwan elections and how it will respond to the new developments in Taipei–Beijing interactions will shape the future trajectory of cross-strait relations as well as U.S.–China relations. Other countries in the region, especially Japan, may also have mixed feelings toward improved Taiwan–China relations. Given the complicated international and regional environment, the Taiwan Strait will not always be tranquil.

Ma's policy of "no unification, no independence, and no use of force" is probably a most practical approach now for both sides to handle the complex cross-strait relations. For the Mainland, how to win the hearts and minds of the Taiwanese remains the biggest challenge. Beijing should get used to Taiwan's robust and often boisterous democracy, where people are not easily cowed.

For Taiwan, the challenge is to maximize Taiwan's interests while taking advantage of the Mainland's rapid reemergence as a great power. It is imprudent and unnecessary to provoke Beijing by pushing for formal Taiwanese independence. Unification is highly idealistic and *de jure* independence remains a difficult dream. Both Taipei and Beijing need to be realistic and pragmatic to stay engaged and build lasting peace and prosperity across the Taiwan Strait.

See: https://www.policyforum.net/building-bridges-or-a-bridge-too-far/.

The Papal Challenge for Taiwan's Next Leader

The Taipei Times, October 7, 2015

Chinese President Xi Jinping has made his first state visit to the U.S. Xi arrived at his first stop, Seattle, on September 22, 2015, the same day that Pope Francis arrived in Washington. Xi's trip was eclipsed by the papal visit, which received far more extensive and enthusiastic coverage by the U.S. media.

Some observers in Taiwan speculated over whether the pope and Xi would meet in the U.S. and possibly discuss establishing diplomatic ties between the Holy See and China. It turned out that the two leaders were never at the same place at the same time.

Expectations were low and pessimism permeated the air in both China and the U.S. before Xi's visit, with some academics saying the relationship was approaching a "tipping point." Though Xi's visit is not a game changer and is not likely to affect the U.S.' views of China, it has arrested further slide of the relationship toward confrontation.

U.S. President Barack Obama and Xi had frank conversations and agreed to work together to constructively manage their differences, and expand and deepen cooperation. A significant development is that the U.S. government announced plans to have one million American students studying Mandarin by 2020.

Though Washington reassured Taipei before Xi's visit that the U.S.' cross-strait policy remains unchanged, the government was worried that a "surprise" might arise. Taipei was relieved that the Taiwan issue did not figure prominently. In fact, in public speeches and during a joint conference with Obama, Xi did not even mention Taiwan. It was Obama who reaffirmed the "one China" policy based on the Three Joint Communiqués and the Taiwan Relations Act.

Taiwan has always been a priority for China in its dealings with Washington. Xi's reticence on Taiwan is unusual. It might suggest that China is extremely confident that time is on its side, while Taiwan has limited options about its future. This would not be good news for Taiwan.

The Taiwan Issue 185

A different challenge for Taipei might come from the Holy See. Pope Francis is known for being eager to reach out to Beijing. Since assuming the papacy in March 2013, Francis has repeatedly expressed his wish to bring about closer relations with China. In August 2014, when he flew over China to South Korea, he sent a message to Xi and Chinese. He reportedly said in South Korea that he would go to Beijing the next day if possible.

On his flight back to Rome from his U.S. trip, the pope told reporters that he would like to be the first pontiff to visit mainland China [having been the first to visit Hong Kong].

China's ambassador to Italy is understood to have maintained close communication with the Vatican. However, the two sides still have huge differences, especially regarding religious freedom and the appointment of bishops in China.

China's estimated 12 million Catholics are divided into two groups. The majority belong to the state-sanctioned Chinese Patriotic Catholic Association, which does not recognize the Vatican as its head. The rest attend so-called "underground churches" that recognize the pope as their leader. The Chinese government insists on having the final say on the appointment of bishops, which falls to the pope elsewhere in the world. However, in August, the two sides were in rare alignment on the appointment of Joseph Zhang Yinlin as bishop for the city of Anyang in Henan Province.

Developments in Taiwan might change the dynamics of the Taipei–Vatican–Beijing relationship. For example, if the new president after next year's election pursues a confrontational policy toward China, creating tensions across the Taiwan Strait, it is not inconceivable that Beijing would persuade Taipei's diplomatic allies to shift their ties to Beijing. The tentative "diplomatic truce" between the two sides might come to an end.

Beijing has turned down the olive branch for diplomatic recognition from several of the nation's allies in the past few years. It does not want to destabilize cross-strait relations because the government is conciliatory toward China by not promoting an independence agenda. If the next administration follows a hostile policy akin to former president Chen Shui-bian's, Beijing is likely to react quickly and

186 A Critical Decade: China's Foreign Policy (2008–2018)

harshly, such as by pouching Taipei's diplomatic allies. Given warming ties between the Vatican and China, the Holy See might become one of the first of Taiwan's 22 remaining allies to switch to Beijing, which would be a huge blow to Taiwan's foreign relations.

It is laudable that Democratic Progressive Party (DPP) presidential candidate Tsai Ing-wen has been cautious in her public statements over cross-strait relations. She has claimed she would become a president for all Taiwanese if elected.

Yet, her comrades within the DPP and her supporters might pose challenges as the January 16 election draws near. For example, Tainan Mayor William Lai's public comment that he supports independence created a dilemma for Tsai. How Tsai handles such pressures and moves her campaign beyond the unification-independence debate will speak volumes about what kind of leader she would be and how cross-strait relations are likely to evolve in the years ahead.

See: http://www.taipeitimes.com/News/editorials/archives/2015/10/07/2003629448/.

The Undoing of China's Soft Power

Beijing is struggling to effectively direct soft power at its cross-strait neighbor.
The Diplomat, August 8, 2014

In a dramatic move, a Chinese official had a single-page advertisement for Taiwan's Chiang Ching-kuo Foundation for International Scholarly Exchange taken out of the program at the 20th conference of the European Association of Chinese Studies (EACS), held at the University of Minho in Portugal on July 22–26, 2014. The Chinese official was reportedly Madame Xu Lin, an adviser to China's State Council and director general of the Chinese National Office for

Teaching Chinese as a Foreign Language, known as *Hanban*. Xu's high-handedness shocked many in and outside of Taiwan, at a time when cross-strait relations are relatively stable. Swift and harsh responses from Taiwanese officials and the public condemned the act and blamed Xu for hurting Taiwanese feelings and harming cross-strait relations. The Minho incident is a blow to China's soft power. It not only widens the political and psychological gap between Taiwan and mainland China, but also risks canceling out much of the goodwill the Chinese government has painstakingly built toward Taiwan in the past few years.

Enhancing China's image abroad has been a key aspect of China's new diplomacy since the beginning of this century. The Confucius Institute (CI), with its primary purpose of promoting Chinese language and culture, has been a major official instrument of Chinese soft power since 2004. According to the *Hanban* website, which oversees CIs globally, as of mid-2014 China has established 443 CIs at colleges and 648 Confucius Classrooms (CCs) at public and private schools around the world. As the head of *Hanban*, Xu has become a symbol of China's soft power efforts. It is perhaps ironic that a Chinese official whose job it is to promote China's soft power has in effect done the opposite.

How effective has the CI been at improving China's soft power abroad? The answer is unclear. Looking at various public opinion polls, such as those conducted annually by the Pew Research Center, one gets the general sense that China enjoys largely positive views in the developing world, especially in Africa, and largely negative views in Western democracies. China's neighbors have more mixed views of China's rise, ranging from extremely positive (such as in Pakistan) to extremely negative (such as in Japan). These results have by and large been consistent over the past few years, and the global expansion of the CIs and CCs seem to have had little impact.

Most perplexing for the Chinese government is that the Taiwanese public's attitude toward the mainland has not improved, and over the last decade the percentage of people who consider themselves Taiwanese has risen sharply, while the percentage of those who consider themselves Chinese has fallen significantly. This identity shift has

188 *A Critical Decade: China's Foreign Policy (2008–2018)*

happened despite the fact that the economies situated on either side of the Taiwan Strait are highly interwoven; the two sides have signed over 20 agreements for economic and cultural exchanges, often with beneficial treatment to Taiwan offered by the mainland. China has failed to win the hearts and minds of the Taiwanese, and in the eyes of most Taiwanese, China is clearly not a country with much soft power. In an early July 2014 poll, conducted by Taiwan's Mainland Affairs Council, only 33.4 percent of Taiwanese surveyed thought the Chinese government was friendly toward the Taiwanese, while 50.3 percent believed it to be unfriendly.

Xu has been in charge of *Hanban* since the first CI was established in Seoul in 2004, and her actions in Portugal definitely harm China's soft power in Taiwan, as well as China's international image in general. In the aftermath of the Minho incident, *Hanban* and the Chinese government should consider how to better promote China's image abroad. Chinese officials and diplomats must also sharpen their public relations skills.

In June 2014, the American Association of University Professors (AAUP) issued a statement calling on universities to uphold the principles of academic freedom by either terminating or renegotiating the agreements that have brought nearly 100 CIs to campuses across the U.S. The AAUP fears that American universities may have sacrificed academic independence and integrity of their institutions and staff by allowing the Chinese government to set guidelines for the recruitment and supervision of academic staff, the design of the curriculum and the boundaries on debate within the CIs.

The AAUP apparently made sweeping judgments before conducting a thorough and objective investigation. Its statement cherry-picked a few examples to make its case while ignoring the larger picture, that the CIs and CCs operate within their host institutions and have helped many universities and school districts in offering in-demand Chinese language and culture-related courses, as testified to by many CI directors and instructors. In a public relations debacle, *Hanban* has yet to come up with a robust rebuttal and convincing response, leading many to believe that the AAUP statement is true.

China has a soft power deficit in the world because of its reluctance to embrace and practice universal values at home, and its presumptuous behavior in dealing with disputes abroad in recent years. The last thing China wants is the undoing of its limited, hard-earned soft power by its own officials.

See: https://thediplomat.com/2014/08/the-undoing-of-chinas-soft-power/.

Obama Learns the Three T's the Hard Way

The Journal (Edinburgh, England), February 17, 2010

Relations between China and the United States deteriorated following the recent U.S. sale of $6.4 billion worth of weapons to Taiwan. China cut off military exchanges with the U.S. and threatened, for the first time, to sanction American companies involved in the arms deal.

U.S. arms sales to Taiwan are not a new issue. When Washington switched diplomatic relations from Taipei to Beijing in 1979, the U.S. Congress passed the Taiwan Relations Act (TRA) to commit the U.S. to the defense of Taiwan by selling Taiwan defensive weapons. Beijing has accused Washington of repeatedly violating the three Joint Communiqués in which the U.S. promised to gradually reduce arms sales to Taiwan, leading over a period of time to a final resolution. For Beijing, Washington's justification of its arms sales to Taiwan based on the TRA is unacceptable because the TRA is a domestic law, which should not be used to defend a policy that has damaged bilateral relations.

Out of its own national interests, the U.S. will continue to sell weapons to Taiwan, regardless of Chinese uproar. The bottom line is that America — particularly its military establishment — considers China to be the greatest potential threat. Growing economic

190 *A Critical Decade: China's Foreign Policy (2008–2018)*

interdependence notwithstanding, strategically the two countries remain deeply suspicious of each other.

China had unrealistic expectations of President Barack Obama. Mr. Obama became the first U.S. President to have traveled to China during his first year in office. He deferred to Chinese wishes before and during his November 2009 visit, most notably by avoiding meeting the Dalai Lama in Washington in October and by allowing the Chinese to stage-manage his speech in Shanghai. Many Chinese think the president is either very friendly to China or very weak in foreign affairs. Almost no one in China had expected Mr. Obama would announce the arms deal so soon. The strident Chinese reaction displays China's frustration and sense of betrayal.

Most observers consider the three T's — Taiwan, Tibet and trade — to be the thorniest issues between China and the U.S.; indeed, these issues have frequently erupted as obstacles. However, the fundamental conflict between the U.S. and China is structural.

China's re-emergence as a great power is not a prediction anymore; it is a reality. Even during the current global economic downturn, China's growth continues to impress the world. China has become an increasingly proud, nationalistic and confident nation. This growing confidence is reflected in its foreign policy. It demands that its core national interests such as Taiwan and Tibet be respected. What the U.S. and the international community face today is a more powerful and assertive China. Neither the U.S. nor China wants to see tensions escalate, and both have a vested interest in a stable relationship. The unprecedented challenge for the two countries is how to adjust to, and cope with, the global power restructuring peacefully.

See: https://www.bucknell.edu/x58348.xml.

Chapter

7

Global and Regional Cooperation

Can the Quad Counter China's Belt and Road Initiative?

For a number of reasons, a proposed plan is unlikely to ever materialize.

The Diplomat, March 14, 2018

The Australian Financial Review recently reported that the United States, Australia, India, and Japan had been considering the establishment of a joint regional infrastructure plan to counter China's multi-billion-dollar Belt and Road Initiative (BRI). Though officials from these countries have hastened to clarify that this plan is not a "rival" but an "alternative" to the BRI, it reflects these countries' dilemma on how to deal with what they perceive as "the China threat."

It's too early to tell how and when this proposed plan may materialize since it is still at the discussion stage. The scope and objectives of this plan are unclear, and no one knows how it is going to be implemented. This is not the first time the four countries, or the "Quad," have teamed up to attempt to develop a common approach

192 A Critical Decade: China's Foreign Policy (2008–2018)

to China. In the recent past they also promoted the concept of "Indo-Pacific" in place of the traditional "Asia-Pacific" (though "Asia-Pacific" remains in active and popular use). One of the purposes behind the "Indo-Pacific" concept is to boost India's status in the United States' Asia policy so that the discourse of "Asia-Pacific" will not be dominated by China.

But China has never claimed to be the center or the hegemon of the vast Asia-Pacific region. Healthy competition between major powers is good for all; grouping countries based on political ideology into opposing camps is detrimental to regional cooperation. Obviously attempts to pit the "Quad" against China go against the trend of globalization and interdependence and are counterproductive.

The proposed plan by the "Quad" to counter the BRI is unlikely to become reality for a number of reasons. First of all, due to their domestic priorities, these four countries have difficulty developing a coherent and consistent approach toward China. A stable relationship with China is crucial to all these economies. Various conservative forces within the "Quad" feel uncomfortable about China's rise and often launch political or ideological campaigns against China, a reemerging power that does not completely share their values. But in the end realism and pragmatism will prevail.

For example, Australian Prime Minster Malcolm Turnbull's administration has sounded tough toward China, slashing Beijing for interference in Australia's domestic politics. However, before his recent trip to the United States, Turnbull set a more conciliatory tone and said China was "not a threat." In Washington he stated that it was inaccurate to paint the United States and its allies like Australia as being against China in some sort of rerun of the Cold War. While acknowledging some "complex and difficult issues" with China, the Australian government has denied a diplomatic freeze or cold war between the two countries.

The Trump administration, on the other hand, prefers bilateral approaches to multilateral agreements in international affairs and seeks a constructive relationship with China despite differences with China on trade and other issues.

Second, China's BRI remains open and inclusive, and China welcomes the participation of all countries, including the "Quad." The idea may have come from China, but it is jointly "owned" by all participating countries and the dividends of development are for everyone to share. Yet, the "Quad" countries have been lukewarm to the BRI from the very beginning, though recently they seem to have become more receptive, and both the United States and Australia sent ministerial level official delegations to the May 2017 BRI Forum in Beijing. Still, suspicions remain high.

India and Japan issued the vision document of their proposed Asia–Africa Growth Corridor (AAGC) in May 2017 and began to promote it to counter the Maritime Silk Road of the BRI. The AAGC vision document uses some of the same keywords as the BRI, such as regional cooperation, quality infrastructure, connectivity, people-to-people exchanges, etc. However, India and Japan have yet to explain, convincingly, why the AAGC is superior to the BRI. As a complement to the BRI, the AAGC should be welcomed by others, including China; as a strategic counterforce against China that raises tensions in the region, it should not be.

Third, even if the proposed plan were to proceed, funding will be a major problem. With Trump's "America First" policy, is the United States willing to invest in such a huge project overseas? And where will the money come from anyway? Japan's Abenomics has achieved some positive results but a long and winding road lies ahead in terms of its economic recovery. India tends to exaggerate China's intentions in South Asia and see itself as a peer to China in every aspect while downplaying its domestic problems. China has been Australia's largest trading partner, largest export market, and largest import source since 2009. It is not in any of the "Quad" countries' interest to disrupt their dynamic and beneficial relations with China and none are likely to come up with the money needed to fund the proposed project.

Ostensibly the proposed plan is an economic project, but in essence it represents these countries' political, strategic, and diplomatic efforts to respond to the rise of China. Some people in the "Quad" have still not become accustomed to the new normal of expanding Chinese power and influence. It is understandable that they may feel uncomfortable about or even threatened by China's massive projects like the BRI. But China's growth has benefited other countries as well.

It is not China's job to evenly distribute the benefits of globalization. The best way to deal with China's rise is not to block it but to work with China and shape Asia's emerging political and economic orders together. Moving forward, both China and the "Quad" must reaffirm their commitment to cooperation as the only way to address their differences and promote common development.

See: https://thediplomat.com/2018/03/can-the-quad-counter-chinas-belt-and-road-initiative/.

China's Deeper Penetration into Africa

e-International Relations, November 10, 2016

The China-funded Addis Ababa–Djibouti Railway, which became operational in October 2016, is Africa's first modern electrified railway. It links Ethiopia's capital city with the port of Djibouti, providing landlocked Ethiopia with railroad access to a vital maritime zone. More than 95 percent of Ethiopia's trade passes through Djibouti. The multi-year, multi-billion-dollar project extends a length of 752.7 km (466 mi). Travelling at 120 km/h, the new service cuts the journey time down from three days by road to about 12 h. Chinese controllers, technicians, and station masters are contracted to manage the services for the next 5 years, during which the Chinese will train their Ethiopian counterparts who will take charge afterward. The project is reminiscent of the Tanzam Railway or TAZARA that China helped build in the 1970s, linking the port of Dar-es-Salaam in Tanzania with the town of Kapiri Mposhi in Zambia's Central Province. China's GDP was lower than many African countries then; today, China is the world's second largest economy with global reach.

What does this new Chinese penetration into the African continent mean? At the onset, the new railway, serving as a catalyst for Ethiopia's and East Africa's economic development, will express how China's engagement with Africa has grown deeper and wider. Ethiopia's economy has been one of the fastest growing in the world recently, lifting millions out of poverty. The Ethiopian government is trying to transform its agriculture-based economy into a modern, industrialized one, with particular focus on infrastructure and other public projects. Thus, this new railway is significant in Ethiopia's economic transformation. With the new rail line, there is bound to be an increase in trade between Ethiopia and the Middle East, Europe, and Central Asia. Djibouti will obviously benefit from the projected trade boom. As a main entry point into Africa for many countries in the Middle East, Djibouti's position in regional and global trade will be further enhanced. There is now a greater chance of conducting business in high value imports like fruits, vegetables and flowers, which makes trade between Africa and the Middle East ever more alluring.

Second, the railway demonstrates not just China's financial and construction prowess but also its huge potential and appetite for bilateral cooperation. It was built between 2011 and 2016 by the state-owned China Railway Group and the China Civil Engineering Construction Corporation. Financing for the new line was provided by the Exim Bank of China, the China Development Bank, and the Industrial and Commercial Bank of China. A total of US$4 billion were invested into the railway. Chinese investment accounted for 70 percent of the total cost. For the experienced Chinese contractors, the construction of a railway with a designed speed of 120 km/h is not difficult, but it is nothing short of a great feat to complete it with no compromise on quality and timeliness, given the inadequacy of construction materials and technical staff in Ethiopia. China is also

196 *A Critical Decade: China's Foreign Policy (2008–2018)*

building major rail projects in several other African countries including Nigeria, Angola, DR Congo, Kenya, and Tanzania. Given China's railway construction expertise and financial prowess, it is no more a mere dream that someday China will help build a trans-continental railway from Djibouti's coast all the way to the Atlantic Ocean.

Third, the railway represents China's new approach to Africa, one that is more sensitive to local needs. China has been criticized for not generating local employment by bringing in its own workers to projects in Africa, and for paying little attention to the environment, labor, and safety issues. For the Chinese firms, the lack of local technical personnel with adequate railway technology knowledge had been a serious hurdle in constructing the Addis Ababa–Djibouti Railway. For example, it took 20,000 workers to complete a specific section of the railway and it would have been impossible to have seen the posts filled entirely by the Chinese. To tackle the challenge, the Chinese firms involved made the training of local technical workers a routine part of their operations in Ethiopia. Thereon, more than 15,000 local workers went through various training programs, thus ensuring enough manpower for railway construction and a talent reserve for future management of railway operations. Environmentally, the Addis Ababa–Djibouti Railway is an electrified, eco-friendly system contributing to the region's green development.

There are many other instances of this new Chinese approach. Chinese companies such as Huawei are partnering with African businesses to accelerate Africa's digital economy. Chinese automotive manufacturer, BYD Motors, has been selected as the preferred bidder to supply a fleet of electric battery-operated buses to South Africa's Cape Town, which will be the first city in Africa to use electric buses for public transport. These clean-running buses will not just help provide its residents with a more sustainable public transport system but also assist the country in achieving its environmental objectives.

Finally, despite the imminent benefits of this railway for Africa, it is unlikely to lower the naysayers' anxieties about China's global ambitions. The question is not whether China's rise poses a threat; rather, it is whether others, especially the United States, are prepared. China wants to be able to protect its interests and investments throughout sub-Saharan Africa. At present, work is underway to construct China's first overseas military base in Djibouti, in close proximity to a key U.S. national security asset: a 4,000-strong American military presence that includes the largest U.S. drone installation outside Afghanistan.

Some observers tend to view U.S.–relations as a zero-sum game. In a March 2015 letter, U.S. Representatives Dana Rohrabacher (R-Ca.) and Chris Smith (R-N.J.) wrote to Secretary of Defense Ash Carter, Secretary of State John Kerry and National Security Adviser Susan Rice to warn them of "China's unprecedented investment in Djibouti and worrisome behavior by the country's longtime leader." The two Congressmen warned that Chinese investment in infrastructure could be "parlayed into investment in strategic influence." "We are worried that our own strategic interests around the Horn of Africa, specifically our critical counterterrorism operations, will be impacted by China's growing strategic influence in the region," wrote Rohrabacher and Smith. It has perhaps not occurred to them how the two powers can work together in Africa in areas such as combating terrorism and piracy and promoting development and peace.

Regardless of its detractors, China's engagement with African countries is likely to deepen as China's Belt and Road Initiative takes off. Chinese–African cooperation is increasingly becoming multifaceted. For instance, China's First Lady, Peng Liyuan, and her Malawian counterpart, Gertrude Mutharika, both known for their devotion to charity, agreed recently to work together to fight against AIDS in Africa. As China inches closer to becoming a global power, the rest of the world, especially critical voices within the U.S., may need to ask themselves: are we ready?

See: https://www.e-ir.info/2016/11/10/chinas-deeper-penetration-into-africa/.

Xi Jinping's UK Visit Raises Questions About How to Deal with a Rising China

e-International Relations, February 13, 2016

When Sir George Macartney, the first British envoy to imperial China, visited Peking in 1793, he reportedly refused to kowtow in the presence of Emperor Qianlong, maintaining the dignity of a British nobleman. How British leaders treat China's rulers today may make Sir Macartney's head spin.

Much ink has been spilled on President Xi Jinping's October 2015 state visit to the United Kingdom. Xi's visit undoubtedly raised the Sino-British relationship to a historic height as Prime Minister David Cameron called Britain "China's best partner in the West." The visit focused on trade and investment, but the long-term geopolitical impact should not be underestimated.

X's visit to the UK raises a critical question for the global community: how to deal with China's rise? Unlike the United States, the UK does not feel threatened by China and, unlike Japan — another key U.S. ally, the UK has a more independent foreign policy and does not have bilateral disputes with China.

Xi traveled to the UK on the heels of his U.S. visit a month earlier. While the UK enthusiastically embraces opportunities associated with China's growth, the United States is more cautious. President Barack Obama's statements such as "we can't let countries like China write the rules of the global economy" reflect deep American anxiety about the growing Chinese power and influence. President Xi's active global diplomacy is not so much about what China wants and does, but how the international community responds to the new China.

The UK occupies a unique position in China's worldview and foreign policy. The first Sino-British Opium War in 1839 marked the beginning of China's so-called Century of Humiliation that ended in 1949 with the establishment of the People's Republic. During the Great Leap Forward (1958–1961), Mao romantically claimed that China could surpass Britain in industrial output in 15 years. In the 1980s, "Iron Lady" Margaret Thatcher worked with Deng Xiaoping and creatively found a mutually acceptable way to end Hong Kong's colonization. Hong Kong's smooth handover in 1997 is a remarkable event in international history. Despite suspicions and concerns about Beijing's commitment to the "one country, two systems" policy, it is obviously in both China's and Britain's interest to maintain Hong Kong's prosperity and freedom.

The British are obviously taking a different approach from that of the United States in coping with China's rise. This approach is based on cooperation, mutual benefits, and inclusive development, which resonates with the "new type of international relations" President Xi is touting. In a rare interview with *Reuters* on the eve of his visit, President Xi commended Britain's strategic choice to become "the Western country that is most open to China." While Xi was not given the opportunity to address U.S. Congress, he was offered the chance to address the British parliament.

Britain's China policy has a demonstrative effect. In 2013, the UK became the first G7 country to create a currency swap line with China. In 2015, it was the first Western country to join the China-initiated Asian Infrastructure Investment Bank (AIIB). All major economies are AIIB members now except the United States and Japan. The UK is also the first developed country where China is helping build a nuclear power plant.

Due to their China-friendly policy, both Prime Minister Cameron and Chancellor of the Exchequer George Osborne have faced sharp domestic criticism for trading principles for economic gains. Even the Dalai Lama chimed in and suggested that the current British government has lost morality in focusing on money.

The Australian scholar and former defense official Hugh White has opined that the United States has three options when dealing with China: resist China's challenge and preserve the U.S. dominance in Asia, step back from Asia and let China establish hegemony, or remain in Asia on a new basis, allowing China a larger role but also maintaining a strong presence of its own. Essentially, he argues that the third option, sharing power with a rising China, is the only viable choice. White's idea remains controversial as the world struggles to adjust to the changing power structure.

Should one counter China's rise, which is virtually impossible and may create a more nationalistic and revengeful China, or should one actively engage China to shape its development into a peaceful and responsible global power? Britain, like many others, seems to have made the decision. One hopes that this proves the right choice for Britain, for China, and for the international community.

See: https://www.e-ir.info/2016/02/13/xi-jinpings-uk-visit-raises-question-about-how-to-deal-with-a-rising-china/.

Testing the Waters in the South China Sea

e-International Relations, November 26, 2015

On October 27, 2015, the U.S. navy conducted a high-profile freedom of navigation operation (FONOP) in the South China Sea. USS Lassen sailed into 12 nmi of Subi Reef controlled by China. China, as expected, protested strongly, including summoning U.S. ambassador in Beijing Max Baucus. U.S. Defense Secretary Ash Carter said the U.S. military would continue to fly, sail, and operate wherever international law allows. Indeed, 2 weeks later two U.S. B-52 strategic bombers flew near artificial Chinese-built islands in the South China Sea.

What do recent events in the South China Sea reveal about U.S.–China relations? What is likely to happen in the near future? First, the South China Sea tension is a case of conflict between an existing power and a rising power. Though China cannot and will not replace the United States as the dominant nation in the international system anytime soon, the power gap between the two countries is being narrowed very quickly. From a power transition perspective, China's rise challenges U.S. supremacy, and the United States will do everything possible to stunt China's rapid growth.

Distrust and misunderstanding run deep in the U.S.–China relationship and sometimes lead to confrontational approaches. Not a claimant to the disputed islands, the United States has conveniently

Global and Regional Cooperation 201

used "freedom of navigation" (FON) to get involved in the South China Sea to halt China's assertive activities there. The United States is deeply concerned about growing Chinese power and influence while China feels uncomfortable about U.S. FONOPs and close-range surveillance along China's coast. The United States is also anxious about the Beijing-initiated Asian Infrastructure Investment Bank (AIIB) and the ambitious Belt and Road program; while China is suspicious of real intentions of U.S. rebalance to Asia and the TPP trade negotiations that have excluded China. In the case of TPP, the Chinese wonder: are countries like Vietnam more ready for such a high-level trade deal than China?

Second, USS Lassen's sail is highly symbolic and not intended to be provocative; China's reaction has been measured, indicating neither side is willing to escalate the tension. The United States demonstrated its will to sail and fly freely in the South China Sea and reassured its Asian allies amid growing fear about forceful Chinese behavior.

The United States is likely to continue FONOPs in the South China Sea routinely. China will protest whenever a U.S. warship or surveillance aircraft enters the area claimed by China, but neither side will deliberately trigger a confrontation. The United States is unlikely to take further actions to stop China's land reclamation in disputed waters. As in trade and cybersecurity, instead of heading toward a collision course, the two countries seem to have established a working protocol for issues they disagree on.

Third, the two countries seem to be adjusting, sometimes clumsily, to the changing global power structure with the aim of avoiding the so-called "Thucydides' trap" associated with power transitions. Through initiatives such as China's "new type of great power relations" and America's "rebalance" to Asia, the two countries are developing new strategies to engage each other, though the true objectives of such strategies are murky.

Freedom of navigation has never been a real problem in the region. The Subi Reef is a low tide elevation and does not enjoy 12 nautical mile territorial waters, and China has yet to announce 12 nautical mile territorial waters for those man-made islands. So this whole episode seems quite theatrical, which prompted U.S. Senate Armed

202 *A Critical Decade: China's Foreign Policy (2008–2018)*

Services Committee Chairman John McCain to ask: is USS Lassen's operation an "innocent passage" or a more provocative act to contest China's sovereignty?

With China's growing power comes its expanding global reach. On September 2, 2015, five Chinese navy ships operated in the Bering Sea off the coast of Alaska for the first time in history. The United States publicly stated that Chinese warships' innocent passage was consistent with international law, but privately the United States has become more vigilant of China's ambitions.

Finally, it is not easy to manage this most complex bilateral relationship, but the relationship has become more mature now. In the past, regular exchanges, especially military ones, often became victim to diplomatic disruptions in the relationship. But this time, military exchanges have continued. Following USS Lassen's sail in October 2015, Chinese navy ships visited Florida and California in early November, and USS Stethem visited Shanghai in mid-November as scheduled. The two navies also conducted a combined search and rescue exercise near Shanghai. Posturing in the South China Sea notwithstanding, the two countries are conducting business as usual.

The U.S.–China relationship is global in nature as their cooperation and competition shift from one region to another. Moves by third parties such as Japan, Taiwan, Russia, or North Korea can pose challenges for the U.S.–China relationship. For example, U.S. encouragement of Japan's patrol in the South China Sea is ill-conceived and will only create new tensions between China and Japan. And if a future leader of Taiwan pushes for *de jure* independence for Taiwan, the United States and China will face a real trouble.

Understanding the inherent risks associated with the unfolding power transition, the United States and China are learning to work with each other. With diplomacy, visionary leadership, and expanded exchanges at all levels, the United States and China will be able to maximize their cooperation, manage their differences, and coexist peacefully in the 21st century.

See: https://www.e-ir.info/2015/11/26/testing-the-waters-in-the-south-china-sea/.

Balancing Act

China is navigating between being a rising power and a developing nation.

Beijing Review, November 5, 2015

The next 5 years will be a crucial period for China's goal of building a moderately prosperous society by 2021 — in celebration of the 100th anniversary of the founding of the Chinese Communist Party (CCP). As the international media focus on China's annual growth rate following the Fifth Plenary Session of the 18th CCP Central Committee in October 2015, little attention has been directed to the daunting challenges in China and the blueprint mapped out at the plenum to tackle them.

China has become a highly influential force in today's world. It's no exaggeration that when China sneezes, the world catches a cold, as *Financial Times'* Martin Wolf once wrote. Can China continue to grow? Will China's economic slowdown trigger a global recession? Has China become more assertive in its foreign policy? These are all legitimate questions but fail to address the real issues China and the international community face. Three major sources of global misconstruction and anxiety over China's economy and foreign policy can be identified.

The Mirror Image

Perception and misperception color our understanding of international affairs. What one country sees in another is often the mirror image of itself. When Western countries reacted strongly to China's market tumble earlier this year, they saw a mirror image of themselves struggling with economic recovery. Westerners, especially Americans, always have a missionary impulse to change China in their image, either to Christianize it in the 19th century or to democratize it in the 21st.

Everyone is used to China's fast growth and is unprepared for anything short of miracles in China. From 1978 to 2011, China experienced unprecedented growth averaged at 10 percent annually. Its growth began to drop in 2012, declined to 7.3 percent last year and will likely continue to fall. China has entered a period of "new normal" of slower growth where it places quality and efficiency over quantity.

China's fast-running engine has hit roadblocks: rising labor costs, inefficiency of state-owned enterprises (SOEs), a deteriorating environment, a shrinking market in the West to absorb Chinese exports after 2008, etc. China's slower growth should not have come as a surprise. Overreacting to China's market fluctuations reflects Westerners' frustrations with their own lackluster economies. The United States worries about being replaced by China as the dominant global power without realizing China's policy priorities and challenges, or America's own staying power.

Conflicting Identities

Is China a global power or a large developing nation? Is China abandoning Deng Xiaoping's *"Tao Guang Yang Hui"* strategy that emphasizes economic development while keeping a low profile in international affairs? Widely perceived as a global power, China is actually still a developing nation with 200 million people living in poverty. It suffers from the same problems other developing nations experience, such as a growing income gap and rampant corruption. China's per-capita GDP ranks about 80th in the world and is only one seventh that of the United States.

China may still be playing second fiddle in international affairs, but it is actively reaching out and projecting itself as a major power. Nevertheless, the fundamental objectives of Chinese foreign policy — to create a stable international environment for domestic growth and to contribute to global peace and development — remain unchanged, as reaffirmed by President Xi Jinping's speech at the UN in October 2015.

The AIIB, with 57 members including several U.S. allies as of now, will become operational at the end of 2015. Another ambitious program, the Silk Road Economic Belt and the 21st-Century Maritime Silk Road, or the Belt and Road Initiative (BRI), which integrates China with countries in Asia, Europe, the Middle East, and

Africa, covers some 70 countries along the routes and has a projected investment of $1.4 trillion, dwarfing the Marshall Plan, America's post-World War II program for European reconstruction. China has not just invested in developing countries; it is investing in the developed world now, from nuclear power stations in the United Kingdom to luxury hotels in the United States.

Many of the infrastructure projects proposed under the framework of the BRI would benefit China's poor inland regions, potentially helping mitigate China's rapidly growing income gap and promote more balanced and sustainable growth. This will also allow China to relocate its labor-intensive and low value-added manufacturing facilities overseas, and thus help resolve the severe environmental problem.

China has dual identities: While it is the world's No. 2 economy, it is also a large developing nation. Its policies are sometimes inconsistent, trying to simultaneously satisfy the two sets of priorities. China's internal debate about its proper role in international affairs is inconclusive. As a result, other countries have difficulty figuring out what its intentions are and how to interpret and respond to its policy initiatives. The challenge for China is to remain focused on development and avoid unnecessary conflicts with other countries.

Economy in Transition

China is undergoing two major transitions: from a planned economy to a market economy, and from the export-oriented, investment-driven growth to a new model based on consumption and innovation. China has room for continued growth. For example, household consumption accounts for 35 percent of China's GDP as opposed to 70 percent in the United States. Meanwhile, private businesses like Alibaba, Baidu, Tencent, Xiaomi, and Didi Kuaidi have become an inspiration for innovation and entrepreneurship. With the aim of making SOEs competitive internationally, China recently pledged measures to modernize SOEs, enhance the management of state assets and promote mixed ownership. These transitions and reforms will create disruptions and dislocations in China, which will inevitably affect other economies in this interdependent world.

Slower growth will create serious challenges to social and political stability in China. For example, there are over 270 million migrant workers who need to assimilate into urban lives. Development in western China needs to be energized to narrow the growth gap between regions. The rapidly aging population needs better healthcare and other social safety nets. The road ahead will not be smooth, but the Chinese government seems determined and has been handling the transitions remarkably well so far. Despite an economic slowdown, China's toolbox is still full with the ability to stimulate continued growth: vast foreign exchange reserves, a huge domestic market, active economic diplomacy to boost export to new markets, etc.

For a long time to come, China's policy priorities will remain domestic. Chinese leaders will be preoccupied with tackling tremendous political, economic, social, environmental, and demographic challenges in the years ahead. China is both a rising global power and a large developing nation. Adapting to the new conditions, challenges, and opportunities associated with its rise is the biggest test for China and the rest of the world.

See: http://www.bjreview.com/Nation/201510/t20151030_8000416 01.html.

Why Does China Still Play Second Fiddle?

Despite its achievements, China is not yet ready to take on more responsibility in international affairs.

The Diplomat, September 19, 2013

China's low profile in the current Syria crisis has earned it criticism, with some observers blaming Beijing for not playing a more positive role as a responsible global power. The oft-cited explanations are that

China has a "non-intervention" policy or that it is following Russia's lead in obstructing America's possible use of force.

Both interpretations are wrong. Yes, "non-intervention" is one of the "Five Principles of Peaceful Coexistence" that have guided China's foreign policy since the early 1950s. China does not interfere in other countries' internal affairs, nor will it tolerate interference in its own affairs by other states. But as China's power grows and its interests extend to every corner of the globe, Chinese foreign policy is gradually departing from this once sacred principle. In fact, China has been practicing what I call "selective intervention" in international affairs.

Chinese leaders are preoccupied with domestic affairs. Tremendous challenges at home — a widening income gap, a deteriorating environment, an aging population and an increasingly volatile society, among other issues — will keep the Beijing leadership busy and sleepless for the foreseeable future. China is not a global military power as it lacks power projection capability. More importantly, China is unwilling to get heavily involved in international affairs lest it will be distracted from economic development.

However, with trade and investment everywhere, China now has global interests. It has begun to demonstrate its growing power in selective regions of critical importance to its national interests such as the Gulf of Aden, East China Sea, and South China Sea, and it has gotten involved in the internal affairs of some countries. For example, China has reportedly interfered in Zambia's presidential elections in recent years to ensure that pro-China candidates win. China allegedly tried to influence voting in Zambia's 2006 and 2008 elections, preventing Michael Sata's from winning. During the campaigns, Sata was highly critical of Chinese activities in Zambia and threatened to establish formal ties with Taiwan. Much to Beijing's relief, Sata, who was finally elected Zambia's president in 2011, became very friendly toward China after the election. In April 2013, on a visit to China, President Sata praised China and its people for always standing with Zambia and helping in its development process even as Western countries withheld aid because of its ability to pay back its debt.

Most notably, the now-defunct Six-Party Talks aimed at curbing North Korea's nuclear programs were initiated and hosted by China. Beijing also pressured North Korea to open up and become a normal member of the international community. Who can deny that China has interfered in North Korea's internal affairs?

China has worked to lower tensions in Syria in its own way. The Chinese government has been in touch will various forces in the Syrian civil war. For example, a delegation of six people sent by an opposition organization called the Syrian National Dialogue Forum visited Beijing in September 2013, meeting with Chinese Foreign Ministry officials to discuss the situation in Syria. Beijing has been working with all relevant parties in Syria in a balanced way to achieve a political resolution of the Syrian issue. To host the visit by the Syrian National Dialogue Forum is part of China's efforts. Another opposition group visited Beijing in February 2012. When China's Middle East envoy Wu Sike visited Syria in October 2011, he also met with opposition leaders as well as Syrian government officials.

The fact that China often coordinates its position with Russia in major international affairs does not mean that China follows Russia's leadership. China and Russia are very different powers, with divergent national interests. China is happy to yield global leadership to the United States. China's opposition to military intervention is also out of its concern that the international community may intervene should conflict erupt in Taiwan, Tibet, or Xinjiang, which China views as internal matters.

Despite the seemingly close relations between China and Russia, the two powers remain suspicious of each other. Just look at how long it has taken for the two countries to negotiate a deal to send Russian gas to China. Though China and Russia have conducted several rounds of joint military exercises as part of the Shanghai Cooperation Organization (SCO) programs, the two powers do not have the same vision for the SCO, and they also vie for leadership within the group. Russia is deeply concerned about China's growing influence in Siberia and central Asia.

So how should we explain China's muted role? Chinese foreign policy, just like Chinese society, is in transition. Deng Xiaoping's admonition that China should "keep a low profile" still shapes strategic thinking, even if it is being challenged by many Chinese, who tend to exaggerate China's power and argue for a bigger role for Beijing in global affairs.

Despite all its achievements, China is essentially still a large developing nation. There is an enormous gap between global expectations of China's leadership role and its own willingness and capability. Until that gap is narrowed, China is not ready to assume more responsibilities in international affairs. For some time to come, China will continue to play second fiddle to the United States.

See: https://thediplomat.com/2013/09/why-does-china-play-second-fiddle-2/.

China's Role in International Affairs: An Interview with Prof. Zhiqun Zhu

Foreign Policy Journal, May 31, 2012

Today, most international relations analysts and experts consider China as the world's most important political and economic power after the United States. China came second in the International Monetary Fund's 2011 ranking of countries by GDP (nominal) and is one of the main producers of agricultural products and industrial commodities and the world's number one exporter. China is the United States' top trading partner, and at the same time its major economic and political competitor.

The politics of China is thoroughly complicated. National interests define the limits of China's foreign policy while some traces of opposition to the Western world in general, and the United States in particular, can always be found in China's attitude toward international affairs.

In order to learn more about the intricacies of China's politics, its foreign policy, and its relations with the United States and the Middle Eastern nations, *The Foreign Policy Journal*'s Kourosh Ziabari interviewed Zhiqun Zhu, Professor of International Relations at Bucknell

University, who specializes in Chinese politics and foreign policy and East Asian international relations. Professor Zhu is the author of several books including *US–China Relations in the 21st Century* (2006) and *China's New Diplomacy* (2013).

Kourosh Ziabari: Dear Prof. Zhu, to the ordinary people, it seems that the United States and China are constantly in a state of rivalry that sometimes amounts to animosity and hostility. What's the main reason behind this continued rivalry and competition? Does the U.S. consider China a threat to its economic and political supremacy? Does China believe that the U.S. wants to derail its political establishment?

Zhiqun Zhu: The conflict between the United States and China is structural. The U.S. is the dominant global power, and China is a rising power. The dominant power always feels uneasy if a new power is challenging its status. This structural conflict marks the current dynamics in U.S.–China relations.

However, I do not think the U.S. government considers China a threat. China is a challenge, especially economically and militarily. The U.S. welcomes China's peaceful development, and has actually contributed to China's rise in the past 40 years. China also considers its relationship with the U.S. the most important one in its foreign policy. Of course, in both U.S. and China, there are conservative and nationalistic scholars and politicians who consider each other as the enemy, but that is not the official policy of the two governments. Even the two militaries are highly professional and are conducting regular exchanges and joint humanitarian exercises now.

So in the future, the U.S. and China will continue to cooperate on many international, regional and bilateral issues. At the same time, they will also compete for resources and influence globally such as in the Middle East and Africa. And in Asia, they will compete for power and leadership. Competition and cooperation are the hallmarks of this relationship.

KZ: Chinese goods and commodities have almost dominated the whole global market. In Iran, at least, we can find a Chinese counterpart for every commodity which the people need; from the foodstuff, medical equipment, and handicrafts to industrial accouterments and automobiles. But the people always complain that the quality of Chinese goods is not commendable. Is there any political reason behind this? Is it a large-scale policy of the Chinese government to export low-quality goods to developing countries such as Iran and export the high-quality commodities to its major trade partners such as Canada and EU?

ZZ: In fact, you can hear complaints everywhere, including developed countries and within China itself, about the poor quality of Chinese goods. I do not think China has an agenda here to differentiate its exports. The real challenge for China is to upgrade its industrial structure and improve the quality of its products. China has to climb up the technology ladder and promote innovation and quality control. Perhaps by learning from Japan and South Korea, China can eventually make more high-quality products for export and for domestic consumption.

KZ: As to what I've noted, the meetings of the U.S. and European officials with the 14th Dalai Lama have usually spurred anger and irritation by the Chinese officials. Has there ever been any effort to settle the dispute between the Chinese government and the separationists of Tibet led by the Dalai Lama?

ZZ: Deep suspicion and distrust still exist between the Chinese government and the Dalai Lama. The two sides talked to each other in the past, but the gap remains huge between them. They see Tibet's history, culture, and current political and economic status very differently. China's strategy appears to be waiting for the Dalai Lama to pass away. Like elsewhere inside China, its current priority in Tibet is to maintain stability while promoting growth.

The government does not consider it a priority now to negotiate with the Dalai Lama or his representatives to narrow the differences between the two sides. Of course the danger of such a wait-and-see strategy is that the Dalai Lama's successors may be more violent and radical and even less willing to cooperate with the Communist Party.

KZ: Today, China is the world's second largest economy and it's possible that it may surpass the United States very soon, as it has done in some areas such as agricultural productions, foreign exchange reserves or exports. What factors have contributed to these outstanding and remarkable achievements? How has China reached this point?

ZZ: China's economy started to take off in the late 1970s when Deng Xiaoping introduced economic and political reforms. Deng is considered the chief architect of China's reform and opening-up. Quite a few factors contributed to China's impressive development, such as political stability at home, a mostly peaceful regional environment, China's ability and willingness to adjust its policies and to learn from others, FDI from major economies, strong work ethic of the Chinese, efficient decision-making by competent Chinese leaders. Very interestingly, these leaders are not elected democratically, but most of them happen to be very competent and committed.

Of course, despite the impressive achievements, China remains largely a developing nation, with tremendous domestic challenges such as a worsening environment, a growing income gap, widespread corruption, and rising social discontents.

KZ: The United States and China have long fought over the independence of the Republic of China (Taiwan) and finally settled the dispute with the declaration of the Joint Communiqué on the Establishment of Diplomatic Relations which was signed in January 1979. What's the current position of the United States over the Taiwan question? What's the stance of the Chinese government? Does Beijing still object to countries which maintain diplomatic or economic relations with Taipei?

ZZ: The U.S. does not have official relations with Taiwan, but it maintains a robust "unofficial" relationship with Taiwan under the Taiwan Relations Act passed by U.S. Congress in 1979. The U.S. treats Taiwan as a sovereign political entity and continues to sell weapons to Taiwan for defensive purposes. Of course China considers this an intervention in its internal affairs.

Global and Regional Cooperation **213**

China does not oppose other countries maintaining economic and cultural relations with Taiwan, but formal diplomatic relations with Taiwan are not tolerated by Beijing. The long-term objective of the Chinese government is to unify with Taiwan, but in the short run, it can live with the status quo. In recent years with the KMT in power in Taiwan, cross-Taiwan Strait relations have drastically improved, with the two economies becoming highly interdependent.

KZ: Since the Tiananmen Square protests of 1989, the United States and its European allies have constantly criticized China's human rights record. What's your take on that? Contrary to its economic and political indicators, China doesn't have good rankings in press freedom and human rights. Do you agree?

ZZ: Yes, China still has lots of human rights problems despite much progress in the past 30 plus years. The Chinese government does not like foreign countries to criticize China, especially its human rights record, but many people both in and outside of China know that there is much to be desired in human rights conditions in China. Recent events such as the harsh treatment of blind lawyer Chen Guangcheng show how basic human rights of ordinary citizens are still not well protected in China.

KZ: What's your evaluation of China's current relations with the European Union? Has it been affected by the recent economic recession in the Eurozone? Which countries are the most important partners of China in the EU?

ZZ: Political and economic relations between China and EU have been stable and close. Eurozone countries are looking to China for help to overcome the current debt crisis. China has good relations with almost all European countries. Economically, Germany, France, and Britain are major partners.

Of course, European countries, just like the U.S., are critical of China's human rights policies. And China has complained about EU's

214 *A Critical Decade: China's Foreign Policy (2008–2018)*

reluctance to lift arms embargo to China. The embargo was imposed on China following the 1989 Tiananmen Square incident. EU countries have not reached a consensus on this, and the U.S. also opposes EU's potential lifting of sanctions against China.

KZ: China is a major importer of oil from Iran. Moreover, it exports a huge amount of goods to Iran and has practically dominated Iran's market. However, it gave green light to four rounds of U.S.-directed sanctions against Iran in the United Nations Security Council. Many Iranians were disappointed at the fact that China joined the U.S., U.K., and France in imposing economic sanctions against Tehran over its nuclear program as they expected that China should veto the resolutions. Why do you think China has made such a decision to give way to the anti-Iranian sanctions? Overall, what's in your view the stance of China over Iran's nuclear program?

ZZ: China is under heavy pressure to behave responsibly as a major power now. I think China is not opposed to Iran's development of nuclear program for peaceful purposes, and Iran has the right to defend itself. But remarks by some Iranian leaders that Iran should wipe out Israel from the map make China and the international community very uneasy and concerned.

China is in a dilemma. China is opposed to proliferation of weapons of mass destruction. Developing nuclear weapons has become very destabilizing for the regions involved. Though China has good relations with both Iran and North Korea, it wants to join the international community and put some pressure on them. This is a responsible behavior by a great power.

On the other hand, China has strong economic interests in Iran and it will not cut its longtime cultural and economic ties to Iran. China considers Iran a major economic partner and has encouraged investment in Iran. To some extent China's Iran policy is illustrative of the contradictions and dilemmas in China's foreign policy.

KZ: And finally, does China support the United States in its efforts to pressure Syria over the conflict and unrest in the country? Russia has categorically rejected sanctions and military intervention in Syria. What's the position of China? It seems that China has preferred to keep a low profile regarding the revolutions in the Middle East because of its close economic ties to the regional countries. What's your idea?

ZZ: In principle, China wishes to keep a low-profile in international affairs. It is opposed to the use of force in international relations. So I think China will likely join Russia in the Syria case.

China is one of the very few powers that maintain good relations with all countries in the Middle East, so obviously the expectations are high for China to play a more active and constructive role, and China can and probably should contribute more to the peaceful resolution of problems in the Middle East.

See: https://www.foreignpolicyjournal.com/2012/05/31/chinas-role-in-international-affairs-an-interview-with-prof-zhiqun-zhu/.

Beijing's Diplomatic Blitz Gathers Pace

Asia Times, February 24, 2009

As the Year of the Ox (2009) rang in, China launched a new wave of top-level diplomacy. In the short span of 2 weeks, Chinese leaders became globe-trotters, with their footprints left in Europe, Latin America and the Caribbean, Africa and the Middle East. The frequency, intensity, and magnitude of China's latest diplomatic moves are unprecedented in contemporary international relations.

This new wave of high-level diplomacy started with Premier Wen Jiabao's attendance at the Davos World Economic Forum in Switzerland on January 28 and his subsequent visits to European Union headquarters in Brussels as well as Germany, Spain, and Britain.

216   *A Critical Decade: China's Foreign Policy (2008–2018)*

Shortly after Premier Wen returned to Beijing, both President Hu Jintao and Vice President Xi Jinping traveled abroad at roughly the same time. Hu made a stop in Saudi Arabia on February 10 before heading to Mali, Senegal, Tanzania, and Mauritius, his sixth visit to Africa in 10 years, underlining the importance of the region in China's geopolitical strategy. Vice President Xi Jinping started his visits to Latin America and the Caribbean in Mexico on February 8 before going on to Jamaica, Colombia, Venezuela, and Brazil. He also visited Malta at the end of this trip. It is the first time both the president and the vice president of China traveled abroad at the same time.

In a unique, double-pronged diplomatic offensive toward Latin America and the Caribbean, Hui Liangyu, the Vice Premier in charge of agricultural and economic affairs, toured Argentina, Ecuador, Barbados and the Bahamas between February 7 and 19 while Xi was in the neighborhood. That two of China's top leaders were in the region at almost the same time highlights Beijing's ongoing efforts to strengthen ties and enhance its influence in Latin America and the Caribbean.

One is dazzled and probably puzzled by this intensive and extensive high-level Chinese diplomacy. What are the purposes of these visits? What messages does China want to convey to the international community?

Before China's top leaders embarked on these visits, Foreign Minister Yang Jiechi began 2009 by visiting Uganda, Rwanda, Malawi, and South Africa in early January. In the past 20 years, it has been a New Year ritual for the Chinese foreign minister to start his annual overseas trips in Africa. Yang's visits, together with the latest highest-level travels, are all part and parcel of China's new diplomacy, which is characterized by its consistency, maturity, breadth, and depth. It reveals how China is presenting its image and asserting its position in the international political economy today.

A Responsible, Cooperative Power

Wen labeled his Europe trip as a "journey of confidence." In Davos, London, Berlin, Brussels and elsewhere, Wen assured European and world leaders that China will help stabilize the global economy by

Global and Regional Cooperation   217

promoting continued growth domestically — a welcoming message as Europe and the rest of the world are struggling to recover from the financial crisis.

The current financial crisis has hit China hard. By mid-2008, nearly 70,000 small- to medium-sized export-oriented businesses in China were forced to close. Over 20 million migrant rural workers have lost their jobs so far and Chinese leaders have warned of labor strife. These and other domestic challenges are staggering. However, with the largest foreign exchange reserves in the world, China is in better shape than many economies to deal with the current economic challenges.

With all eyes on China for the salvation of the global economy, Beijing has acted responsibly. During Wen's Europe tour, China helped to stimulate European economies by signing business deals to purchase goods and services worth 15 billion yuan ($2.1 billion). Some in the West have unwisely pressured China to let the yuan appreciate further to help reduce trade deficits with China.

Despite the domestic call for the government to weaken the currency in order to help Chinese exports, China has maintained a stable currency in the past 3 years after a rise of over 20 percent, helping to stabilize the global economy — a fact not very much appreciated in the West. A floating yuan now may lead to the fall of the U.S. dollar and create inflationary pressure in the United States and elsewhere. China's recent announcement of spending $123 billion to establish universal health care by 2011 for the country's 1.3 billion people is another effort to stimulate domestic consumption. With their health taken care of, the Chinese may decide to save less and spend more. Though Wen remarked modestly that China could only save itself, not the world, it is clear that the country is ready to weather this financial storm together with the rest of the international community.

A Friend in Need

China and other developing countries have helped each other in times of need. Before he traveled to Africa, President Hu paid an official visit to Saudi Arabia. Besides the fact that Saudi Arabia is the largest supplier of crude oil to China, a special purpose for Hu's visit, according to Chinese media, was to thank the Saudi government for providing the largest donation to China after the 2008 Sichuan earthquake.

Partially in response to charges that China is only interested in resources in Africa, Hu visited several relatively resource-poor nations this time. His trip is designed to reassure Africa and other developing regions that China's interests extend beyond oil and mining.

To ward off criticism that Beijing exploits the world's poorest continent, China has reaffirmed that it would not cut financial aid and loans to African countries during hard economic times. During his visit to Mali, Hu laid the first brick of a "Friendship Bridge" in its capital. The 2.6 km, $74.9 million "Sino-Malian Friendship Bridge" over the Niger River in Bamako will be the largest project carried out in West Africa as a Chinese donation. China's investments and loans have benefited other developing regions. In January 2009, China became a member of the Inter-American Development Bank, pouring $350 million into the bank's coffers for infrastructure spending in the region.

Africa, like other developing regions, is welcoming Beijing's new diplomatic moves not just because of its rich resources but also because of its strong support for China in international affairs. The UN Human Rights Council reviewed China's human rights record in early February 2009. Some Western countries criticized China on issues such as Tibet as well as civil and political rights in China, while developing countries generally praised China for its economic development and efforts to eliminate poverty.

With strong support from developing countries, the UN Human Rights Council concluded that China's human rights record was "on track." Differences between developed and developing nations over the human rights issue will remain. China will continue to rely on support from the developing world as a counter force to Western pressure on human rights.

Less Dependent on the U.S., Europe

In the Chinese language, the word "crisis" consists of two characters *wei* (danger) and *ji* (opportunity). China is attempting to convert the

Global and Regional Cooperation 219

global financial crisis into an opportunity to improve its long-term economic advantage and energy security. China's exports to Europe and North America have shrunk substantially as a result of declining demand in these markets. China is desperate to open up and maintain new markets in Africa, Latin America, and elsewhere. China's trade with Africa and Latin America has both soared to over $100 billion in 2008.

Some worry that China may sell U.S. Treasury bonds as a way to consolidate its own economy. The fact is selling a large part of U.S. holdings will be counterproductive because it would probably cause bond prices and the dollar to fall sharply, which will immediately reduce China's own foreign exchange reserves.

The Chinese government has indicated that it will continue to purchase U.S. Treasury bonds, but obviously it will no longer put all of its eggs in one basket. Its active diplomacy around the world is part of its strategy to diversify investment risks. Recent Chinese investments and purchases have taken place in Africa, Latin America, Central Asia, Russia, the Middle East, and Southeast Asia, among others.

An episode during Wen's visit to London is revealing of Chinese leaders' confidence and maturity. While speaking to students and faculty at Cambridge University, a student from the audience threw a shoe at Wen, mimicking the now famous Iraqi journalist's act during a press conference between former President George W. Bush and Iraqi Prime Minister Nuri al-Maliki in December 2008. "This despicable behavior cannot stand in the way of friendship between China and the U.K.," a very calm and collected Wen said to loud applause before continuing with his speech.

Chinese leaders never forget to promote China's "soft power" abroad these days. During his visit to Jamaica, Vice President Xi found time to attend the opening ceremony of the Confucius Institute on the Mona Campus of Jamaica's prestigious University of the West Indies, in Kingston. So far, China has set up over 300 Confucius Institutes worldwide, promoting Chinese language and traditional culture.

As a growing power China will continue to pursue active diplomacy and play a bigger role in international affairs. China's expanding trade, aid and investments around the world are evidence of its strength in today's troubled global economy. As Chinese leaders have suggested, maintaining the stability of the Chinese economy is a great contribution to the recovery of the global economy.

China's new diplomacy undoubtedly serves its own national interests first, but it is also conducive to global development. During her maiden trip to Beijing as America's top diplomat, U.S. Secretary of State Hillary Clinton remarked that the United States and China must cooperate and lead the global recovery. China has become an indispensable player in world affairs.

The world will enter a new "Chimerica" era, as Harvard history professor Niall Ferguson has suggested. One should welcome China's full participation in the international political economy and encourage its transition to a more transparent and democratic system. One hopes that China's development will continue to be stable, peaceful, and beneficial to the rest of the world.

See: https://www.bucknell.edu/news-and-media/op-ed-columns/beijings-diplomatic-blitz-gathers-pace.html.

Part III
Challenges and Prospects

Chapter

8

Geostrategic Challenges
of the Belt and Road Initiative

Introduction

On September 7, 2013, in a speech at Nazarbayev University in Astana, Kazakhstan, Chinese President Xi Jinping proposed building a "silk road economic belt," in order to enhance economic and trade cooperation between China and Central Asian countries. During his visit to Southeast Asia in October the same year, Xi proposed building a 21st century "maritime silk road" in a speech at the Indonesian parliament. "One Belt One Road" or the Belt and Road Initiative (BRI) has become China's most important foreign policy undertaking since then. Spanning globally and with projected investments of up to trillions of U.S. dollars, the BRI is aimed at promoting commercial and people-to-people exchanges and building infrastructure to connect China to a range of Southeast Asian, Central Asian, Middle Eastern. African, and European countries. Through extension, the BRI has made inroads into Latin America, the Caribbean, and South Pacific, where many countries wish to jump onto the wagon of

223

China's fast development. To promote the BRI, Beijing hosted the first Belt and Road Forum in May 2017, which was attended by representatives from more than 130 countries and over 70 international organizations.

Along with the BRI, China developed the Asian Infrastructure Investment Bank (AIIB) in 2015. The AIIB largely serves as the financing arm of the BRI, with the starting capital of $100 billion. In addition to economic benefits, the AIIB and BRI will significantly facilitate the movement of goods, services, and people across national borders. The number and scale of the projects proposed under the BRI are truly breathtaking. By the end of 2018, trade between China and the BRI partner countries had exceeded $6 trillion, and China had already invested over $80 billion in countries along the Belt and Road, creating 240,000 jobs for them.[1] The BRI has stimulated both awe and deep worries among Chinese and foreign observers. For some countries, the BRI presents an alternative model of development and a great opportunity for expanding trade and upgrading infrastructure. Others view it with suspicion and concern and some even see it as a threat and a new form of colonialism.

The BRI is not just China's major economic diplomacy today, it is also a mechanism for promoting China's own growth and projecting its soft power globally. How to turn concepts such as "win–win" and "community with a shared future" into reality will be a major test in China's foreign relations. Over the past two decades, China has contributed substantially to building infrastructure or "hardware" for many developing nations, but it remains short of "software" or soft power. Beijing hopes that its new initiatives, such as the BRI and AIIB, along with a non-coercive, non-military approach, will help enhance its international image as a responsible global power. The AIIB and BRI are also important steps to realizing President Xi's "Chinese Dream."

---

[1] Foreign Minister Wang Yi's speech at the 2018 Forum on International Situations and Chinese Diplomacy, Beijing, December 11, 2018. https://www.fmprc.gov.cn/web/wjbzhd/t1620761.shtml.

The significance of the BRI should not be underestimated. This is the first time that China as a developing country has proposed a new model on the international stage in modern times. Comparatively speaking, even hosting the Olympics and World Expo is not that significant since they are models developed by others (Luo, 2017). The key words used in the BRI include belt, road, bridge, and corridor, without naming China as the "center," which affirms China's proclaimed commitment to fairness, equality, and inclusiveness of the initiative. This chapter will discuss key geostrategic challenges of the BRI at the international and domestic levels.

Key Geostrategic Challenges

1. *The international level*: The BRI is likely to face some bumps in the road for a variety of reasons. The first geostrategic challenge is the potential clash between the "Chinese Dream" and America's long-standing policy of maintaining global dominance. The United States allegedly tried to keep its allies from becoming founding members of the AIIB, but South Korea, Australia, and the United Kingdom, among others, defied the United States and became founding members. The United States and Japan are still not AIIB members as of this writing, though their stance has become more moderate and may join at a future date. Likewise, the United States has not fully embraced the BRI, which it suspects to be a strategic scheme, but it has not publicly opposed it either. The U.S. position on the BRI has been ambiguous and confusing. Matt Pottinger, Special Assistant to President Donald Trump and National Security Council (NSC) Senior Director for East Asia, attended the Belt and Road Forum in Beijing in May 2017 and said that the United States would welcome efforts by China to promote infrastructure connectivity as part of its BRI and U.S. companies could offer top value services (*Reuters*, 2017). However, in practice the U.S. government remains lukewarm to and suspicious of the BRI. Fundamentally, it is uncomfortable with the economic and diplomatic clout China is gaining through the BRI and other initiatives.

226 *A Critical Decade: China's Foreign Policy (2008–2018)*

The U.S.'s concerns are twofold. First, the United States views the BRI as a threat to the existing international economic and political order dominated by the West. Secretary of Defense James N. Mattis remarked during a congressional hearing in October 2017: "Regarding 'One Belt, One Road,' I think in a globalized world, there are many belts and many roads, and no one nation should put itself into a position of dictating 'One Belt, One Road.' That said, the 'One Belt, One Road' also goes through disputed territory, and I think that in itself shows the vulnerability of trying to establish that sort of a dictate."[2] Taking a jab at the BRI, Vice President Mike Pence said during the 2018 Asia-Pacific Economic Cooperation (APEC) summit, "We don't drown our partners in a sea of debt. We don't coerce or compromise your independence" and "We do not offer a constricting belt or a one-way road (Shih, 2018)." Pence also mentioned that the United States had stepped up development financing programs and doubled its financing capacity to nearly $60 billion to drive private sector investment in the Asia Pacific region in a bid to counter the BRI. The United States is undoubtedly alarmed by China's expanding influence in different regions of the world, including in its backyard Latin America, and will continue to push hard to counter it.

Second, the United States is particularly sensitive to the maritime Silk Road's challenge to its sea power — a reason why it has been so active in the South China Sea recently. The United States will simply not yield its maritime dominance to anybody, and in the name of defending freedom of navigation, it will continue to challenge China's activities in the South China Sea and elsewhere. The 21st century maritime Silk Road, if successfully implemented, will make the so-called first island chain and second island chain irrelevant in the U.S. attempt to block China's power projection. It is expected that U.S.–China rivalry in the South China Sea will intensify since the BRI directly challenges U.S. sea power, which is likely to be the biggest geostrategic challenge China has to face in the years ahead. To resist

---

[2] James N. Mattis, Hearing before the Senate Armed Services Committee, Washington, DC, October 3, 2017.

perceived "China threat," the United States has beefed up its presence in the Indo-Pacific region and strengthened ties with its maritime allies and partners including Australia, Japan, the Philippines, India, and most notably Taiwan.

The BRI has become a symbol of China's global ambitions. Whether China intends to replace the United States as the dominant power in the international system or not, the BRI presents a serious challenge to the U.S. leadership in international political economy — a key reason why the United States will not enthusiastically support the initiative. President Donald Trump may be retreating from globalization and withdrawing from some international organizations and agreements, but the United States is unlikely to yield its global leadership to someone else, especially China, which does not share its values. In fact, a domestic consensus is being formed in the United States: after some 40 years of development, China has not moved in the direction the United States has desired. Hence the "China worry," "China threat," and "China bashing" in the United States now.

The second geostrategic challenge comes from China's regional competitors India and Japan. India has publicly voiced its opposition due to the China–Pakistan Economic Corridor (CPEC) from Kashgar to Gwadar, as part of the BRI, which passes through the controversial Kashmir region. In fact, India and Japan worked together and developed a different proposal — the Asia–Africa Growth Corridor (AAGC) to counter the BRI. One week after Beijing hosted the first Belt and Road Forum, Japan and India unveiled the AAGC Vision Plan during the African Development Bank annual meeting on May 22–26, 2017 in Ahmedabad, India. Interestingly, the theme of the AAGC Vision Plan is very similar to that of the BRI, both of which emphasize quality infrastructure, inclusiveness, sustainable development, and people-to-people connectivity.[3] It is disappointing that the three Asian powers have not worked together and supported each other on these projects. With skillful diplomacy, perhaps the three

---

[3] Full text of the AAGC Vision Document can be found here at: http://www.eria.org/Asia-Africa-Growth-Corridor-Document.pdf. Accessed on June 11, 2018.

228 *A Critical Decade: China's Foreign Policy (2008–2018)*

powers can find a way to promote common development for themselves and for other countries.

Will the "Chinese Dream" clash with the "Indian Dream"? South Asia used to be India's sphere of influence. With growing Chinese economic expansion in South Asia as part of the BRI, India feels its interests are being challenged by China. Chinese investments in Pakistan, Sri Lanka, Maldives, Nepal, and Bangladesh have fueled concerns in India about losing its traditional sphere of influence. India also aims to become a global power, and South Asia is its power base, which must not be eroded in its efforts to achieve its global ambition. Sri Lanka, for example, has long been in India's orbit, but its relationship with China has strengthened in recent years. Perceiving a threat to its regional hegemony, India has watched with suspicion as cranes operated by Chinese firms began to dot the skyline in Colombo, Sri Lanka's capital. To counter the imbalance, India has partnered with Japan to develop a port on Sri Lanka's eastern coastline, and it has entered into talks to invest in an airport near Hambantota.[4] Obviously China must work with India to ensure that India does not feel threatened by Chinese activities in its neighborhood.

In recent years, China has been working to improve relations with Japan and India, hoping that they will work with China and enjoy the benefits of the BRI. President Xi invited Prime Minister Narendra Modi for an "informal" meeting in Wuhan in April 2018, while Premier Li Keqiang visited Japan in May 2018, ending the nearly 8-year freeze of top-level exchanges between Japan and China. Prime Minister Modi met with President Xi again during the Shanghai Cooperation Organization (SCO) summit in Qingdao, China on June 8–10, 2018. Unfortunately, India still did not endorse the BRI during the SCO summit, with Modi speaking of the need to "respect sovereignty" in dealing with infrastructure projects, clearly signaling India's objection to the CPEC (Dasgupta, 2018). During Premier Li's visit to Japan, he proposed the "China, Japan, and Korea plus X" model for economic cooperation and community building. This is an

---

[4] *Ibid.*

idea for promoting regional cooperation and development, consistent with the inclusive nature of the BRI.

Japan, on the other hand, has gradually moved to support the BRI despite its lingering ambivalence about China's long-term intentions and its uneasiness about competition from China. Japan used to be one of the most vehement critics of the BRI; however, its position gradually softened. On April 15, 2018, Chinese and Japanese officials pledged to enhance their countries' economic cooperation under the framework of BRI during Chinese Minister of Commerce Zhong Shan's visit in Tokyo. Japan got onboard partly because the BRI helps its multinationals expand in other countries and it does not want to miss the opportunities or benefits associated with the BRI. Meanwhile, Japan clearly sees the BRI as part of Beijing's broader strategy to enhance regional influence and leverage, and Japan wants to counter it (Jennings, 2018). During his long-delayed visit to China in October 2018, Japanese Prime Minister Shinzo Abe promised to work with China on the BRI, especially investing in infrastructure in third countries. Japan's decision to join the BRI reflects Abe's pragmatic approach to China and his desire to improve strained relations with President Xi, but strategic rivalry may hamper deeper bilateral cooperation.

The third geostrategic challenge is security along the Belt and Road, which go through some regions that are hotbeds for terrorism, civil conflicts, and piracy. As part of the BRI, China will build 81,000 km (about 50,000 mi) of high-speed railway, more than the current world total. Who is going to protect so many projects, across so many countries? The CPEC links Western China and Pakistan with roads and pipelines and will send electricity to Pakistan. The route passes through some of the world's most vulnerable and conflict-ridden territory. What will be the cost of maintaining security for the highways, railways, and pipelines, which could all be held ransom to strife? A major goal for China is to link its landlocked western region to a deep-water port at Gwadar, so that oil and other goods from the Persian Gulf can avoid the "choke point" of the Strait of Malacca, which is patrolled by foreign navies. Security challenges will make it difficult for China to overcome the so-called "Malacca dilemma."

Along the CPEC, China has pledged to spend $63 billion to bolster Pakistan's power plants, ports, airports, expressways, and other infrastructure. A terror attack on the Chinese consulate in Karachi by the Balochistan Liberation Army (BLA) in November 2018 is just one of the violent actions aimed at the Chinese. In August 2018, the BLA reportedly launched a suicide attack on a bus carrying Chinese engineers who were working on a Balochistan mining venture. Balochistan, which is on the borders of Afghanistan and Iran, has rich mineral and natural gas reserves but is Pakistan's poorest province. Separatists there have for decades resisted and campaigned against what they see as the unfair exploitation of resources. China is unlikely to be deterred by such terror attacks, but security concerns will continue to accompany Chinese projects along the Belt and Road.

The fourth geostrategic challenge has something do to with potential debt burdens of some developing countries. Many recipient countries in Asia have poor credit, which means some projects may be promising at the beginning but will be difficult to pursue and complete. Agreement and consensus are reached at the top levels of government, but implementation is at the local level. In some countries, local governments may simply not care about the central government's policies and do not always cooperate with foreign investors.

Some developing countries along the Belt and Road are already facing debt problems. For example, Sri Lanka, unable to pay back the debt it owed to Chinese state-owned enterprises (SOEs) for building major infrastructure on its territory, had to agree to lease its port in Hambantota to China for 99 years. The Chinese-financed Hambantota Port in southern Sri Lanka had been underused since it opened in 2010, prompting the Sri Lankan government to sell a 70 percent stake to state-run China Merchants Port Holdings for $1.1 billion in July 2017. In December 2017, the Sri Lankan government completed the handover of the port to two state-controlled entities run through China Merchants Port Holdings. Sri Lanka reportedly owed more than $8 billion to Chinese state-controlled firms (Schultz, 2017). The port is just a few hundred miles off the shores of India and sits along a critical commercial and military waterway. Unsurprisingly, India is worried that the port may be used to host Chinese naval vessels (Campbell, 2017).

Hambantota reminds people of Hong Kong, which was leased by the Qing Dynasty to the British in circumstances that epitomize colonialism. Critics said the Hambantota lease could set a precedent for Sri Lanka and other countries that owe money to China to accept deals that involve concessions of sovereignty. After the original port deal was signed in July 2017, Namal Rajapaksa, a Member of Parliament and son of the former president, asked whether the government was "playing geopolitics with national assets (Schultz, 2017)." Also in Sri Lanka, the Exim Bank of China put up $190 million with a concessionary loan to help the construction of the $209 million Mattala Rajapaksa International Airport, Sri Lanka's second international airport. The airport has become "the world's emptiest international airport" because it has no regular daily flights now (Yamada and Palma, 2018).

In Pakistan, some people worry about what may happen if it is unable to repay its debt. Pakistan's trade deficit with China has been rising. As with other countries that have benefited from Beijing's largesse, some in Pakistan are concerned that the price of such investment could be a huge debt burden (Yamada and Palma, 2018). Concerns about unmanageable debts to China have also surfaced in the Maldives and Laos. As these countries become indebted to China, some of them may be forced to give up part of their sovereignty in their relations with China. In taking control of these countries' properties, China has become vulnerable to charges of being a new colonial power, which constitutes a fatal blow to China's international image.

Change of government in some recipient countries may also complicate the BRI implementation. Malaysia and Myanmar reportedly are reconsidering whether to go ahead with new China-financed projects. Malaysia's finance minister announced plans in June 2018 "to report to the anti-graft agency upfront payments of billions of ringgit the previous administration made to a Chinese firm for two pipeline projects that have barely begun," reported the *South China Morning Post* (2018). Mohamad Mahathir, Prime Minister of Malaysia from 1981 to 2003, was reelected in June 2018 and is likely to scrutinize Chinese projects more closely than his predecessor. "Mahathir sees China as increasingly more of a geopolitical threat than an economic opportunity," according to a Manila-based scholar (Heydarian, 2018). Nevertheless, Malaysia is not going to reject the BRI or confront China; it wants more "free and fair trade" with China and it wants better deals from the BRI. In fact, the newly reelected prime minister paid a friendly visit to China in August 2018, where he convinced Chinese leaders that Malaysia was not being hostile to China but needed to put a number of China-financed mega projects on ice due to genuine financial concerns.[5] During a news conference in Beijing with Chinese premier Li Keqiang, Mahathir also warned China against a "new version of colonialism."[6]

In Myanmar, a planned $10 billion deep-water port to be built by China at Kyaukpyu was announced in 2007. Myanmar "became sensitive about being indebted to China," and the project was under government review as of 2018 (Lintner, 2018). In Nepal, the country's deal with a state-owned Chinese firm to build a massive dam with a price tag of $1.8 billion "would be canceled and Nepal would fund the projects itself (Lo, 2018)." At the end of 2018, a new government in Maldives was reportedly seeking help from India and the United States to climb out from under a mountain of Chinese debt (*Channel NewsAsia*, 2018).

China needs to ensure that the Belt and Road only travels to where it is needed, cautioned IMF Managing Director Christine Lagarde in a speech in Beijing in April 2018 (Lagarde, 2018). To alleviate local concerns about debt or governance problems, Chinese businesses will need to follow international practices and share more corporate social responsibilities (CSR) in developing countries and become more active members of local communities.

Finally, among big powers, Russia's role in Chinese foreign policy should not be overlooked. Potential clashes of Chinese and Russian

---

[5] See comments of Mahathir with Malaysian journalists upon his return from the China trip. https://www.kinitv.com/video/6496OO8. Accessed on November 26, 2018.

[6] Clips of video can be viewed at: https://www.ft.com/video/5f04f120-6491-4d68-bca3-14a9cfec9ca6. Accessed on November 26, 2018.

Geostrategic Challenges of the Belt and Road Initiative   233

interests will be the fifth geostrategic challenge. With President Xi and President Putin forming strong personal ties and with no immediate departure of the two strong leaders from the top positions of their respective countries, it seems China–Russia relations will be very close in the years ahead, at least at the official level. But deep down, suspicions toward each other always exist. Russia has historically dominated Central Asian and Eastern European affairs. With the BRI, these traditional Russian spheres of influence may gravitate toward China. To what extent will Russia tolerate it? Will this create tensions between Russia and China down the road?

In fact, mutual mistrust and cultural insensitivity already threaten to undo the careful diplomatic work of Xi and Putin. For example, residents on the shores of Siberia's Lake Baikal have become a lightning rod among Russian nationalists after Chinese investors purchased properties on the lakefront. Russian newspapers have inflamed public opinion over the town of Listvyanka, running headlines about a Chinese "invasion," "conquest" and even China's "yoke" — a reference to the Mongol invasions of the Middle Ages (Clover and Zhang, 2018). In another case of Russians' uneasiness about Chinese investment, a local Russian court ruled on June 14, 2018 to forbid a Chinese company from making bottled water with the Lake Baikal water (*Voice of America*, 2018a). This happened shortly after President Putin returned from the SCO summit in Qingdao, China. Interestingly, South Korean companies also produce bottled water along Lake Baikal, but have not received much local attention or resistance. Media reports also suggest that Russia, cognizant of its declining influence in Africa, is competing with China there for nuclear energy deals and arms exports (*Voice of America*, 2018b). To some extent, Russia's and China's strained relations with the United States pushed Russia and China together. How long their friendship will last is hard to tell.

2. *The Domestic level*: Geostrategic challenges also have domestic dimensions. First, there is little evidence suggesting that the Chinese government had done much feasibility study or risk

234 *A Critical Decade: China's Foreign Policy (2008–2018)*

assessment of the BRI before President Xi proposed the idea. Since 2013, the official label of the project has swung between "initiative" and "strategy," indicating that the government is perhaps uncertain how and to what extent this idea should be carried out. The idea came from the very top, and it must be implemented. This top-down approach is a distinct Chinese characteristic. China is on horseback, charging ahead. It simply cannot climb down without hurting itself. National laws and rules regarding Chinese investment and other activities along the Belt and Road are yet to be stipulated.

Second, there is little reliable information about how the BRI is unfolding in aggregate, and there is no agreed-upon definition for what qualifies as a BRI project. Over 70 countries are participating in the BRI. Yet, there are Chinese-funded projects in non-participant countries that share many of the same features. The BRI was officially launched in 2013, but projects started years earlier are often counted as well. The BRI banner hangs over a wide and ever-expanding list of activities, such as BRI fashion shows, concerts, and art exhibits. By design, the BRI is more a loose brand than a program with strict criteria (Hillman, 2018). Everything can be put under the umbrella of the BRI. People outside China may ask, "What is the BRI?" Inside China, people are asking, "What is not the BRI?"

Third, Chinese projects seem less open to local and international participation. According to a CSIS study, of all the Chinese-funded projects across the Eurasian continent, 89 percent are operated by Chinese companies, 7.6 percent are local companies, and 3.4 percent are foreign companies. In comparison, out of the contractors participating in projects funded by the multilateral development banks, 29 percent are Chinese, 40.8 percent are local, and 30.2 percent are foreign. These findings suggest that it should not come as a surprise that Chinese companies are winning more contracts for Chinese-funded projects. Despite official rhetoric about the BRI being open, inclusive, and global, it seems to be a China-centric effort (Hillman, 2018). The Chinese government has not published any official report regarding the extent of foreign involvement in all of the BRI projects, but this is likely to be scrutinized by foreign businesses and governments in the years ahead.

Fourth, domestic support for the BRI could decline over time. The BRI is constrained by China's domestic political imperatives. It aims to increase the flow of goods and people, but China's overbearing security presence near border areas may impede commercial activities. Chinese capital controls, while favoring outbound investment for BRI-related projects, are still inefficient and overly restrictive for inbound investments. The BRI aspires to promote the exchange of ideas and knowledge, but Chinese censorship is increasing. These trends all contradict the BRI's expressed goal of improving global connectivity. Beijing's dilemma is that greater connectivity requires giving up some control (Hillman, 2018).

Some analysts suggest that the AIIB and BRI are direct responses to the Obama administration's rebalance to Asia, while others consider them as examples of a more confident China attempting to reshape the global order. These may be important factors, but there is a much more significant domestic impetus. For example, many of the infrastructure projects proposed under the BRI could benefit China's poor inland regions, integrating them with the global economy and helping to mitigate China's rapidly growing wealth gap. They will also contribute to more balanced and sustainable development and allow China to relocate its labor-intensive and low value-added manufacturing facilities overseas, helping solve the severe environmental problems facing China today. Local and provincial governments in China may also wish to take advantage of the initiative and seek the central government's support and subsidies as they become actively involved.

No matter how outside observers view Chinese politics and foreign policy, China's focus remains on domestic affairs. Despite massive projects such as the BRI, the Chinese leadership continues to be distracted by challenging domestic problems, including rampant corruption, a widening income gap, an aging population, and a deteriorating environment. China may be the second biggest economy in the world today, but in terms of GDP per capita, it ranks about 80th, and China's vast central, western, and northeastern regions are even poorer. According to Chinese Premier Li Keqiang, some 200 million Chinese still live in poverty, which is equivalent to the population of France, Germany and the United Kingdom combined (*The New York Times*, 2014). To what extent the BRI can help these underdeveloped regions is unclear. Before long, people will ask: why spend so much in other countries when China's own poor regions need investment and development?

Discussions

Despite many challenges, there is a growing sentiment at home that China is powerful enough now to be more active in international affairs and aggressively push forward its foreign policy initiatives such as the BRI. Some preliminary studies have been conducted about the outcomes of the BRI. Outside assessment tends to be critical, such as U.S. Vice President Mike Pence's accusation of China's use of "debt diplomacy"[7] to expand its influence and India's assertion that the BRI harms its sovereignty. A March 2018 *Nikkei Asian Review* report examined how BRI projects were unfolding in eight countries — Indonesia, Sri Lanka, Kazakhstan, Bangladesh, India, Poland, Laos, and Pakistan — and identifies key problems related to the BRI, including project delays after initial fanfare, heavy debt burdens for recipient countries, and sovereignty concerns such as in Sri Lanka and India (Yamada and Palma, 2018). The Chinese edition of *The Financial Times* also ran a series of interviews in 2018 with scholars and policymakers to critically evaluate the BRI on its fifth anniversary (*The Financial Times*, 2018).

Many see the AIIB and the BRI as part of China's effort to boost influence in the Asia-Pacific region once dominated by the United States and Japan. While Asian Development Bank (ADB) and AIIB have jointly financed some projects, the AIIB is viewed as a rival to

---

[7] See Pence's speech at the Hudson Institute on October 4, 2018, the text can be found here at: https://www.whitehouse.gov/articles/vice-president-mike-pence-china-meddling-americas-democracy/.

the Manila-based ADB, in which Japan and the United States are the largest stakeholders. At an ADB conference in Manila in early May 2018, Chinese Deputy Finance Minister Yu Weiping called on the ADB to "increase the linkage between the Belt and Road Initiative and other regional cooperation programs." However, Japanese Finance Minister Taro Aso, who spoke before Yu, said the ADB should shift its emphasis from "quantity to quality" financing, even as developing Asia and the Pacific needs $1.7 trillion annually to build infrastructure. The United States underscored sustainable development including "strong environmental and social safeguards," which the United States views as "underpinning high-quality projects," said Geoffrey Okamoto, the U.S. temporary alternate governor at the same conference (Venzon, 2018). In practice, the AIIB and the ADB are complementary despite their differences.

China's official assessment of the BRI tends to be more upbeat. Contrary to Western critical narratives, roads and power plants built and financed by Chinese companies are not known for being of lower quality compared to others. Some of the standards Chinese companies set and follow are actually world leading. Green financing policies implemented by the China Banking and Insurance Regulatory Commission, for instance, are considered as an example for others to adopt (Yu, 2018). International reception of the AIIB gradually moved from suspicion to acceptance. The "big three" credit rating agencies, Moody's, Fitch, and Standard & Poor's (S&P), all gave the AIIB the highest rating in 2017 and noted the strength of the AIIB's governance framework. Western views of the BRI could also change as the BRI yields more positive outcomes.

Chinese officials have refuted Western accusations and argued that economic cooperation has strongly promoted the economic and social development of countries along the Belt and Road and improved the wellbeing of the people. According to Chinese Foreign Ministry spokesperson Lu Kang, China-related cooperation projects only account for a very small part of the debt of the related regions and countries, and not a single country is caught in the "debt trap" due to cooperation with China. The China-financed Mombasa–Nairobi railway, for example, created nearly 50,000 jobs for Kenya. The CPEC contributed 2.5 percentage points to Pakistan's GDP growth in 2016. By the end of 2017, China's loans accounted for only about 10 percent of Sri Lanka's foreign debt. China's total loans to the Philippines were less than 1 percent of its foreign debt (Zhang, 2018). At the 2018 Beijing Summit of the Forum on China–Africa Cooperation and the 73rd session of the UN General Assembly, many African leaders voiced their objections to the fallacy that China–Africa cooperation has worsened the debt burdens of the continent. The Sri Lankan ambassador to China said the allegation that the Chinese government had dragged Sri Lanka into the "debt trap" was completely wrong. The Pakistani finance minister also refuted the U.S. statement that the construction of the CPEC triggered a debt crisis in Pakistan (Zhang, 2018).

China is on a learning curve and faces many geostrategic challenges in implementing the BRI. Countries like the United States and India remain non-committal to the initiative, although their support is not indispensable; China can carry out the initiative without their participation. However, the participation of these countries is important for China since it will help improve the coverage of the initiative and give it added legitimacy. China considers the BRI as a new forum for regional cooperation. Thus, it must work harder to encourage the United States and India to participate as two major economies.

India can and will play a bigger role in the newly named Indo-Pacific region. China feels the heat of India not being onboard with the BRI. A big neighbor and emerging power voicing concerns and opposing the initiative profoundly challenges the goal of creating a "community with a shared future." Nevertheless, China is all set to play a decisive role in Asian political economy, whether New Delhi likes it or not. Meetings between Xi and Modi in 2018 reset the relationship after the two countries faced off at the Doklam/Donglang area for nearly 2 months in 2017. During the Wuhan "informal" meeting in April 2018, India and China agreed for the first time to implement a joint economic project in war-torn Afghanistan. Indian and Chinese officials will identify the project and work out the modalities of cooperation. The Sino-Indian agreement may rile Pakistan, which has consistently tried to exclude India from a region it considers as its strategic area of influence.

Managing relations with countries along the Belt and Road requires diplomatic skills. In an effort to balance its relations with India and Pakistan, Chinese Vice President Wang Qishan, widely believed to be the second most powerful figure in China today, met with visiting Pakistani Foreign Minister Khawaja Muhammad Asif on April 24, 2018 in Beijing, vowing to promote bilateral ties to a new high. Wang confirmed Pakistan as China's "all-weather strategic cooperative partner," adding that China will continue to regard Pakistan as "a priority" in its neighboring diplomacy (*China Daily*, 2018). The CPEC was making good progress and several projects have either been completed or are under implementation. Meanwhile, China supported both India's and Pakistan's membership in the SCO. Both India and Pakistan are important neighbors of China and are along the BRI. It is in China's interest to maintain good relations with both and promote friendly ties between them.

Integrating North Korea into regional development is another challenge for China. North Korea's application for the AIIB was turned down due to its low financial standards, but little has been done to help North Korea to be part of the dynamic Asian economic development. As North Korea moves toward denuclearization, it is important for China and others to support North Korea's efforts to modernize its economy and integrate into regional development. China's industrial overcapacity can be transferred to help North Korea, as the impoverished country moves out of the nuclear shadow.

China is transitioning from export-oriented growth to a new model based on consumption, innovation, and outward investment. This process accelerated after the 2008–2009 global financial crisis, which sharply weakened the ability of Western countries to absorb Chinese manufacturing products and to invest in developing

240 *A Critical Decade: China's Foreign Policy (2008–2018)*

countries. China is not just investing in developing countries; it is investing in developed economies as well. According to the National Committee on United States–China Relations and Rhodium Group, Chinese direct investment in the United States grew from far less than $1 billion before 2008 to more than $46 billion in 2016, mostly due to new establishments and acquisitions. At the end of 2017, Chinese-affiliated companies in the United States directly employed more than 139,600 Americans. If the United States continues to be a major recipient of China's booming outward investment, it could receive between $100–200 billion of investment by 2020. This would increase the number of full-time U.S. jobs provided by Chinese U.S. affiliates to somewhere between 200,000 and 400,000.[8]

The United States is not the only country that has absorbed billions of dollars of Chinese investment. The European countries, among others, have embraced Chinese investment and often compete to attract Chinese businesses. For years the United States and its European allies have called China a "free rider," and urged Beijing to shoulder more international responsibilities. When China attempts to do so, the West becomes suspicious of China's intentions and concerned about its growing influence — in short, "Damned if you don't, and damned if you do." Statements such as former U.S. President Barack Obama's "we cannot allow China to set trade rules" are arrogant from the Chinese perspective. Obviously a new era is dawning. Both the West and China need to adjust to the new global reality in which China is playing a more active role in international political economy. The international community should welcome China's positive contributions to global development and peace.

Since 2017, the Chinese government has tightened control of capital outflow. Big investors such as Dalian Wanda and Anbang have

---

[8] "New Neighbors: Chinese Investment in the United States by Congressional District," A Report by the National Committee on US–China Relations and Rhodium Group, May 2015. https://www.ncuscr.org/sites/default/files/Chinese-FDI-in-US_Exec-Summary-2015-NCUSCR.pdf, and "New Neighbors: 2018 Update" at: https://rhg.com/research/new-neighbors-2018. Accessed on November 27, 2018.

undergone financial investigations by the Chinese government. Along the Belt and Road, SOEs have become more cautious, uncertain about the benefits from their potential investment. They have become more reluctant to directly invest in unfamiliar countries. Private businesses have been encouraged to go first. After their initial success, SOEs may step in and continue to invest by merging with or acquiring the private businesses.[9] Guidelines on investment along the Belt and Road are still lacking.

Deng Xiaoping insisted that China should "hide our capacities and bide our time; be good at maintaining a low profile, and never claim leadership." Those days seem to be gone under the strong leadership of Xi Jinping. The BRI represents China's ambitious transition from a regional power to a global power, with the potential to reshape the international order, and Xi has officially been promoted to be the "chief architect" of the BRI, reminiscent of Deng's title as the "chief architect" of China's "Reform and Opening up." Whether the BRI will succeed or not is far from clear. While China's infrastructure building capacity is first-rate and very attractive to other countries, some are less sure about the BRI's impact on local politics, economics, and ecology. China has yet to convince all countries involved that this is indeed a win–win initiative. In addition, few have studied whether the BRI will create the dilemma of "imperial overstretch" for China.

China has quickly moved from a bystander in world politics to an active participant and a rule-maker of the international system today. The BRI, with its many faces, is neither a nefarious plot for world domination nor the answer to all the world's problems. We should evaluate its projects individually and hold them to the goal that the broader initiative has set for itself: to build a better future modeled on an idealized past (Millward, 2018). China insists that the BRI idea may have come from China, but the benefits will be extended to all continents. If so, China should not go at it alone and must work with others to ensure the success of the BRI, including managing relations

---

[9]This is based on a conversation with a Chinese IR scholar in Nanjing, China, June 15, 2018.

with key partners such as India, Japan, and the United States, sharing more global responsibilities in governance and sustainable development, and paying more attention to local economic and ecological concerns in countries along the Belt and Road.

References

Benabdallah, Lina, 2019. "Contesting the International Order by Integrating It: The case of China's Belt and Road initiative." *Third World Quarterly*, Vol. 40, Issue 1, pp. 92–108.

Channel NewsAsia, "India's Modi Embraces Maldives' as New Leader Takes Office, China out of Favor," November 17, 2018. https://www.channelnewsasia.com/news/asia/india-s-modi-embraces-maldives--as-new-leader-takes-office--china-out-of-favour-10938846.

Campbell, Charlie, "China's Belt and Road Initiative Stands to Boost Beijing's Geopolitical Clout as the U.S. Retreats from Its Global Leadership Role," *Time*, October 23, 2017.

Cheng, Dawei, *Belt and Road Initiative: China's Trade Governance and Policy* (Abingdon, UK: Routledge, 2018).

China Daily, "Chinese Vice President Meets with Pakistani FM," April 24, 2018.

Chong, Alan and Pham Quang Minh (eds.), *Critical Reflections on China's Belt & Road Initiative* (New York: Palgrave Macmillan, 2019).

Clover, Charles and Archie Zhang, "China Land Grab on Lake Baikal Raises Russian Ire," *The Financial Times*, January 4, 2018.

Dasgupta, Saibal, "India only SCO Member to Oppose BRI," *The Times of India*, June 11, 2018. https://timesofindia.indiatimes.com/india/india-stays-out-of-move-to-support-chinas-bri-at-sco-meet/articleshow/64533390.cms.

Feng, Bing, *One Belt and One Road: The Chinese Logic for Global Development*, Chinese Edition (Beijing, China: China Democracy and Rule of Law Publishing House, 2015).

Ferdinand, Peter, 2016. "Westward ho — the China dream and 'one belt, one road': Chinese foreign policy under Xi Jinping," *International Affairs*, Vol. 92, No. 4, pp. 941–957.

Heydarian, Richard Javad, "What Mahathir's Return Means for China and the Region," *China-US Focus*, June 5, 2018.

Hillman, Jonathan E., "China's Belt and Road Initiative: Five Years Later," Washington, DC: Center for Strategic & International Studies, January 25, 2018.

Holslag, Jonathan, *The Silk Road Trap, How China's Trade Ambitions Challenge Europe* (Polity, 2019).

Islam, Md. Nazrul, *Silk Road to Belt Road: Reinventing the Past and Shaping the Future* (Springer, 2019).

Jennings, Ralph, "Japan Is Committing to China's Belt & Road Initiative, But What's In It for Them?" *Forbes*, April 17, 2018.

Lagarde, Christine, "Belt and Road Initiative: Strategies to Deliver in the Next Phase," IMF–PBC Conference, Beijing, China, April 12, 2018.

Li, Xing, *Mapping China's 'One Belt One Road' Initiative* (New York: Palgrave Macmillan, 2019).

Lim, Tai Wei, Henry Hing Lee Chan, Katherine Hui-Yi Tseng and Wen Xin Lim, *China's One Belt One Road Initiative* (London, UK: Imperial College Press, 2016).

Lin, Minwang, (林民旺).《"一带一路"与南亚地缘政治》(*The BRI and South Asian Geopolitics*) (Beijing: 世界知识出版社 World Affairs Press, 2018).

Lintner, Bertil, "Myanmar Risks Falling into a China Debt Trap," *Asia Times,* June 5, 2018.

Lo, Kinling, "Fate of US$1.8bn Chinese Dam Project up in the Air after Nepal Ministers Send Mixed Signals," *The South China Morning Post*, June 6, 2018.

Luftm, Gal, *Silk Road 2.0: US Strategy toward China's Belt and Road Initiative* (Atlantic Council Strategy Papers Book 11, 2017).

Luo, Shiqing, (罗仕清). "一带一路'建设的重大战略意义," (Major Strategic Significance of the Construction of "One Belt One Road") 东方网 (Eastday.com), May 19, 2017.

Mayer, Maximilian (ed.), *Rethinking the Silk Road: China's Belt and Road Initiative and Emerging Eurasian* (New York: Palgrave Macmillan, 2018).

Miller, Tom, *China's Asian Dream: Empire Building along the New Silk Road* (Zed Books, 2017).

Millward, James A., "Is China a Colonial Power?" *The New York Times*, May 4, 2018.

Ranjan, Rajiv, "Wuhan: A Tale of Extraordinary Willpower and Realpolitik," *Hindustan Times*, April 30, 2018. https://www.hindustantimes.com/

editorials/wuhan-a-tale-of-extraordinary-willpower-and-realpolitik/story-D2eDZZATvhnwSwSiWSQ3AP.html.

Reuters, "United States Says It Supports China's Infrastructure Connectivity Plan," May 14, 2017.

Rolland, Nadège, *China's Eurasian Century? Political and Strategic Implications of the Belt and Road Initiative* (Seattle and Washington, DC: National Bureau of Asian Research, 2017).

Schultz, Kai, "Sri Lanka, Struggling With Debt, Hands a Major Port to China," *The New York Times*, December 12, 2017.

Sharma, Bal Kishan and Nivedita Das Kundu (eds.), *China's One Belt One Road: Initiative, Challenges and Prospects* (Vij Books India, 2017).

Shih, Gerry, "Pence and Xi Deliver Dueling Speeches Despite Signs of Trade Détente," *The Washington Post*, November 17, 2018.

The Financial Times, "一带一路"五年评估全球访谈之一：郑永年," July 20, 2018.

The New York Times, "Despite Poverty Efforts, China Still Faces Income Gap," October 17, 2014.

The South China Morning Post, "Malaysia to Probe US$2 billion in Payments Made to Chinese Pipeline Firm Under Ousted Ruler Najib Razak," June 5, 2018.

Venzon, Cliff, "China urges ADB to back Belt and Road Initiative, AIIB," *Nikkei Asian Review*, May 5, 2018.

Voice of America, (白桦). "普京访华后俄禁止中国在贝加尔湖取水," (Russia Forbids China from Obtaining Water from Lake Baikal after Putin's Visit to China), June 17, 2018a.

Voice of America, (白桦). "俄加快重返非洲脚步 与中国争夺非洲核能项目," (Russia Steps up Efforts to Return to Africa, Competing with China on Nuclear Energy Programs), December 5, 2018b.

Wang, Yiwei, *The Belt and Road: What Will China Offer the World in Its Rise* (New World Press, 2016a).

Wang, Yiwei, 世界是通的：一带一路的逻辑 (The World is Connected: The Logic of One Belt One Road) (商务印书馆 Beijing: The Commercial Press, 2016b).

Yamada, Go and Stefania, Palma, "Is China's Belt and Road Working? A Progress Report from Eight Countries," *Nikkei Asian Review*, March 28, 2018. https://asia.nikkei.com/Spotlight/Cover-Story/Is-China-s-Belt-and-Road-working-A-progress-report-from-eight-countries.

Yu, Ye, "China's Response to Belt and Road Backlash," *East Asia Forum*, December 15, 2018.

Zhang, Jianfeng, "China Refutes U.S. Allegation of 'Debt Diplomacy'," *Xinhua*, October 17, 2018.

Zhang, Yunling, 2015. "One Belt, One Road — A Chinese view," *Global Asia*, Vol. 10, No. 3, pp. 8–12.

Zou, Lei, *The Political Economy of China's Belt and Road Initiative* (World Scientific Publishing, 2018).

中国一带一路网 (Belt and Road Portal): https://eng.yidaiyilu.gov.cn/

Chapter

9

Going Global 2.0: China's Growing Investment in the West and Its Impact[*]

Introduction

China's post-Mao "Reform and Opening up" started in December 1978 with the conclusion of the third plenary session of the 11th Chinese Communist Party (CCP) national congress. The reforms spearheaded by China's then paramount leader Deng Xiaoping contained two integral parts: *yin jin lai* (引进来 bringing in) and *zou chu qu* (走出去 going out).

At the beginning of the reform era, China's policy focus was understandably on *yin jin lai* — bringing in foreign direct investment (FDI) and foreign management skills — due to China's lack of funds and backwardness in industry and technology. To attract FDI, China established four Special Economic Zones (SEZs) on the southeast

---

[*]An earlier version of this article was published in *Asian Perspective*, Vol. 43, No. 2. Copyright © 2018 by Institute for Far Eastern Studies, Kyungnam University. Reprinted with permission of the publisher.

coast. This first phase of reforms lasted roughly from 1978 to 1990. After 1990, China has continued to be a major destination of global FDI, but concurrently it began to implement "*zou chu qu*" — going out in terms of investing overseas. Now China is not just a major FDI recipient, it has become a net investor in the global economy.

Between 1990 and 2005, China's outward direct investment (ODI) covered mostly developing countries, particularly Africa, Latin America, Southeast Asia, the Middle East, and Central Asia. This is Going Global 1.0. Ample research has been done about phase one of China's ODI in the developing world and its impact on international political economy.[1]

The year 2005 was a turning point when a Chinese company attempted but failed to purchase a money-losing California oil company, Unocal. The $18.5 billion deal was blocked by US Congress on national security grounds, but China's global ambition was not blunted; instead, China's reach into Western markets has actually accelerated since then, with mergers and acquisitions (M&As) in all major Western economies.

The year 2015 was also a milestone in China's economic ambitions globally: China's ODI surpassed inbound FDI for the first time and the International Monetary Fund (IMF) approved the Chinese *yuan*'s inclusion into its basket of reserve currency. China's role as a major economic power and global investor had taken a solid foothold.

Going Global 1.0 (1990–2005)

During the first phase of "going out," China concentrated its investment in the developing world with tremendous amounts of trade, energy deals, and infrastructure projects. China's appetite for natural resources seemed insatiable, which propelled it to reach out to resource-rich countries. Many countries in Africa, Latin America, and the Middle East became major sources of raw materials and energy to

---

[1]For example, Shambaugh (2014); Dollar (2016); Wolf *et al.* (2013); and Zhu (2013).

sustain China's rapid economic growth. As a manufacturing power, China was also looking for export markets for its products.

In 1991, the trade volume between China and the Association of Southeast Asian Nations (ASEAN) was only $8 billion. It rose to $40 billion in 2000 and China has been the region's largest trading partner since 2009. In 2014, China's total goods trade of $480 billion was more than twice the U.S. goods trade with ASEAN of $220 billion. The United States has a free trade agreement with only one ASEAN nation, Singapore, while China has a free trade agreement with all 10 ASEAN countries. China and ASEAN have agreed to boost trade to $1 trillion by 2020. Two-way investment will reach $150 billion by 2020 (*Xinhua*, 2014). Already the provider of more loans to developing countries than the World Bank, China finances numerous agricultural, hydropower, housing, railway, road, and mining projects in Southeast Asia. With the establishment of the Asian Infrastructure Investment Bank (AIIB) and the implementation of the Belt and Road Initiative (BRI), China's investment in Southeast Asia is expected to further increase in the years ahead.

In Africa, China pursued a political agenda in the 1960s and 1970s, supporting rebel movements and Maoist forces in competition with the Soviet Union and winning over countries that recognized the Republic of China (ROC) in Taiwan. In the 1970s, China began to invest in several African countries, including the 1,160 mile Tanzam Railway linking Tanzania and Zambia. But it was after 1990 that China's trade with and investment in Africa has grown significantly. In 1995, China–Africa trade volume stood at $4 billion. Ten years later, it reached $40 billion. By 2015 it had topped $300 billion (*China Daily*, 2015). China is seeking to raise the volume to $400 billion by 2020. In comparison, U.S.–Africa trade is under $100 billion now. Though Chinese investment is welcomed by various African governments, Chinese indifference to the recipient countries' environment and rule of law has elicited some criticism from the West, as well as within some African nations (Brautigam, 2011).

Trade between Latin America and China jumped from less than $3 billion in 1988 to over $240 billion in 2011. Trade between China and Latin America multiplied 22 times between 2000 and 2016, a stark contrast to Latin American trade with the United States and Europe, which merely doubled in the same time period (Melguizo, 2017). To facilitate bilateral trade and investment, China has signed free trade agreements with Chile, Peru, and Costa Rica. China–Latin America business relations also encompass finance — FDI and loans. In 2015, while visiting Latin America, President Xi Jinping pledged to invest $250 billion in the region over the next decade. In 2016 alone, Latin American countries received $21 billion in loans from Chinese banks. China has several ambitious, but challenging, investment projects in Latin America such as a railroad stretching 3,300 miles, from Brazil's Atlantic coast to Peru's Pacific Coast, and a canal stretching across Nicaragua that will rival the Panama Canal if completed.

Despite China's expanding investment in Latin America, its influence in the region remains limited. Studies have found that Sino-Latin American economic ties may not be dramatically reshaping the host country's foreign policy toward China, that positive political relations are not sufficient to ensure smooth economic relations, and that the activities of Chinese firms in Latin America may be shaped by the host country's institutional environment and their own operational interests rather than by any dictates from Beijing (Blanchard, 2016).

The rapid growth during Going Global 1.0 turned China into a major trading power, especially after its admission into the WTO in 2001. After years of working with developing countries, China accumulated business experience and appeared prepared to enter the more sophisticated markets in the West. It continues to invest in developing countries, but its eyes are on the developed Western markets now.

Going Global 2.0 (2005–present): Rationale

In the Going Global 1.0 phase, Chinese trade and investment in the developing world served several non-economic purposes, such as projecting China's global image, competing for influence with other powers, namely the United States and Japan, and limiting the international space for Taiwan whose diplomatic allies are all located in the developing world except the Vatican (Zhu, 2013). In Going Global

2.0, the rationale for Chinese investment seems different from the previous phase and focuses more on conventional economic and political considerations. Due to China's global power status, Chinese ODI in the West will have significant impact on international political economy, and Western countries tend to view Chinese investment from both economic and strategic perspectives.

Structural reforms in the Chinese economy mean that China's growth will move away from manufacturing toward consumption and innovation, and China's appetite for raw materials has diminished, which makes the developing market less attractive. It's only natural that China is turning to developed markets as its economy undergoes qualitative changes. China's total global ODI has increased more than tenfold since 2005 (Figure 1).

Despite being the second largest economy in the world, China's FDI stock is not yet commensurate with its newfound global economic status. However, Chinese ODI is growing quickly now. In 2005, the total volume of China's outbound acquisitions was just a little over $10 billion. In 2014, its outbound investment flows totaled $116 billion, inching ahead of Japan to take the world's number 2

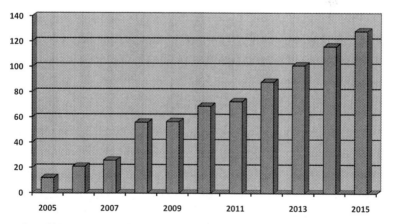

Figure 1: Chinese Outward Investment Since 2005 (in billions of dollars)

Sources: "World Investment Report," UN Conference on Trade and Development and Ministry of Commerce of the PRC, various years.

position, just behind the United States. Chinese ODI steadily increased, and by 2015 it had topped $120 billion.

In 2016, China struck a staggering $225 billion in deals to acquire companies abroad, almost doubling 2015's total. Such a sudden jump in overseas investment not only surprised many outside of China but also alarmed Chinese regulators. Chinese Commerce Minister Zhong Shan said in March 2017 that Chinese officials planned to intensify supervision of Chinese companies to curb "blind and irrational investment" (Bradsher, 2017, B1).

1. *The government push*: As China's economy becomes more mature, developing markets can no longer satisfy China's needs for upgrading its economy. As a result, the Chinese government has encouraged businesses to look for new opportunities in the West. But it was not until the 2010s that the focus of Chinese investments began to diversify from emerging and frontier markets to advanced markets.

   The 3rd plenary session of the 18th Central Committee of the CCP in November 2013 strongly endorsed globalization of the Chinese economy, calling upon "Enterprises and individuals to directly invest abroad." The resolution added, "Enterprises and individuals are permitted to develop overseas investment based on their own advantages. They are allowed to take risks in all the countries and regions to develop engineering or labor coopera-tion projects. And they can use innovative methods to undertake overseas expansion involving greenfield investment, mergers and acquisitions, securities investment, joint venture investments, and the like."[2]

   For the Chinese government, going out to the West has helped jumpstart long-stalled reforms of state-owned enterprises (SOEs). SOEs generally lack efficiency and competitiveness, and some have become heavily indebted, with many still receiving government subsidies to offset such disadvantages in the global market. When

---

[2]The resolution can be found in a *Xinhua* report, http://news.xinhuanet.com/politics/2013-11/15/c_118164235.htm

SOEs compete overseas, they lose the monopoly and privileges they enjoy at home and are forced to improve their performances and establish their competitiveness in the international market.

While the BRI focuses on the developing world, it involves accelerating outward investment, shifting excess industrial capacity and infrastructure projects into other regions such as South Asia and Europe, creating new markets, upgrading its own industries, and stimulating domestic growth. The land-based "Silk Road Economic Belt" goes through Central Asia and Russia, all the way to Europe, thus facilitating and servicing further Chinese investment in Europe. Different from investing in the developing world, where rule of law tends to be weak and policies are often non-transparent, investing in the West represents a giant leap forward for Chinese businesses toward becoming a major force in international political economy. Chinese business activities will be under tight scrutiny by Western governments and Chinese companies will have to follow international norms and practices such as assuming more corporate social responsibilities (CSR). The Chinese government's push for global investment demonstrates its growing confidence. All of this is also in line with President Xi Jinping's "Chinese Dream," which seeks to turn China into a powerful and wealthy nation.

Chinese investment in the West is at its incipient stage and has not received much attention from mainstream economists in China (Wang 2014, XI). Despite the government's calls for West-bound investment, the Chinese government has few specific guidelines or rules. Most of the investment and other commercial activities have been initiated by companies and individuals themselves. More official and scholarly efforts are needed to analyze both successful and failed cases, collect data, and produce high quality research to provide guidance for Chinese businesses.

2. *Demand in the West*: The global recession that began in the United States in 2008 provided China with an opportunity to move into Western markets since China's economy remained

robust. Against the backdrop of a slowly recovering global economy, new modes of economic cooperation and industry transfer are brewing, and countries around the world have high expectations for capital inflows from China. With over $3 trillion in foreign exchange reserves, China is taking the opportunity to develop FDI, both as a way of conforming to the needs of economic development at home and meeting global demands. One way to protect the value of China's foreign exchange reserves is to use them to buy real assets, like property or shares in companies in the United States and other developed markets. Such acquisitions could make China's dollar holdings less vulnerable to the volatile gyrations of financial markets (Schuman, 2011).

European countries have actively sought Chinese investment. Without Chinese investment, the Greek economy may still be stuck in a deep hole. From London to Paris, from Rome to Madrid, European governments are not only welcoming Chinese investment but also enticing Chinese tourists whose spending power often awes local residents.

Former British Prime Minister David Cameron and Chancellor of the Exchequer George Osborne hoped to bring forth a "golden era" in Sino-British relations and warmly welcomed President Xi in October 2015. Britain was the first Western country to sign up to join the China-led AIIB in 2015. Prime Minister Theresa May's delayed approval in September 2016 of the $24 billion Hinkley Point nuclear power station is telling of Britain's policy, however. The Hinkley Point nuclear power station is a Franco-Chinese joint investment that raised some security concerns in the United Kingdom. When May held up the project temporarily, China hinted that its cancellation would inevitably affect its future economic relations with Britain (*The Guardian*, 2016). May wrote a letter to Xi before attending the September 2016 G-20 summit in Hangzhou, China, affirming her then new government's intention to maintain strong ties with China. Shortly after her return from China, she approved the project. Clearly May, who had criticized the Cameron–Osborne approach toward China, did not wish to jeopardize economic ties with China and lose investment from China either (*The Guardian*, 2016).

Germany did not attract much investment from China in the past, but now it has become a major destination of Chinese ODI. In May 2017, BaFin, Germany's financial watchdog, welcomed Chinese investment into the German banking sector, a week after it was revealed that Chinese conglomerate HNA had become the biggest single investor in Deutsche Bank (Shotter, 2017). Another high-profile deal was a $5 billion bid in 2016 by the Midea Group, a Chinese appliance maker, for robotics specialist Kuka AG. Other proposed or completed Chinese deals include China National Chemical Corporation's $1 billion takeover of KraussMaffei Group, a cutting-edge equipment maker that processes plastics and rubber, and Beijing Enterprise Holdings Ltd.'s $1.59 billion takeover of EEW Energy from Waste, which operates high-tech waste incineration plants that produce electricity, heat and steam for industrial use (*The Wall Street Journal*, 2016b).

A U.S. Congressional Research Service report in 2008 highlighted the importance of China in dealing with the financial crisis. "China is a major economic power and holds huge amounts of foreign exchange reserves, and thus it could play a major role in responding to the current crisis (Morrison, 2008)."

3. *Domestic imperative to upgrade the economy:* China's growth has slowed down considerably since 2010, from double-digit growth annually before 2010 to 6.7 percent in 2016. Certain sectors such as steel and coal are experiencing overcapacity. Diminishing returns and limited attractive opportunities as a result of decades of over-investment in real estate and infrastructure at home compel Chinese businesses to look for new markets. The industrialization phase of Chinese growth is yielding to a new era focused on efficiency, innovation, and consumption. The new mindset among Chinese investors reflects the recognition that while China is no longer a capital scarce country, it is still "a relatively technology-scarce economy (Paulson, 2016, 6)."

256   *A Critical Decade: China's Foreign Policy (2008–2018)*

China now sees ODI as an integral part of transforming and upgrading its economy. This strategy helps China to expand its room for development in a globalized world, improve the level of its international competitiveness, and promote sustainable growth. Acquiring assets in the West helps Chinese businesses to diversify into more mature markets with stable regulations and to build global brands. Chinese companies can learn how multinational corporations mobilize global resources in order to become more competitive globally.

After successes at home, businesses like Alibaba are seeking new opportunities abroad. Since its share went public in New York in 2014, Alibaba has acquired major deals in Singapore, Macao, Japan, Hong Kong, and the United States, including the acquisitions of TangoMe ($280 million) and Magic Leap ($794 million) in the U.S. in 2014 and 2016, respectively (The Wall Street Journal, 2016a). In January 2017, Alibaba's Jack Ma met with President-elect Donald Trump and promised to create one million jobs for the United States.

Many consumers in the West still hold negative views of Chinese products. To overcome this global branding deficit, Chinese businesses have purchased valuable Western brands, such as Lenovo's acquisition of IBM's PC division, Geely's buyout of Sweden's Volvo, and Haier's takeover of GE's appliances division. Establishing global brands and strengthening innovation capacity have been major objectives of China's outbound investment.

Top Destinations of Chinese West-bound ODI

The United States, Australia, and Canada were the top three recipients of Chinese ODI between 2005 and 2016. In Europe, Britain, Russia, Italy, France, Switzerland, and Germany have been the largest destinations of Chinese investments since 2005 (Figure 2). Competition has been intensifying among EU countries in attracting Chinese investment. For example, Chinese investors have sought to acquire German companies at a rate of roughly one a week in 2016, according to data provider Dealogic (*The Wall Street Journal*, 2016b).

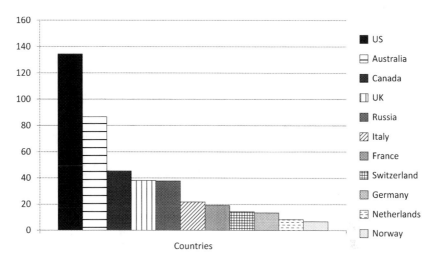

Figure 2: Top Western Destinations of Chinese Investment (2005–2016, in billions of US$)

Source: "China Global Investment Tracker," The American Enterprise Institute, www.aei.org/china-global-investment-tracker. Accessed on October 1, 2017.

Germany attracted more investment from China than any other European country in 2016.

According to "China Global Investment Tracker," maintained by the U.S.-based think tank, the American Enterprise Institute, Chinese investments and contracts in the United States have topped $134 billion since 2005. If the United States continues to be a major recipient of China's investment, it could receive another $100–$200 billion from China by 2020, according to a study by the Rhodium Group and the National Committee on United States–China Relations. This would increase the number of full-time jobs to somewhere between 200,000 and 400,000 Americans, according to some estimates (Rhodium Group, 2016).

Chinese investors, whether SOEs, private businesses, or individuals, are pouring billions of dollars a year into the U.S. to buy real estate just like the Japanese did in the 1980s and early 1990s. Notable big purchases include Anbang's purchase of the Waldorf Astoria in New York for $1.95 billion in 2014, Lexmark's purchase by a consortium of Chinese companies for $3.6 billion in 2016, and Wanda's acquisition of Legendary Entertainment for $3.5 billion in 2016. In February 2016, Chongqing Casin Enterprise Group signed a definitive agreement to acquire the 134-year old Chicago Stock Exchange (CHX). The deal, which was cleared by the interagency Committee on Foreign Investment in the United States (CFIUS) in December 2016, was blocked by the U.S. Securities and Exchange Commission (SEC) in February 2018 in the midst of growing trade tensions between China and the United States. If successful, this would have been the first sale of a stock exchange in the United States (*The Washington Post*, 2017).

Chinese investors, much like their counterparts from Japan, Europe, and elsewhere, view the United States as one of the most stable and dynamic markets in the world. As former U.S. Secretary of Treasury Henry Paulson remarked, Chinese direct investment "reflects a vote of confidence in the American market and its workers and a belief in the long-term resilience of the U.S. economy (Paulson, 2016)."

China has also invested in Western media firms and startups. Examples include Snapchat and Lyft, and China has purchased mobile gaming firms like Supercell of Finland and Playtika of Israel. Chinese internet giant Tencent Holdings and its partners agreed to buy "Clash of Clans" creator Supercell Oy for $8.4 billion in July 2016. A Chinese consortium of 11 investors led by Shanghai Giant Network Technology Co. agreed in August 2016 to purchase an Israeli games business for $4.4 billion in cash. The consortium will purchase a 100 percent stake in Caesars Interactive Entertainment's subsidiaries (*The Wall Street Journal*, 2016c). Chinese companies acquired 25 firms based in the United States and Canada in 2015, compared to just four in 2014 and nine in 2013.

Australia maintained its position as the second largest recipient of aggregated Chinese ODI between 2005 and 2015 (KPMG and the University of Sydney, 2016). Chinese investment in Australia reached $11.1 billion in 2015, the second highest in the past 10 years following 2008, when Chinese investment peaked at $16.2 billion due to the mining boom. Investment in real estate continued to dominate, accounting for $6.85 billion, or 45 percent, of total Chinese investment in Australia. Chinese investment in Australia has also expanded into other areas such as healthcare, energy, mining, infrastructure, and agribusiness. The free trade agreement signed between the two countries in June 2015 made it easier for Chinese businesses to enter the Australian market.

Features of Chinese Investment in the West

1. *Most of China's investment in the West is through M&A, rather than greenfield investment.*

   In the past, the vast majority of Chinese capital flows into the U.S. market were paper transactions involving the purchase of securities, particularly U.S. Treasuries, not direct investments that involved hiring of American workers and the operating of businesses in the U.S., but this is quickly changing. Chinese companies consider M&A in the West a short cut to upgrade technology. For example, after its failed 2005 acquisition of Unocal, the state-owned China National Offshore Oil Corporation (CNOOC) successfully acquired Canada's Nexen oil-sands facility at $15 billion in 2013.

   China's FDI in the U.S. soared to $45.6 billion in 2016 — triple the total from the year before, up from $15 billion in 2015 and $11.9 billion in 2014. In 2013, China's Shuanghui Group acquired Smithfield Foods, the world's largest hog processor, at $4.7 billion. Smithfield has continued to operate its business as usual and maintained its US-based farm supply chains. The Shuanghui–Smithfield deal underscores a key rationale behind Chinese investment: acquiring managerial and technical expertise from Western businesses.

2. *Chinese investment is concentrated in certain sectors, such as energy, entertainment, real estate, sports, agriculture, and technologies.*

   Chinese money has flooded into European soccer clubs since Xi Jinping came to power in 2012. Xi is a soccer fan and has expressed interest in China hosting a World Cup. While visiting the

UK in October 2015, Xi made a high-profile stop at the Manchester City football club. To realize Xi's "soccer dream," Chinese tycoons are purchasing soccer clubs overseas. In December 2015, a consortium of Chinese investors obtained a 13 percent stake in City Football Group, Manchester City's parent company. Two teams in central England — Aston Villa and Wolverhampton — were also purchased by Chinese investors. A consortium of Chinese companies have sought to buy the Liverpool Football Club at roughly $1 billion from its US owner Fenway Sports Group. The family holding company of former Italian Prime Minister Silvio Berlusconi agreed in August 2016 to sell the Italian soccer club AC Milan to Chinese investors. Chinese investors and firms have also been acquiring stakes in soccer clubs in Spain, France, Netherlands, and the Czech Republic (*BBC*, 2016).

Chinese insurance companies have been active in purchasing abroad. Some of the most high-profile purchases include Anbang's purchase of the Waldorf Astoria Hotel and Taikang's 13.5 percent stake purchase in Sotheby's. With an investment of $233 million announced in July 2016, Taikang is now the largest shareholder of Sotheby's (Yan, 2016b, 2). In August 2016, Ping An joined a small group of Western bidders to acquire CIT Group Inc., a U.S. lender for aircraft leasing, to satisfy the growing demands of Chinese travelers.

Dalian Wanda, primarily a commercial property developer, has become an aggressive buyer of entertainment assets in the West. It now owns control of AMC Entertainment Holdings Inc., the second-largest cinema chain in the US, and acquired the Ironman triathlon series of races in 2015. In July 2016, it was in final talks to buy a 49 percent stake in Viacom Inc.'s Paramount Pictures, a major Hollywood movie studio, for a value of between $8 billion and $10 billion (*The Wall Street Journal*, 2016d). In September 2016, it reached an investment partnership with another major Hollywood studio, Sony Pictures. Wanda already bought Legendary Entertainment in early 2016. Famous Chinese film director Zhang Yimou directed his first English-language film, "The Great Walls," with Legendary. The $150 million production is hailed as the costliest ever U.S.–China co-production (Chow, 2017).

3. *Chinese private businesses and individuals have become a powerful force in overseas consumption and purchases.*

    China does not publish detailed figures about its capital outflows, but according to an estimation by Goldman Sachs in July 2016, there were $372 billion in outflows by Chinese residents spent on foreign assets in the second half of 2015, and another $108 billion left the country in the first quarter of 2016 (*South China Morning Post*, 2016).

China imposes strict capital control on residents, allowing each individual to buy no more than $50,000 in overseas assets annually. Nonetheless, there are policy loopholes which people use to disguise their capital flight. A widely used method is to fake invoices, such as overstating the value of imports. Although the Chinese banking regulatory system has tightened the scrutiny of residents' overseas transactions, it has been hard to eliminate those activities, and Hong Kong is being used to disguise such capital outflows as well (*South China Morning Post*, 2016).

According to an American Enterprise Institute study, overseas investment by Chinese private enterprises is now larger than that by SOEs (Scissors, 2016). Private Chinese investments are increasing because firms want to get the money out of China due to the weakness of the *yuan* and, some speculate, political and economic uncertainty in China. It is also suspected that some SOEs or companies with close ties to the Chinese government use front companies and individuals to launder money abroad in order to evade taxes or for other illicit purposes.

The Impact of China's Investment in the West

On February 17, 2017, during a national security seminar in Beijing, President Xi Jinping suggested that China should "guide the international community to jointly shape a fairer and more just new world order" and "guide the international community to jointly safeguard international security" [两个引导] (Xi, 2017). It's a clear indication that Xi intends to shape the future of the international system. Soon afterward Prime Minister Li Keqiang gave his annual work report at

262 A Critical Decade: China's Foreign Policy (2008–2018)

the National People's Congress in March. The report included an unusually long passage about foreign policy and mentioned *quanqiu* (global 全球) or *quanqiuhua* (globalization 全球化) 13 times. That compares with only five such mentions the previous year (*The Economist*, 2017). As China keeps growing, its voice in international affairs will become louder and its influence bigger, whether the West likes it or not.

Chinese investors face many hurdles in the West. Just like Japan's investment and purchases in the United States in the 1980s, it is China now that is causing anxiety among Americans as Chinese investment increasingly moves to the United States. Japanese presence in the United States triggered widespread fears and "Japan is buying up America" perception began seeping into American culture. Japan's successes and America's worries were reflected in Professor Ezra Vogel's 1980 book, *Japan As Number One*.

China faces more challenges than Japan did since it is the first non-democratic, non-Western power challenging the dominance of the West in international political economy spheres. Different from international reactions to China's investment in the developing world, which focus on issues such as the environment, labor standards, and local governance, Western countries pay greater attention to jobs and national security when they examine Chinese investment in the West. Such concerns are often highlighted during an election year, as was the case in the 2016 U.S. presidential election.

In addition, the U.S. government fears that some Chinese companies may engage in industrial espionage and steal high technology for military purposes. Huawei has been singled out for having ties to the Chinese military, since its President, Ren Zhengfei, was a former PLA officer. Huawei has strongly denied any links to the Chinese government. Large private businesses such as Huawei and ZTE are often perceived by Western governments as state-owned or state-controlled, creating obstacles in their normal business activities. In December 2018, Ren's daughter Meng Wanzhou, Chief Financial Officer of Huawei, was arrested in Canada at the request of U.S. authorities ostensibly because Huawei violated the U.S. export ban and sanctions against Iran. However, many believe this was not simply a financial case but had something to do with the long-standing U.S. view of Huawei as a national security threat.

It's not just security concerns that are driving the increased backlash against Chinese investment abroad, it's also the suspicion that China is gaming the system by snapping up foreign firms in key areas while blocking others from doing the same in China. On the other hand, the Chinese government has already begun to regulate overseas investments.

Some foreign businesses complain that it's more difficult to invest in China. David Dollar of the Brookings Institution asserts that China "remains the most closed to foreign investment of the G-20 countries." "This creates an unfairness in which Chinese firms prosper behind protectionist walls and expand into more open markets such as the U.S. (*Bloomberg*, 2016)." For example, since the launch of the "going out" strategy, many international energy companies have played important roles in their Chinese partners' growing overseas investments, including jointly tapping into oil and gas explorations in many parts of the world. But they have made little headway over the years, with oil majors, such as Shell and BP, still complaining about unfriendly energy policies and limited business opportunities in China (*Bloomberg*, 2016). As Henry Paulson recommended, China and the United States should avoid putting entire sectors off-limits from foreign investment, and apply national-security reviews in a fair and transparent manner (Paulson, 2016). The United States and the European Union were still interested in negotiating a bilateral investment agreement (BIT) with China as of 2018. A successfully concluded BIT may help rectify some of the problems and concerns mentioned above.

China is a favorite punching bag of some Western politicians, especially during elections, but facts speak louder than words. According to McKinsey Global Institute, only around 700,000 of the 6 million manufacturing jobs lost in the U.S. between 2000 and 2010 went to China (*Time*, 2016, 34). In recent years there has been some resurgence of manufacturing jobs in the US: one million jobs have returned to the U.S. since 2010. A joint study by the National Committee on United States–China Relations and the Rhodium Group indicates, in 2010 fewer than 15,000 Americans were on Chinese company payrolls, and in 2016 Chinese companies employed about 140,000 Americans with Chinese companies operating in 98 percent of congressional districts nationwide.[3] As Americans debate the risks of growing Chinese investment in the U.S., it is important that the American public and policy community not lose sight of the benefits these investments can generate for local economies.

The CFIUS is perhaps the most famous governmental organization that reviews foreign investment in the United States. In August 2016, the state-owned China National Chemical Corporation (ChemChina) received clearance from CFIUS for its $43 billion acquisition of Syngenta, a giant in farm chemicals and seeds, removing one of the biggest challenges to the deal. Chinese investment is not necessarily more scrutinized by Western governments than that of other nations, but certainly some large projects or companies like Huawei often get a lot of media attention, helping politicize negotiations, review processes and lending to the appearance that China's investment is likely to hurt the economy and national security of the recipient country.

While contributing to recipient countries' economies, Chinese investment faces three kinds of hurdles in the West. First, some policymakers, regulators, media, and scholars question the motives of Chinese investment. They think it's not pure commercial activity but a policy tool of the Chinese government. Second, they believe Chinese businesses, especially SOEs, are supported and subsidized by the Chinese government and engage in unfair competition with foreign companies. Third, they criticize Chinese firms for lacking CSR (Wang and Lu, 2016, 2).

Indeed, Chinese investors face restrictions in the West. For example, in Vancouver, a favorite destination for individual Chinese investments, the British Columbia government announced that starting August 2, 2016, it would begin to charge an additional transfer tax of

---

[3]This information comes from "New Neighbors: Chinese Investment in the United States by Congressional District," a joint report released on April 25, 2017 by the Rhodium Group and the National Committee on U.S.–China Relations, which can be found at: www.ncuscr.org/content/new-neighbors-chinese-investment-united-states-congressional-district-0

15 percent of a property's value to foreign buyers, as a way to limit foreign money coming into real-estate markets to rein in home prices (*The Wall Street Journal*, 2016e). In January 2018, Ant Financial, owned by Alibaba, failed to acquire U.S. money transfer company MoneyGram International because CFIUS feared customer data could be used to identify U.S. citizens, creating a national security concern.

In Australia, the government blocked China's state-owned State Grid Corporation and Hong Kong's Cheung Kong Infrastructure Holdings Ltd. from taking a controlling stake in the country's largest state-owned electricity network, Ausgrid, citing national security considerations. Though the Australian government said that the national security concerns are not country-specific, the failed Australian deal is a major upset for State Grid, the world's largest electricity provider by revenue. In May 2016, Australia blocked a Chinese consortium led by Shanghai Pengxin Group from buying an 80 percent stake in Kidman & Co — the world's biggest cattle farm — on concerns that it would not be in the national interest.

Using a national security rationale to block outbound investment from China is far more confrontational than a trade dispute. It suggests that China is untrustworthy and has potentially nefarious intentions, commented James Laurenceson, deputy director of the Australia–China Relations Institute at the University of Technology in Sydney (*Bloomberg*, 2016). Bilateral relations are likely to suffer in the long-term due to such distrust.

National security remains the top U.S. concern regarding Chinese investment, especially from Chinese state-owned or state-controlled enterprises. In a September 15, 2016 letter to the Comptroller General of the US Government Accountability Office (GAO), a group of 16 members of Congress raised concerns about security challenges posed by foreign ownership in sector sectors such as the telecommunications, media, and agriculture, especially from Chinese companies designated as "state champions" that often benefit from illegal subsidies designed to gain strategic access to markets like the U.S. They mentioned ChemChina's $43 billion acquisition of Syngenta (for food security and safety implications) and Dalian Wanda's acquisition of major American movie studios (for concerns about China's efforts to shape American media and culture). The letter requested a review report from the GAO on the CFIUS to determine whether its statutory and administration authorities have effectively kept pace with the growing scope of foreign acquisitions in strategically important sectors in the U.S. Among a list of recommendations, the members of Congress urged the GAO to consider whether the CFIUS membership should include the Director of the FBI, the Chairman of the Federal Communications Commission, and the Secretary of Agriculture, and whether foreign acquisitions from designated countries should be subject to mandatory, rather than voluntary, notification to CFIUS.

In its 2017 annual report, the U.S.–China Economic and Security Review Commission, an advisory body to U.S. Congress, recommended prohibiting the acquisition of U.S. assets "by Chinese state-owned or state-controlled entities," and ensuring a strict review process for all significant Chinese investments in the U.S., including licensing agreements and any deals that enable Chinese entities to "determine the disposition of any asset."[4]

One needs not exaggerate the obstacles facing China's overseas investment. As Rhodium Group's Thilo Hanenmann suggested, for every sensitive deal that draws opposition, there may be ten that go through (*The Economist*, 2016, 44). Strict reviews by CFIUS have not deterred Chinese firms that are eager to enter the U.S. market. How Chinese investment can benefit both China and the recipient without creating concerns about national security or jobs continues to be a question worth exploring.

Concluding Remarks

China has undoubtedly become an economic powerhouse today and has deepened its participation in global governance. From the

---

[4]The report which was released on November 15, 2017 can be found at: www.uscc. gov/Annual_Reports/2017-annual-report?utm_source=October+Sweeps+-+Smaller+ List&utm_campaign=77a672c7da-20171116-422++ToughLoveForChina&utm_ medium=email&utm_term=0_76dd808eaf-77a672c7da-164890617

World Bank to the United Nations, from APEC to the Davos Forum, China's voice has become clearer and louder, which means that the existing international institutions will not be able to address global issues properly without taking China's views into account. More importantly, China is contributing to global governance through innovative measures to strengthen international cooperation such as the establishment of AIIB and the launching of the BRI.

China's rise and its global economic activities challenge traditional patterns of international political economy. Chinese trade and overseas investment do not always follow existing norms and practices such as ignoring the environment, local culture, or CSR, and restrictions on foreign businesses including international media have not been lifted. Meanwhile, China under President Xi has become more confident, with Xi proclaiming in his 19th Party Congress report in October 2017 that the "China model" can be an alternative to international development. Whether China is a revisionist power or a status quo power or whether China intends to replace the current international system is in the eye of the beholder, but the fact is China's rise has already created unprecedented challenges to the global economic and political orders established and maintained by Western powers. China has repeatedly called for a more just and fairer international order. Since such challenges are new to the West and China alike, the international system may need to undergo some transformation or modification in the years ahead reflecting the changing reality. However, it is premature to conclude that China's challenge to the existing international order will necessarily precipitate a conflict between China and the West.

Indeed, since China's investment in the West is a relatively new phenomenon, mutual learning and adjustment are required for both China and the West to fully understand its causes and consequences. For example, in compliance with international norms and practices, Chinese firms need to assume CRS while aiming at their direct business interests. Western governments and public, on the other hand, must avoid knee-jerk reactions simply because an investment comes from "communist" China. They need to get to know and work with globally ambitious Chinese companies and seek new opportunities to expand their businesses in their home country, in China, and elsewhere. Western countries must also reconcile the tensions that sometimes emerge between the central government that focuses more on national security issues and the local government that cares more about economic development.

Investment is a two-way street. To address outside concerns about restrictions for investment in China, the Chinese government has repeatedly reassured foreign governments and foreign investors that China's door remains open. It is encouraging that in November 2017, China's State Council announced a new financial market liberalization policy, easing limits on foreign ownership of financial services groups. According to the new policy, foreign firms will be allowed to hold a majority stake in joint ventures with Chinese securities companies and life insurers. In addition, caps on foreign banks' stakes in Chinese banks and asset managers are to be removed (*Financial Times*, 2017). The new policy was immediately welcomed by Western businesses such as JPMorgan Chase & Co, Morgan Stanley, Goldman Sachs, UBS, and Citigroup.

For China, investing in the West is not just a simple commercial act; it is a milestone in its pursuit of great power status. With its contributions to the development of the Western world, China is moving closer to becoming an indisputable global power. China's investment in the West will fundamentally change the traditional global economic and political orders dominated by the West, and its impact will be significant and transformative. Much of the angst about China's investment in the West boils down to the fundamental question: Is China's rise an opportunity or a threat? How company executives, politicians, economists, and other stakeholders can encourage, secure, and ultimately leverage Chinese investments will continue to be a topic of discussion and debate in the future.

It seems clear that Chinese investments abroad are poised to grow, albeit under tighter scrutiny by both Western countries and China itself. The rest of the world will need to get used to it and adopt legal and regulatory adjustments to make the most out of it.

China has entered uncharted territory in international business and global outreach. Chinese companies investing in advanced economies will likely reshape the global business landscape irrevocably. While major international concerns about Chinese investment in the developing world are typically related to human rights and environmental protection, concerns about Chinese investment in the West focus primarily on national security and global order. Western countries will increasingly have to balance their national security concerns with their economic ones.

For China, following internationally accepted norms in global business and launching public relations campaigns may help erase some of the concerns about China's investment. Greater transparency from Chinese companies on their finances and ownership would help dispel fears about their motives. China can also diversify investment destinations and enhance investment in areas or sectors that are less likely to generate national security or employment concerns. In the final analysis, both China and the West need to become accustomed to the growing power and influence of China through mutual socialization.

References

Bartz, Diane, "Exclusive: U.S. Lawmakers Urge AT&T to Cut Commercial Ties with Huawei," *Reuters*, January 16, 2018.

BBC, "Chinese Firm 'Eyes Liverpool FC Stake,'" August 21, 2016.

Blanchard, Jean-Marc F. 2016. "The Political Economy of China's Contemporary Latin American Relations: Issues, Findings, and Prospects." *Asian Perspective:* October–December, Vol. 40, No. 4, pp. 553–578.

Bloomberg, "Chinese Takeovers Trigger Global Backlash Ahead of G-20 Summit," August 25, 2016.

Bradsher, Keith, "After $225 Billion in Deals Last Year, China Reins In Overseas Investment," *The New York Times*, March 12, 2017.

Brautigam, Deborah, *The Dragon's Gift: the Real Story of China in Africa* (New York: Oxford University Press, 2011).

China Daily, "China–Africa Trade Approaches $300 Billion in 2015," November 10, 2015.

Chow, Vivienne, "China Should Persist With Co-Productions, Say Experts," *Variety*, March 13, 2017.

Dollar, David, *China's Engagement with Africa: From Natural Resources to Human Resources* (Washington, DC: The Brookings Institution, 2016).

Financial Times, "China's Financial Groups Opened to Foreign Owners," November 12, 2017.

Financial Times, "Chinese Investment is Welcomed by the West with Caution," March 27, 2016.

Huang, Yukon, *Cracking the China Conundrum: Why Conventional Economic Wisdom Is Wrong?* (New York: Oxford University Press, 2011).

KPMG and the University of Sydney. 2016. "Demystifying Chinese Investment in Australia," April. http://demystifyingchina.com.au/reports/demystifying-chinese-investment-in-australia-april-2016.pdf.

Melguizo, Angel, "It's Time for a New Era of China–Latin America Business Relations," The World Economic Forum, March 27, 2017.

Merle, Renae, "Chinese Bid to Buy Chicago Stock Exchange Stirs Security Fears," *The Chicago Tribune*, September 5, 2017.

Morrison, Wayne M., "China and the Global Financial Crisis: Implications for the United States," Congressional Research Service Report to Congress, November 17, 2008.

Paulson, Henry M. Jr., "Demystifying Chinese Investment in the United States," Paulson Papers on Investment, The Paulson Institute, September, 2016.

Schuman, Michael, "Will Asia 'Buy up' America?" *Time*, August 30, 2011.

Scissors, Derek, "The Year China Inc. Bet Big on the U.S.," *The Wall Street Journal*, July 15, 2016.

Shambaugh, David, *China Goes Global: The Partial Power* (New York: Oxford University Press, 2014).

Shotter, James, "German Watchdog Welcomes Chinese Investment in Banks," *The Financial Times*, May 9, 2017.

South China Morning Post, "How Wealthy Chinese Move Hundreds of Billions abroad to Buy Assets," August 9, 2016.

Time, "Is China Stealing US Jobs," April 11, 2016, p. 34.

The Economist, "Chinese Investment: Not So Gung-ho," August 6, 2016.

The Economist, "Is China Challenging the United States for Global Leadership?" April 1, 2017.

The Guardian, "Beijing tells Theresa May not to close door on China amid Hinkley Point tensions," September 1, 2016.

The Rhodium Group. 2016. "New Neighbors 2016: Chinese Investment in the US by Congressional District," April 12. http://rhg.com/reports/new-neighbors-2016.

The Wall Street Journal, "Alibaba Looks beyond China," August 13, 2016a.

The Wall Street Journal, "China's Deal Makers Have German Tech Firms in Their Sights," June 9, 2016b.

The Wall Street Journal, "Chinese Group Buys Israeli Games Business," August 1, 2016c.

The Wall Street Journal, "Chinese Eye Stake in Viacom Studio," July 14, 2016d.

The Wall Street Journal, "Foreigners Targeted by Home Tax," August 11, 2016e.

The Washington Post, "Why a Chinese bid to buy Chicago Stock Exchange stirs security fears," September 1, 2017.

Wang, Huiyao and Miao Lu, *China Goes Global, The Impact of Chinese Overseas Investment on Its Business Enterprises* (London: Palgrave Macmillan, 2016).

Wang, Mei, *China Overseas Investment.* 王梅: *中国投资海外* (Beijing: China Citic Press, 2014) 中信出版社.

Wolf, Charles, Xiao Wang and Eric Warner, *China's Foreign Aid and Government-Sponsored Investment Activities: Scale, Content, Destinations, and Implications* (Washington, DC: RAND Corporation, 2013).

Xi, Jinping, "习近平首提 "两个引导" 有深意," *中国干部学习网*. February 21, 2017. http://www.ccln.gov.cn/hotnews/230779.shtml.

Xinhua, "ASEAN–China Trade Expected to Reach \$500b by 2015," November 14, 2014.

Yan, Sophia, 2016a. "Chinese Flock to America to Work for Companies They've Bought," CNN Money, July 22.

Yan, Sophia, 2016b. "Chinese Firm Buys Big Stake in Auction House Sotheby's," July 28.

Zhu, Zhiqun, *China's New Diplomacy: Rationale, Strategies and Significance* (Burlington, VT: Ashgate, 2013).

Chapter

10

Pitfalls in China's Soft Power Promotion

China's rapid rise as a major power in the early 21st century has generated both admiration and apprehension around the world. As China's economic, diplomatic, and military strengths continue to grow, many people wonder how China will project or use its newfound power. A major concern from China's neighbors and other countries is the assertive tendency in Chinese foreign policy since 2010. This final chapter will not summarize what has already been discussed in previous chapters in order to draw a definitive conclusion, nor will it serve as a prediction about future trajectories of Chinese foreign policy. Instead, it will focus on China's international image and some major "pitfalls" in its soft power promotion. This topic is important for China since it cares deeply about its international image and has been attempting to improve its soft power abroad since the beginning of the 21st century.

Indeed, despite its growing economic, diplomatic, and military powers, China remains deficient in soft power. Assertive policies abroad and tight social and political controls at home severely hurt

China's international image. Several "pitfalls" or problems in China's soft power promotion practices must be fully understood in order to learn why China does not enjoy a very high approval rating in many parts of the world. The Chinese government must properly address such problems in order to avoid further damage to China's international image.

Pitfalls in Soft Power Promotion

1. *The mismatch between hard power and soft power: Amazing China* (厉害了，我的国) is a 2018 Chinese documentary that displays and applauds China's achievements in science, technology, industry, and poverty reduction since Xi Jinping became General Secretary of the CCP at the Party's 18th National Congress in 2012. "厉害了，我的国," roughly translated as "My country is awesome, formidable, or amazing," has become an expression by nationalist Chinese, especially 愤青 (angry youth) in recent years. It conveys a strong sense of national pride to the point of being chauvinistic. The underlying message is that China is very powerful now and is doing better than many other countries in this world full of uncertainties and turbulences.

The inconvenient truth is that China's soft power does not match its expanding hard power. There is also a huge gap between how China's soft power is perceived internally and externally. In fact, even China's hard power is not that "amazing;" after all, the Chinese government itself still calls China a large developing nation, which is true. For a long time to come, China's focus will remain on domestic development before it really becomes a modernized, prosperous, and evenly developed society. Nevertheless, many Chinese believe that since China will soon be the largest economy in the world, it can and should play a bigger role in international affairs. Some Chinese scholars and officials have suggested that China should ditch Deng Xiaoping's strategy of keeping a low profile externally and focusing on growth internally, which has prompted Deng Xiaoping's son Deng Pufang to urge current Chinese leaders to pull back as China pursues an ambitious foreign policy. The transcript of a speech, reportedly given by Deng Pufang in September 2018, suggests that China "should neither be overbearing nor belittle ourselves" and it should "know its place in the world (Yan, 2018)." Indeed, many observers in and outside of China believe that China should not punch above its weight in international affairs now. Veteran China expert and former U.S. Deputy Assistant Secretary of State Susan Shirk has cautioned China against "premature triumphalism" (*Voice of America*, 2018). On the other hand, Shirk warns the U.S. against exaggerating and overreacting to China's capabilities and influence. "If we inflate the threat we raise the risk of a 'red scare' ... that harms us as a free and open society," says Shirk in her response to a November 2018 report titled "Chinese Influence & American Interests: Promoting Constructive Vigilance," which was jointly issued by the Hoover Institution and the Asia Society (Hornby, 2018).

Many Chinese who believe China is already a very powerful and perhaps well-liked country in the world will come to a rude awakening that China's international image is very mixed, and remains largely poor in the West. According to the Pew Research Center's Global Indicators Database on China, the Chinese themselves view China extremely positively. From 2006 to 2017, the overwhelming majority of the Chinese (in most years over 95 percent) viewed China favorably. On the other hand, global views of China were very mixed. In Pakistan, Russia, and most African countries, favorable views of China were above 50 percent in most years, but in the United States, much of Europe and Latin America, favorable views of China were mostly below 50 percent. Most strikingly, several of China's neighbors, particularly Japan, Vietnam, and India, held highly unfavorable views of China. For example, in 2017, only 26 percent in India, 13 percent in Japan, and 10 percent in Vietnam had favorable views of China.[1]

China began to realize the importance of soft power in its foreign policy in the early 2000s, with the establishment of the first Confucius Institute in Seoul, South Korea in 2004, hoping to boost its overseas

---

[1] The Global Indicators Database on "Opinion of China" can be accessed at: http://www.pewglobal.org/database/indicator/24/survey/19/. Accessed on November 5, 2018.

image through promoting Chinese language and traditional culture. By the end of 2018, over 500 Confucius Institutes had been established across the world. However, in recent years, the Confucius Institutes have become a subject of criticisms, concerns, and controversies during their international expansion. While most Confucius Institutes continue to be welcomed on the college campuses where they operate, some have been forced to close or have faced other challenges. Lack of academic freedom is often cited as a major problem. In June 2014, the American Association of University Professors (AAUP) issued a statement which said that "Confucius Institutes function as an arm of the Chinese state and are allowed to ignore academic freedom" and called on colleges across the United States and Canada that operated Confucius Institutes to cease their relationship with the Chinese government or renegotiate their practices to support greater transparency and academic freedom (Graham, 2014).

Academic freedom is not the only concern regarding Confucius Institutes. Some Western politicians tend to inflate the perceived "China threat" and seem to lack confidence in democratic institutions and values. In April 2018, Texas A&M University, at the recommendation of U.S. Representatives from Texas Henry Cuellar (D) and Michael McCaul (R), terminated its agreement to host the Confucius Institute out of concern that the Chinese-government backed Confucius Institutes were "platforms for political propaganda and espionage" (Redden , 2018). Such politically tinged accusations are tenuous at best and are not supported by solid evidence; however, the Chinese government has yet to present a powerful and effective rebuttal, and the damage has already been done to regular educational and cultural exchanges between the two countries.

Confucius Institutes are not the only target in the renewed debate about China's soft power. In October 2018, Cornell University suspended a couple of undergraduate exchange programs with Renmin University of China in Beijing, accusing Renmin University of cracking down on student groups advocating workers' rights (Weiss, 2018). Declining academic freedom in China in recent years has also become a major concern for many China observers in and outside of China. Studies of the Xi Jinping Thought have grabbed the lion's share of state funding. Nearly all the proposals approved by China's National Social Sciences Fund in recent years deal with examining the impact of Xi's thoughts or ideology on various aspects of Chinese politics.

It's certainly true that some politicians and academics in the West are highly ideological and have knee-jerk reactions to anything that is supported by the Chinese government, and they tend to exaggerate the so-called "China threat." Nevertheless, as China turns more conservative at home and assertive abroad, it is clearly a big challenge for the Chinese government to project and enhance the country's soft power around the world, especially in the West.

2. *Soft power can or should be "promoted" by the government*: According to Joseph Nye, a country's soft power comes from three broad sources: its culture (in places where it is attractive to others), political values (when it lives up to them at home and abroad), and foreign policies (when they are seen as legitimate and having moral authority) (Nye, 2004). How much soft power China has today based on its traditional culture, current policies, and political values its political system represents is in the eye of the beholder.

A dilemma the Chinese government faces is that obviously the West in general suffers from an "information deficit" about China since voices from the Chinese government and Chinese scholars are seldom heard in the West; yet, no one seems to know how to best or most effectively introduce Chinese perspectives to the West. Somehow the Chinese government believes that soft power can and must be promoted by the government, without realizing that soft power comes from within and barely needs official propagandizing. Since the early 2000s, the Chinese government has spent billions of dollars in its propaganda overseas to help polish China's image. The so-called "big overseas propaganda (大外宣)" has involved all major state-owned media outlets such as *Xinhua, China Daily, People's Daily, Global Times,* and *China Global Television Network* (CGTN) in an effort to present China's voice and compete with the West for the so-called "power of discourse" or "pouvoir du discours (话语权)." In March 2018, the Chinese government consolidated all TV and radio international programs and merged them into a new single network named "Voice of China" in order to better tell "the China story" and win favorable views of China by foreigners. It does not seem to be aware that when the CCP reasserted its control on every aspect of the Chinese society, including cyberspace, schools, and economic sectors, after the 19th Party Congress in 2017, it became increasingly difficult to sell China's soft power overseas.

To a large extent, a country's soft power is also reflected in the behavior of its citizens. During the 2018 World Cup in Russia, the Japanese national soccer team did not make it to the final 16 after failing to be one of the top two in its group. Yet, Japanese soft power greatly enhanced during the World Cup due to the awe-inspiring behavior of the Japanese team and the Japanese fans. Before they left the stadium, the Japanese team would clean their locker rooms and leave a note saying "Thank you" in Russian, and the Japanese fans at the games would pick up the trash and clean up their sections of the stadium. This is particularly remarkable as they did so after their team lost the matches. Most countries do not actively promote their national images abroad. The Japanese government, for example, does not need to promote its overseas image; through the deeds of ordinary Japanese, Japan's soft power remains high globally.

In recent years, a new term has emerged to describe an authoritarian government's activities abroad to achieve its foreign policy objectives. "Sharp power" is the use of manipulative diplomatic policies by one country to influence and undermine the political system of a target country (Walker and Ludwig, 2017). Sharp power can include attempts by one country to manipulate and manage information about itself in the news media and educational systems of another country, for the purpose of misleading or dividing public opinion in a target country, or for masking or diverting attention away from negative information about itself. Both China and Russia have been accused of using their "sharp power" to meddle in other countries' internal affairs.

Instead of promoting soft power through official propaganda, the Chinese government should consider involving more ordinary citizens in public diplomacy and expanding public space for individuals and non-governmental organizations at home. Public diplomacy, with its emphasis on cultural, educational, and other people-to-people exchanges, is much more effective than the official propaganda. When China ranks a dismal 176 out of 180 for media freedoms (*Reporters sans Frontieres*, 2018) and comes in last in an 88-country ranking for Internet freedom (Crouch, 2015), it is simply a terrible idea for the government to use official media to promote soft power abroad. As Joseph Nye commented, there is little international audience for brittle propaganda (Nye, 2013). For China, probably the best overseas propaganda is no official propaganda at all.

3. *Watch the company you keep*: During Mao's time, China used to claim that "We have friends all over the world" (我们的朋友遍天下), which was one of the first sentences Chinese students would learn from their English textbooks. Does China have friends all over the world now? Despite its independent and non-alignment foreign policy, it is quite embarrassing that China has very few true friends today. A friend in need is a friend indeed. As China is embroiled in territorial disputes with its neighbors in the South China Sea, the East China Sea, and along its borders, almost no country has stepped up to defend China's position.

Which countries can China count as its close friends? Perhaps North Korea, Cuba, Myanmar, Cambodia, Pakistan, Venezuela, Zimbabwe, Russia, etc.? Unfortunately, all of these countries also suffer from poor images on the international stage due to suppressive policies at home. Despite China's long-standing "good neighbor" policy, China continues to have difficult relations with some important neighbors such as India, Japan, and Vietnam. Its friendly relations with South Korea were deeply wounded due to its high-handed opposition to South Korea's decision to allow the United States to deploy the Terminal High Altitude Area Defense (THAAD) system against missile threats from North Korea.

Russia was one of the imperialist powers that forced China to pay large amounts of reparations, open up ports for trade, cede territories, and make various other concessions of sovereignty following military defeats during the "Century of Humiliation." Today China continues to hold grudges against Western powers and Japan for their bullying of China roughly from 1839 to 1949, but it seems Russia's inglorious past is completely erased by the Chinese government. Though China–Russia ties have become much stronger in recent years, through holding joint military exercises and joining hands in opposing U.S. hegemony in international affairs, few believe China and Russia are true friends given their mutual suspicion derived from history and their conflictual interest in Central Asia and elsewhere. China and Russia are leaders in the Shanghai Cooperation Organization (SCO), but Central Asia is Russia's backyard. With every new wave of Chinese expansion to Central Asia through trade and investment, especially with the BRI, many Russians are deeply concerned about their declining influence in the region.

While China is not exporting any political or economic model, Chinese leaders have become increasingly confident in talking about China's development as an alternative growth path for other developing countries. Since the 19th Party Congress in 2017, the Chinese government has called for Party members, government officials, and the Chinese public to be "confident in our chosen path, confident in our political system, confident in our guiding theories, and confident in our culture." But such confidence cannot conceal the many flaws and challenges China's development entails, such as damage to the ecological system and sharp decline in social morality. Even developing countries that enjoy the benefits from China's growth may not wish to mimic China's development model.

4. *Do big bucks talk?*: Since the early 2000s, visits of top Chinese leaders overseas have always included pledges of huge economic aid and loans. Such style of giving large sums of money to other countries has been ridiculed by the Chinese public as "大撒币" (da sa bi), which is pronounced the same as another Chinese expression meaning "big idiot."

There are plenty of cases of China throwing out money without much deliberation. Mattala Rajapaksa International Airport (MRIA) is widely considered a white elephant project by Sri Lanka's former President Mahinda Rajapaksa (2005–2015). It is supposed to serve southeastern Sri Lanka and is the country's second international airport. As of June 2018, there were no flights to and from the airport due to lack of business and other reasons. Nicknamed "the emptiest airport in the world," MRIA was financed by Chinese loans. The first phase of the airport cost the Sri Lankan government $209 million, $190 million of which came as loans from the Export–Import Bank of China (Shepard, 2016). Without regular flights, it has been proposed that the airport offer long-term aircraft parking services as well as creating flying schools and maintenance services. As of July 2018, India and Sri Lanka were reportedly going to operate the airport as a joint venture (*The Hindu*, 2018). It's unknown whether China has learned any lesson from this failed case.

Other Chinese investments have also turned sour in Sri Lanka, leading some Sri Lankan officials to warn of a looming debt crisis as the country struggles to pay back the loans. In August 2017, China took over the loss-making deep-sea port of Hambantota in the south of Sri Lanka on a 99-year lease under a $1.1 billion deal, sparking particular concerns in neighboring India, a regional rival of China. Apparently some of China's development loan programs have not helped recipient countries, nor achieved its purpose of projecting its soft power. The United States has criticized such Chinese investment in developing countries as a form of "debt diplomacy."[2] Certainly, the questions of whether China is a predatory lender in developing countries and whether China has created debt crisis in some countries have to be answered objectively and by these developing countries themselves. As Deborah Brautigam and Kevin Gallagher, who have conducted balanced studies of Chinese investment in Africa and Latin America, argue, the United States cannot just point a finger at China without offering alternative, viable options for developing countries that need investment and development (Brautigam and Gallagher, 2018).

---

[2] See U.S. Vice President Mike Pence's speech on China at the Hudson Institute, October 4, 2018. The text and video can be found at: https://www.hudson.org/events/1610-vice-president-mike-pence-s-remarks-on-the-administration-s-policy-towards-china102018.

282 *A Critical Decade: China's Foreign Policy (2008–2018)*

China's overseas investment needs to be better managed. "Money talks" often drives Chinese activities overseas. From loans and investments to "big overseas propaganda (大外宣)," flows of massive Chinese funds overseas have not helped China improve its international image. Instead, Western countries and international organizations have cautioned China to focus on sound fiscal policies of itself and recipient countries with loans and investment in infrastructure, especially as it implements the BRI in different parts of the world. At an IMF conference in Beijing on April 12, 2018, IMF Director Christine Lagarde suggested that one of the biggest challenges for China's BRI is to ensure that "the Belt and Road only travels where it is needed" (Lagarde, 2018). Lagarde also urged China to be transparent in decision-making and provide clarity to all stakeholders with its foreign aid programs.

5. *Problematic rhetoric*: Chinese Foreign Ministry officials, state media, and some public intellectuals often use inappropriate, offensive, unrefined, or boastful language when commenting on international affairs and Chinese policies. Here is a partial list of such expressions in the official and popular vernacular.

- 搬起石头砸自己的脚 — Lift a rock only to drop it on one's own feet.

  This is used to condemn other countries for their wrongdoings against China and warn them of severe consequences. Are these countries really so unwise and do they not know how to protect their own interests?
- 悬崖勒马 — Rein in one's horse at the edge of a cliff; stop on the precipice.

  This is a serious warning to foreign countries that if they do not stop harming China's interests, China may retaliate soon. China seems very nice to give them a warning before retaliation. The question is: if they are your enemies hurting your interests, why don't you just push them down the cliff and solve the problems once and for all?

- 披着羊皮的狼 — A wolf in sheep's clothing.

  This is almost reserved for the 14th Dalai Lama, who is also called a splittist. These Chinese officials do not seem to understand how the Dalai Lama is revered globally. Such repulsive language will instantly nullify any good image China may enjoy overseas.
- 中国又创世界第一，西方胆战心惊 — With another world record of achievement in China, the West trembles in fear.

  This is a boastful claim of China's achievement in certain areas. It views the world in a realist zero-sum perspective, creating concerns and trepidation around the world about China's continued rise and contributing to the "China threat" narrative.
- 我们的拳头还不够硬 — Our fists are not hard enough.

  It seems China is always ready to fight. This is a self-reflection of China's limited power — the implication is that in the future we will be powerful enough to do what we want.
- 帝国主义亡我之心不死 — Imperialists always harbor the intention of exterminating our nation.

  This is often used to imply that the West, particularly the United States, intends to overthrow the Chinese government led by the Communist Party. Do Western countries really have such ulterior motives? And is the Chinese government so fragile?
- 伤害了14亿中国人民的感情 — hurting the feelings of the 1.4 billion Chinese people.

  This is used to accuse foreign countries of harming Chinese national interests through words and deeds, especially on issues regarding history and sovereignty. Chairman Mao said, the Chinese people have stood up. The Chinese people are proud, confident and tough today; their feelings are really not that delicate and so easily hurt.
- 引领 — guide and lead.

  Chinese officials and media increasingly use this word to suggest that China is standing at the forefront of our times. Xi Jinping's "two guides" [两个引导] — China should "guide the international community to jointly shape a fairer and more just new world order" and "guide the international community to jointly safeguard international security" — are such examples.

Is China able and ready to play such a leadership role? Does China intend to revamp the current international order and replace it with a new one under its leadership?

- 中国是最大的赢家 — China is the biggest winner.

China oftentimes sees the world in zero-sum terms despite its repeated championing for peace and win–win cooperation in international affairs.

- "应约" 通电话 — (The Chinese president) had a phone conversation at the invitation or request of (a foreign leader).

In official Chinese media reports, phone conversations between a Chinese leader and a foreign leader almost always take place at the invitation of the foreign leader, which seems to hint that the Chinese leader has a higher status. Chines leaders like to put on airs. Does this suggest that foreign leaders still need to kowtow to Chinese leaders today? On issues of great concern to both sides, why can't Chinese leaders initiate the conversation? For instance, the highly anticipated December 2018 meeting between President Xi and President Trump in Buenos Aires on the sidelines of the G-20 summit took place "at the invitation" of Trump, according to the Chinese media. When the two countries were engaged in a high-stakes trade war and when North Korea's denuclearization reached a critical junction, why couldn't China take the initiative? Such *Xinhua*-style reporting of conversations or meetings between Chinese leaders and their foreign counterparts also typically heavily focus on what Chinese leaders say, with little coverage of foreign leaders' remarks, giving readers an impression that Chinese leaders always dominate such dialogues and even lecture foreign leaders.

Moving Forward

There is no doubt that the Chinese government and the Chinese people have much to celebrate and to be proud of. It's little short of a miracle for China to be transformed from a backward, weak, underdeveloped, and isolated country in 1978 to a powerful, prosperous, open, and continuously progressing country in 2018. It is hard for young people in China today to imagine that their parents and grandparents were once so poor that they could barely fill their stomachs. Since 1978, more than 700 million Chinese have been lifted out of poverty. China's middle class keeps expanding, and living conditions continue to rise for most Chinese. China's modern infrastructure is first-rate in the world, and Chinese people are generally happy at a time when people in many other countries are experiencing uncertainty, insecurity, economic stagnation, desperation, conflicts, and even wars. In the 30 years from 1949 to 1978 when China was largely closed, only 200,000 Chinese people traveled abroad. In 2017 alone, they made 130.5 million trips overseas, while foreigners made 139 million visits to China (Huang, 2018). These statistics speak volumes about how China has transformed and become highly interdependent with the rest of the world.

Still, as the world's largest developing nation, China has much room to grow in terms of both hard power and soft power. China's poor human rights record is probably the single most important factor that shapes external views of China. Its iron-fist control on ethnic minority regions, including widely reported mass detention of Xinjiang Uyghur muslims in "educational camps" in 2018, has raised serious human rights concerns (Beydoun, 2018). The Chinese government continues to follow its own policies and practices, brushing off outside concerns as interference into China's internal affairs. It is in China's own interest to improve human rights conditions for the Han Chinese and for all ethnic minority groups. There are several things that the Chinese government can do immediately to help enhance its overseas image, among which having a meaningful dialogue with the Dalai Lama and lifting media censorship are perhaps the most significant.

Few people inside China know that the 14th Dalai Lama enjoys tremendous popularity and commands immense respect outside of China. Indeed, the Dalai Lama is widely viewed and revered as a symbol of non-violence, peace, humility and reconciliation. There was a time when the Tibetan goal was independence from China. Since the 1970s, the Dalai Lama has sought redress through negotiations. In the late 1980s, he proposed the Middle Way Approach (中间道路) as a path toward genuine Tibetan autonomy within China. The Chinese government tends to consider the Dalai Lama part of the

286 A Critical Decade: China's Foreign Policy (2008–2018)

problem in Tibet without realizing that he may well be part of the solution. The Dalai Lama has in recent years clearly expressed his stand that he does not seek independence for Tibet, only greater development for Tibet and protection of Tibetan culture (*The Times of India*, 2017). As ranking members of U.S. Congress Nancy Pelosi and James McGovern opined, "Imagine the world's reaction if Chinese authorities were to affirm the right of the 14th Dalai Lama to return to his homeland if he so desires. Imagine if they were to afford His Holiness the respect he deserves as a man of peace. Imagine if through good-faith dialogue they sought to ease tensions, rather than implementing policies that exacerbate them. Imagine" (Pelosi and McGovern, 2018).

It is unfortunate that the Chinese government does not trust the Dalai Lama and is perhaps waiting for him to pass away. The Chinese authorities seem to believe that with his eventual, inevitable passing, they will be assured of consolidating their hold on Tibet. However, the next generation of Tibetans might not be as accommodating, and the Beijing-sanctioned reincarnation of a new Dalai Lama might not even be recognized by the Tibetans. Should the Chinese government talk to the Dalai Lama while he is able and willing? Is China prepared to deal with a potentially more radical and violent Tibetan independence movement after the current Dalai Lama is gone?

Censorship is another dark spot in Chinese politics and society. Media censorship, including control of free speech in cyberspace, reflects the CCP's lack of confidence. What is the Party afraid of? China's achievements under the leadership of the Party since 1978 have been well-known. The Party deserves credit and should be proud of itself. Why will the Party be afraid of its own people, most of whom feel grateful to be living a much better life than their parents? It is the information age now, and there are about 800 million Internet users in China. Restricting the free flow of information through internet censorship does not make sense at all. The majority of the Chinese masses probably do not care about such sensitive issues like Taiwan or Tiananmen, and those who want to learn about the outside world already can through international travels and through bypassing the "Great Firewall" with VPNs. While media regulation is understandable in certain areas such as limiting access to pornography, prohibiting speeches of hatred, and banning terrorism-related activities, it only hurts China's international image if the Chinese government continues to censor the free flow of information in the 21st century. Limiting people's rights to free speech and information goes against the global tides and against China's own ambition to become a democratic, advanced, civilized, and beautiful nation by the mid-21st century.

In the final analysis, foreign policy is an extension of a country's domestic politics. Whether a country's foreign policy can succeed and whether it will have a positive international image largely depend on how well it handles domestic affairs. There is a reason why some people in and outside of China are disappointed that China's economic miracle has not brought it closer to political democracy even if they are amazed by China's rapid progress in many aspects. Political and economic reforms should go hand in hand, but China's economic achievements are so phenomenally ahead of its lagging political development. Before too long, something has got to give. As veteran journalist and scholar Tom Plate commented, "If Beijing wants to maximize international support and minimize resistance to its rise, the government needs to accept that the way it looks at itself is not always the way others look at it" (Plate, 2018). Diplomacy is a two-way street. Chinese leaders have proposed a few new initiatives in China's foreign policy since 2000, but as a large developing nation, China must also remain humble and continue to learn from the rest of the world in its politics and foreign relations. In 2018, China commemorated the 40th anniversary of "Reform and Opening Up" spearheaded by Deng Xiaoping. It is high time China revisited Deng's vision and reflected upon what China has achieved in both economic and political reforms, as well as where it is headed in the years ahead.

References

Beydoun, Khaled A., "China Holds One Million Uyghur Muslims in Concentration Camps," *Al Jazeera*, September 13, 2018.

Brautigam, Deborah and Gallagher, Kevin, "Trump Team Bashes China but Offers No Alternative in African Countries," *The Hill*, March 15, 2018.

Crouch, Erik, "China Ranks Dead Last on Global Internet Freedom Survey," *Tech in Asia*, October 28, 2015. https://www.techinasia.com/china-freedom-house-ranking.

Graham, Edward J., "Confucius Institutes Threaten Academic Freedom," *AAUP News*, September/October 2014, https://www.aaup.org/article/confucius-institutes-threaten-academic-freedom#.W-CsGiBRdhE.

Hornby, Lucy, "China Did Not Interfere Directly in US Elections, Report Says," *The Financial Times*, November 29, 2018.

Huang, Cary, "Rising Giant Stretches Its Arms Across the World," *The South China Morning Post*, November 12, 2018, pp. A4–A5.

Lagarde, Christine, "Belt and Road Initiative: Strategies to Deliver in the Next Phase," IMF–PBC Conference, Beijing, China, April 12, 2018.

Nye, Joseph, *Soft Power: The Means to Success in World Politics* (New York: Public Affairs, 2004).

Nye, Joseph, "What China and Russia Don't Get About Soft Power," *Foreign Policy*, April 29, 2013. https://foreignpolicy.com/2013/04/29/what-china-and-russia-dont-get-about-soft-power/.

Pelosi, Nancy and McGovern, James, "Let the Dalai Lama Go Home," *The Boston Globe*, July 13, 2018. https://www.bostonglobe.com/opinion/2018/07/12/let-dalai-lama-home/KaYlKtEdwE4pHmoljAAMeL/story.html.

Plate, Tom, "Why China Should Care About Its Image in the West," *The South China Morning Post*, April 23, 2018.

Redden, Elizabeth, "Closing a Confucius Institute, at Congressmen's Request," *Inside Higher Ed*, April 9, 2018.

Reporters sans Frontieres, "Classement mondial de la liberté de la presse 2018," https://rsf.org/ranking#!/. on November 6, 2018.

Shepard, Wade, "For Sale: The World's Emptiest International Airport," *Forbes*, July 18, 2016.

The Hindu, "India to Operate 'World's Emptiest Airport' in Sri Lanka," July 6, 2018.

The Times of India, "Tibet Wants to Stay with China, Says Dalai Lama," November 24, 2017. https://timesofindia.indiatimes.com/india/tibet-wants-to-stay-with-china-says-dalai-lama/articleshow/61775261.cms.

Voice of America, "谢淑丽：中国对外政策转变导致美中关系紧张," (Susan Shirk: Changes in China's Foreign Policy Led to Tensions in US–China Relations), November 23, 2018.

Walker, Christopher and Ludwig Jessica, "The Meaning of Sharp Power: How Authoritarian States Project Influence," *Foreign Affairs*, November 16, 2017.

Weiss, Jessica Chen, "Cornell University Suspended Two Exchange Programs with China's Renmin University. Here's Why," *The Washington Post*, November 1, 2018.

Yan, Sophia, "Deng Xiaoping's Son Urges China to 'know its place' in Counterpoint to Xi's Expansionist Foreign Policy," *The South China Morning Post*, October 30, 2018. https://www.telegraph.co.uk/news/2018/10/30/deng-xiaopings-son-urges-china-know-place-counterpoint-xis-expansionist/.

Index

A
1994 Agreed Framework, 126, 135

Addis Ababa–Djibouti Railway, 194–196

Africa, 5, 7–9, 28, 50, 52, 59–62, 77, 83, 142, 187, 194, 196–197, 205, 210, 218, 223, 227, 248–249, 275, 281

Air defense identification zone (*see also* ADIZ), 161–162, 165

America First, 77, 193

American Association of University Professors, 188, 276

American Institute in Taiwan, 14, 168

Asia–Africa Growth Corridor (*see also* AAGC), 7, 193, 227

Asia-Pacific Economic Cooperation (*see also* APEC), 143, 150, 159, 226, 267

Asian Infrastructure Investment Bank (*see also* AIIB), 5, 28, 75, 83, 142, 145, 147, 183, 199, 201, 224, 236–237, 249, 254, 267

Association of Southeast Asian Nations (*see also* ASEAN), 65, 103, 249

B
Beijing Consensus, 38, 104

Beijing Olympics 2008, 16

Belt and Road Forum, 224–225, 227

Belt and Road Initiative (*see also* BRI), 28, 49, 67, 69, 75–76, 138, 143, 145, 191, 197, 204, 223, 237

Big overseas propaganda, 277, 282

Bush, George W., 56, 134, 152, 219

Byungjin, 75, 119, 122

C

1992 Consensus, 7, 178, 183
Carter, Jimmy, 99, 115, 134, 197, 200
Censorship, 84, 88, 235, 285–286
Century of Humiliation, 29, 198, 279
Chen Shui-bian, 101, 170, 185
China National Offshore Oil Corporation (*see also* CNOOC), 17, 259
China threat, 10, 50, 191, 227, 276–277, 283
China–Africa Cooperation Forum, 238
China–Pakistan Economic Corridor (*see also* CPEC), 7, 138, 143, 227
Chinese Dream, 4, 224–225, 228, 253
Clinton, Bill, 13, 102, 133
Committee on Foreign Investment in the United States (*see also* CFIUS), 168, 258, 264–266
Community with a shared future for mankind, 4, 19
Confucius Institute(s), 51, 187, 219, 275–276
Constructivism, 23
Corporate social responsibilities (*see also* CSR), 232, 253, 264, 267

D

Dalai Lama, 283, 285
Davos World Economic Forum, 215
de jure independence, 173, 183, 202

Debt diplomacy, 13, 236, 281
Democratic Progressive Party (*see also* DPP), 170, 181, 186
Deng Xiaoping, 4, 10, 19, 22, 45, 50, 83, 99, 134, 198, 204, 208, 212, 241, 247, 274, 287
Diaoyu/Senkaku (*see also* Senkaku/Diaoyu), 18, 85, 160, 162, 164–166
Doklam/Donglang (*see also* Donglang/Doklam), 7, 137, 141, 238

E

East China Sea, 6, 122, 124, 144, 162–163, 166, 207, 279
Economic Cooperation Framework Agreement (*see also* ECFA), 171

F

Financial crisis, 82, 103–104, 217, 219, 239, 255
Five Principles of Peaceful Coexistence, 11, 22, 32, 141, 207
Four tigers, 164
Freedom of navigation, 165, 200–201, 226

G

Going Global, 61, 247–248, 250
Great Firewall, 286
Gunboat diplomacy, 94

H

Hambantota, 138, 228, 230, 281
Hanban, 187–188
Hard power, 180, 274, 285

Hu Jintao, 4, 10, 87, 90, 97, 99, 216
Huawei, 85, 168, 196, 262–264

I

Indo-Pacific, 7, 139–141, 192, 227, 238
International political economy, 3, 12, 21, 54, 69, 100, 216, 220, 227, 240, 248, 251, 253, 262, 267
International security, 8, 19, 48, 118, 178, 261, 283

J

Jack Ma, 168, 256
Jiang Zemin, 4

K

Kim Jong-un, 74, 78–80, 105–108, 111, 116, 118, 122–124, 127–129, 132, 134
Kim Jong-il, 90–91, 102–103, 106, 126, 128–129, 131–132, 134
Kim Jong-nam, 79, 81
Kissinger, Henry, 15, 33, 176
Kuomintang (*see also* KMT), 101, 171, 213
Korean Peninsula, 6, 10, 32, 57, 59, 74–75, 80–81, 90–92, 100, 105, 109, 113, 115, 119, 124, 129, 132–133

L

Latin America, 5, 8–9, 48, 50, 59, 63, 65–66, 83, 139, 142, 159, 215–216, 219, 223, 226, 248–250, 275, 281

Li Keqiang, 82, 145, 228, 232, 236, 261
Lips and teeth, 110, 123, 130

M

21st Century Maritime Silk Road, 5, 204, 226
Ma Ying-jeou, 101, 170–171, 181
Malacca dilemma, 11, 229
Mao Zedong, 16, 45, 99, 134
Mar-a-Lago resort, 81
Meng Wanzhou, 262
Middle East, 65, 83, 195, 204, 208–210, 215, 219, 223, 248
Ministry of Foreign Affairs, 30–31, 34
Modi, Narendra, 138, 146, 228
Moon Jae-in, 74, 109, 113

N

2018 National Defense Authorization Act, 168
National Committee on United States–China Relations, 82, 240, 257, 263
National People's Congress (*see also* NPC), 4, 99, 262
New type of great power relations, 6, 19, 83, 201
Nixon, Richard, 14, 33, 99, 112, 117, 155, 164, 169, 175
Nobel Peace Prize, 12, 110

O

Obama, Barack, 14, 84–86, 88–90, 92, 97, 99, 111, 119, 121, 125, 132, 135, 152, 176, 184, 189–190, 198, 235, 240

294 *Index*

"One China" policy, 174–176, 184
Outward direct investment (*see also*
  ODI), 248, 251–252, 255–256,
  258

P

Paris Agreement, 110
Park Geun-hye, 79, 123
Paulson, Henry, 15, 258, 263
Peaceful development, 5
Pence, Mike, 13, 117, 226, 236
People-to-people diplomacy,
  155–156, 159
Ping Pong diplomacy, 112,
  155–156
Pivot, 48, 83, 121, 140, 150–151,
  166
Power of discourse, 12, 277
Power transition, 6, 21, 53–54, 56,
  84, 91, 162–163, 165, 200–202
Putin, Vladimir, 119, 233

Q

Quad, 7, 191–194

R

Reform and Opening up, 21–22,
  35, 212, 241, 247, 287
Regional Comprehensive Economic
  Partnership (*see also* RCEP), 75,
  182
Ren Zhengfei, 168, 262
Rhodium Group, 82, 178, 240,
  257, 263
Rodman, Dennis, 111, 113–114

S

Selective intervention, 207

Shanghai Cooperation Organization
  (*see also* SCO), 6, 11, 28, 75,
  138, 142, 147, 208, 228, 233,
  239, 280
Sharp power, 278
Shinzo Abe, 7, 77, 119, 121, 123,
  150, 156, 159, 162, 164, 229
Silk Road Economic Belt, 5, 204,
  253
Six Assurances, 175
Six-Party Talks, 12, 94, 102, 114,
  118, 124, 207
Sleeping dragon, 63
Soft power, 8, 28, 30, 50–52, 156,
  180, 186–187, 189, 273,
  277–278, 281
South China Sea, 4, 6–7, 10, 14,
  17, 45–46, 77, 81, 85, 122, 124,
  143, 148, 151, 169, 174,
  200–201, 226, 279
Special Economic Zones (*see also*
  SEZs), 247
Sri Lanka, 138, 143, 228, 230,
  236, 238, 280–281
State-owned enterprises (*see also*
  SOEs), 17, 204–205, 230, 241,
  252–253, 257, 261, 264
Strategic rebalancing, 86, 151
Summer Olympics, 3, 115

T

Taiwan Relations Act (*see also*
  TRA), 168, 184, 189, 212
Taiwan Strait, 6–7, 10, 40, 43,
  100–101, 178, 181, 183, 185,
  188, 213
Taiwan Travel Act, 7, 14, 167–168
Taiwanese independence, 183

Tao Guang Yang Hui, 4, 10, 19, 23, 204
Terminal High Altitude Area Defense (*see also* THAAD) System, 79–80, 116, 121, 279
Think tanks, 16–17, 31, 39, 41
Thucydides' Trap, 6, 21, 53, 201
Tiananmen Square, 44, 157, 164, 213–214
Tibet, 9, 16, 29, 84, 87, 96, 104, 179, 190, 208, 211, 218, 286
Trans-Pacific Partnership (*see also* TPP), 182, 201
Trump, Donald, 6–7, 13–15, 73–75, 77–78, 80, 105, 108–111, 117–119, 168, 174, 176, 178–181, 284
Trump–Kim meeting (*see also* Kim–Trump meeting), 73, 75, 80, 105–108
Tsai Ing-wen, 172, 174, 178–179, 182, 186
Two Centenary Goals, 4
Two guides, 19, 283

U
U.S. Congress, 7, 88, 103, 134, 147, 152, 189, 199, 212, 266, 286

U.S. Treasury bonds, 98, 103–104, 219

W
Washington Consensus, 104
Wang Yi, 119, 176
White-eyed wolf, 79
World Trade Organization (*see also* WTO), 11, 15, 69, 98, 144, 250

X
Xinjiang, 9, 16, 208, 285
Xi Jinping, 3–5, 15, 19–20, 47–48, 78, 91, 105, 108, 122–123, 138, 147, 153, 159, 165, 176, 180–181, 216, 223, 241, 250, 259, 261, 276

Y
Yasukuni Shrine, 150, 152, 154, 157, 160–162, 164–165
Yin jin lai, 32, 247
You Suo Zuo Wei, 4

Z
Zhongnanhai, 10, 84
Zhou Enlai, 99, 141, 165
Zou chu qu, 17, 32, 247–248